YOU AND YOUR CHILD'S PSYCHOTHERAPY

The Essential Guide for Parents and Caregivers

Michael O. Weiner, LCSW

and

Les Paul Gallo-Silver, LCSW-R

OXFORD
UNIVERSITY PRESS

OXFORD

UNIVERSITY PRESS

Oxford University Press is a department of the University of
Oxford. It furthers the University's objective of excellence in research,
scholarship, and education by publishing worldwide.

Oxford   New York
Auckland   Cape Town   Dar es Salaam   Hong Kong   Karachi
Kuala Lumpur   Madrid   Melbourne   Mexico City   Nairobi
New Delhi   Shanghai   Taipei   Toronto

With offices in
Argentina   Austria   Brazil   Chile   Czech Republic   France   Greece
Guatemala   Hungary   Italy   Japan   Poland   Portugal   Singapore
South Korea   Switzerland   Thailand   Turkey   Ukraine   Vietnam

Oxford is a registered trademark of Oxford University Press
in the UK and certain other countries.

Published in the United States of America by
Oxford University Press
198 Madison Avenue, New York, NY 10016

© Oxford University Press 2015

Library of Congress Cataloging-in-Publication Data
Weiner, Michael O.
You and your child's psychotherapy : the essential guide for parents and caregivers /
Michael O. Weiner, LCSW, and Les Paul Gallo-Silver, LCSW-R.
pages cm
Includes bibliographical references and index.
ISBN 978–0–19–939145–5 (paperback)
1. Child psychotherapy—Parent participation.   2. Parent and child.   3. Psychotherapist
and patient.   I. Gallo-Silver, Les Paul.   II. Title.
RJ505.P38W45 2015
618.92'8914—dc23
2015007876

9 8 7 6 5 4 3 2 1
Printed in the United States of America
on acid-free paper

To our loving wives and the remarkable children in our lives

CONTENTS

HOW TO USE THIS BOOK

It is the intention of this book to be a supportive document used in the fashion that you feel would be most helpful.

This is not a textbook. We include theory as a way to demonstrate where our ideas come from. We have included the name of the theorist in parentheses. The bibliography can provide you with ways to learn more about that particular theorist. Where we do use a professional term, we offer an explanation. To that end, we have included a glossary of terms at the end of the book.

You may read this book by picking and choosing those chapters that address your current concerns and questions, by reading it cover to cover, or by browsing the chapter summaries as a way of getting a brief overview. You can always return to this book to read or re-read a chapter that addresses issues that have become more meaningful to you as your child's situation changes. There is merit in all of these options and, of course, how you use the book may change over time.

However you choose to make your way through this book, we recommend that you read the Introduction. It is an account of what you may be experiencing and was written to help you organize your thoughts as you begin this journey.

We seek to provide you with a very complete understanding of the way child psychotherapy works as well as your valuable contributions to the therapeutic process.

Introduction

A Framework and Rationale for This Book

This book is for all parents—mothers, fathers, LGBT, single, separated or divorced, widowed, adoptive, relatives, foster, medically ill, and of any cultural and ethnic background. Loving and caring for a child connects all of us to each other. If you find yourself reading this book, then you are a parent who is already considering the possibility that your child may need psychotherapy.

You may have started psychotherapy with your child and now may be unsure how to proceed. Perhaps you are thinking about psychotherapy and are not sure where to begin. The thoughts, issues, and difficulties that bring you and your child to this moment may already be creating increased feelings of stress or confusion. These feelings may be contributing to a reduced sense of control and more anxiety for you, your child, and your family. Wherever you are at this moment, let us, for the sake of all being on the same page, start at the beginning.

If you have not participated in psychotherapy before, you may be uncertain about what kind of help this is and how it helps children. You may have heard things from your friends or family, or you may have seen things on television or in movies that have created some ideas about what psychotherapy is all about. You may have many kinds of images and stereotypes of what a therapist looks like and acts like—the couch, the soft speech, and the calm. These images come in many forms.

If you have participated in your own psychotherapy or if your child has seen a therapist, knowing about therapeutic processes through your own experiences will shape how you understand your child's needs in psychotherapy and how to address those needs. Unlike the parent who has never engaged in psychotherapy before (their own or their child's), you may have specific ideas about types of psychotherapy, how to interact with a therapist, the language used, the duration of treatment, the focus, and so on. If the experience was a positive one, helpful and enlightening, you may see engagement in psychotherapy as straightforward and easy. If the experience was not a positive one, you may be skeptical about psychotherapy and about how a therapist could help the situation with your child. For both groups, it is the goal of this book to create a deeper understanding of the process.

We would like you to think about typical types of choices we make in life and how we prepare for these. Let us use the idea of engaging in an activity that is unfamiliar to people when first attempted. You can choose one—picking out where you want to live, considering taking a pregnancy test, deciding on what car to buy, determining if you want to change jobs, or selecting which school you want your child to attend. These are activities that you can have much more control over by getting information about them ahead of time. Learning as much as you can about these activities helps you to know your options and to make good choices for yourself. If you do not feel prepared, these types of processes and the decisions you will have to make to accomplish them can very easily feel overwhelming. Whatever you are thinking about psychotherapy, the following discussion will focus your thoughts in such a way as to make psychotherapy with your child more manageable.

There are different models of understanding difficulties and problems in a child. Typically, health professionals use the **medical model** owing to our country's historic esteem for physicians and the ever-present focus on (and advertising of) medications as remedies. The medical model almost exclusively looks at symptoms, diagnosis, and treatment concepts as a way of addressing problems. This book offers an alternative viewpoint—an extension of the **humanistic model**, or the **person-in-environment model**. The humanistic model is based on an understanding of a person's strengths, her psychological makeup, the positives and negatives of her social supports, the environment in which she lives, and her cultural background. The humanistic model values the role of diagnosis and the possible use of medication but sees this as a part of a **holistic perspective** of understanding and helping an individual.

Adding to this idea of different stances in treatment is an examination of perception. **Perception** is the act of using one's senses to know something. Logically, there are many ways to perceive something. Each person, based on his or her own unique qualities, experiences, and ideas, perceives things differently. Applied to your child and her or his difficulties, this idea of differences in perception becomes important. What you sense is a problem, others may not. You may have, with no input from others, decided to pursue psychotherapy for your child because of something you have noticed that concerns you. Alternatively, what others see as a problem, you may have yet to observe. You may be familiar and comfortable with a behavior that others find problematic. The way in which a child's issues are viewed and the way in which therapy is suggested as a course of action can affect the entire process—like the old adage about making a first impression.

The reality is that, although many people have some knowledge about how psychotherapy works for children, most do not know all of its nuances. Some people who suggest psychotherapy for children do so with good intentions, but with only a partial awareness of other issues that can cause problems with the referral. They may have

- an incomplete amount of information about a child's problems;
- a limited grasp of a child's overall needs;
- a personal agenda based the policies of the organization making the referral; or
- a medical model point of view regarding how treatment works and the ways that it can be useful.

For instance, sometimes individuals make a diagnosis without a full assessment of the child's strengths, his psychological makeup, the positives and negatives of his social supports, the environment in which he lives, and his cultural background. They may recommend **psychotropic medication** (psychiatric medicines that alter chemicals in the brain affecting mood and behavior) to address problematic issues even before other types of therapy have been attempted. Sometimes their own emotions—worries about or frustration with your child's behavior—are the basis for their suggestions. They may not have the skills or may not have taken the time to consider other ways to assist your child. Sometimes they confuse types of treatment. They may think that individual therapy and individual school counseling are the same. Similarly, they may think that group psychotherapy and socialization groups operate under the same set of rules. Sometimes, they may make a referral to treatment in such a way that a parent may feel that the "option" is actually mandatory—a disciplinary consequence for her child's problematic behaviors.

The following are some examples of the reasons for recommending child psychotherapy to caregivers. The list comprises most of the reasons for referrals. The entries all include the individual making the referral and the purpose for each referral:

- By you in connection with concerns you may have about your child
- By a school mental health professional who feels that this is not an issue that can be handled exclusively within the structure of school
- By a teacher because of a problem in the classroom that is causing disruption
- By a school official as a policy requirement connected to a behavior problem at school
- By a relative/friend after seeing you struggling with your child
- By a pediatrician as part of a doctor's appointment that includes reference to problems at home or at school
- By a healthcare professional in connection with a significant life-changing social, medical, and/or environmental situation
- By a psychologist as a part of psychological testing that has been administered to your child
- By a psychiatrist in conjunction with a psychotropic medication evaluation
- By a child welfare agency case worker as a legal requirement
- By a family court judge as a legal requirement.

Do you feel that your child's situation is on this list? Do you feel you have a choice? Does the suggestion of therapy feel helpful? Does it feel critical? Do you feel it is appropriate, or is it an over-reaction? Do you feel it should be part of a larger caregiving discussion? Do you feel the person is focusing on something other than the needs of your child?

The above list of referral scenarios ranges from ones that can leave us feeling very inspired and cared for to those that can leave us discouraged and saddened—from upset to worried to angry.

Take a moment to imagine your child going to psychotherapy. Try to see him entering the building or office with you, introducing yourselves to the therapist, separating from each other for the session, and the reuniting after the session. Envisioning your child in the psychotherapy process can generate a variety of new and unexpected feelings.

Some questions that go along with this experience are the following:

- Am I good enough?
- Can I do this?
- Why is this happening?
- How can I best help my child?
- What did I do wrong?
- Why do I feel so helpless?
- What will happen next?
- Will my child be okay?
- When is this going to be over?

All parents, with or without psychotherapy experience, have many of the same concerns, thoughts, and fears. It is important to realize that your child will be seeing the problems from his or her own viewpoint, not yours. We are making this point to emphasize the idea of maintaining a separation between your perceptions on what has brought you to this point and those of your child. Emotional distance can give you the clarity you need to see the situation with more accuracy.

There are two concepts that we feel are important to know at this moment. The first concept is **projection**. Projection is giving the ownership of feelings or ideas that you are having to someone else.

Frank and Henry's Battle at Bedtime

Frank struggles with putting his son, Henry, to bed every night. Each night, there is great tension leading up to bedtime. There are fears and negotiations that lead to anger, yelling, and a contentious "good night." Frank feels that Henry just will not go to bed. This is a story that we hear often. Missing from the telling is Frank's ideas about saying good-bye to Henry each night. Frank, in this story, has his own strong and difficult feelings about "letting go" of his son each night and he **projects** *them onto Henry. Unaware of this process, Frank has difficulty coping with his own feelings of anxiety and loneliness that he experiences, so unknowingly he passes them on to his child. In those moments, it is easier to be angry and frustrated about the behavior of his acting-out child than to feel his own anxiety of separation.*

The second concept is **displacement**. Displacement is transforming a feeling or idea about one thing into a feeling or idea about something else.

A Child Gets Lost

*A child goes missing in a store. When they are reunited, his mother screams at him for walking away. The child, feeling scared and humiliated, cries. Where is the expression of relief of a safe reunion of parent and child? What we see instead is the mother's expression of fear and anxiety about having lost a child **displaced** and transformed into the mother's anger at the behavior of the child. The parent yells because she cannot cope with just how scared she really was during those moments when her child was missing. In that moment, it is easier to be angry with a child than it is to feel the terror of having lost that child.*

We sometimes use both of these concepts when something we are coping with is too uncomfortable or stressful for us to manage. These are **defenses** or **defense mechanisms**, and most of the time people are unaware that they are using these defenses. What we mean by unaware is that these ways of helping ourselves are below the surface of our awareness. In these stressful moments, we do not know we are using them. Why are we not aware of our defenses? Simply put, they would not be effective if we were aware. Think of it this way. Would you ever find yourself thinking, "I am going to take this feeling that I cannot handle and give it to someone else?" That said, without being aware of it, this is exactly what we do sometimes. It protects us and helps us to balance our thoughts, and to remain in control by keeping feelings that are overwhelming at a distance (below the surface of our awareness). Usually our defenses help us cope; at times, though, they do not serve their purpose and can cause additional problems for us.

We bring up the concepts of **projection** and **displacement** in the introduction of this book to assist parents. We hope that being aware of the possibility that parents may experience strong feelings, worries, and ideas—and that these may trigger their own defense mechanisms—will help parents to acknowledge and think about the feelings, instead of projecting or displacing them. A more self-aware parent is a stronger and more effective parent.

Our children are separate people, but they are also a part of us. We give birth to them, adopt them, or accept them into our homes. We choose to care for them and raise them. They may look like us, act like us, and often respond to things the way we do. In short, they remind us of little versions of us. On a day-to-day basis, we are not always aware of this connection and extension, but it is always present. This connection to our children is most noticeable to us in times of tension and stress—when they have problems, we can feel these problems as our own.

During a moment of particular tension, you may have used the phrase "my child knows how to push my buttons." These "buttons" are actually connections to your memories of difficult situations.

Our children can do things and say things that create links to our past, and what comes through the connections are often deep feelings that are difficult to describe in words. Sometimes we know what they are all about, and sometimes they are confusing and unexpected. These feelings often affect our reactions and behaviors. As we all know, someone can press our buttons at any time. When your children are struggling with a big problem or difficulty, you can be certain that one of those times is on the horizon, and the bigger the problem, often the bigger the button.

We are forecasting that you, in all likelihood, will experience a version of these intense reactions. This is where courage comes into play. It is important for us to acknowledge that it requires courage to choose psychotherapy for our children. To *knowingly* and *willingly* engage in a process in which our buttons will be pushed requires making a choice to be challenged in personal ways that we cannot anticipate. Preparing you for this will not stop it from being taxing, but it can alter and ease its impact on you.

It is a reality that we are sometimes hesitant to address emotional or psychological problems in our children. We may believe that it reflects on us as parents. We may feel doubt, guilt, regret, and responsibility. We realize that these disapproving thoughts can easily lead to a certain level of self-criticism. We would ask you to recognize that this is how all parents feel at times like these. These typical reactions are the most normal ones because they represent the frustrating and painful truth that caregivers cannot prevent every bad thing that happens to their child—that there is vulnerability in being a parent.

Providing parents with knowledge undermines this vulnerability. We have found that the actual steps that parents take in obtaining psychotherapy for their children are often made more complicated simply because the steps are unknown and unpredictable. Obtaining explicit concrete information gives you, as the parent, more control, greater input, and an increased ability to participate. This is common sense. It is why we go on the Internet to get information about illnesses. We want to know what is happening; it helps manage our worry and concern. It also helps us feel less alone. In this book, we go through every step, from choosing a therapist to separating from psychotherapy, so that you feel engaged and in charge of your child's psychotherapy throughout.

With this knowledge of the process comes your responsibility to use this information to optimize and improve the overall experience. There will be the understanding that the therapist cannot "solve" your child's issues alone but that you, as the most important person in your child's life, will become partners with the therapist. Your child's therapist will need you; you are the expert on your child, although you may not feel that way to start. The therapist may be an expert on child development, child thought processes, and engaging children in communicating their thoughts and feelings, but child psychotherapy needs a team approach—child, parent, and therapist—to be most successful.

This book will cover all three phases of psychotherapy: the engagement phase, the work (or middle) phase, and the termination phase. In the engagement phase, or at the start of psychotherapy, your child, you, and the therapist will begin to build a therapeutic relationship. You and your child will begin to figure out how to work with this therapist, how to trust this unknown person, how to talk to and interact with him or her, and how to begin to understand the issues that are facing you and your child. Depending on each child and parent and their ideas about building trust, sharing, and communicating, this phase can last a short period of time (several sessions) or much longer (months). One cannot rush this phase because all the work and changes that can happen in psychotherapy are dependent on you and your child feeling comfortable enough to open up with the therapist.

The middle phase is where much of the "work" of psychotherapy takes place. With the therapist's assistance and guidance, your child and you will face, challenge, and attempt to address the issues that required psychotherapy. The precise workings of the middle phase will depend on your child's age and developmental stage, how your child feels most comfortable communicating, what the specific issues are that he or she is struggling with, and the style of your child's therapist. These same criteria form the basis for the extent of your participation.

The termination phase, or ending phase, is where you, your child, and the therapist say goodbye. There is a review of the work and of the progress. The progress and skills learned in psychotherapy are called **therapeutic gains**. Your child takes what he or she has learned in psychotherapy as his or her own.

He or she has experimented with therapeutic gains all during the work phase (between weekly sessions and over vacations, etc.). With the end of psychotherapy, the experimenting ends and the gains take on authenticity. It is similar to driving for the first time, or walking to school for the first time, or taking a bus for the first time. We believe we have the skills, but are never completely certain until we use them independently. Without an ending, neither you nor your child would have confidence that things have truly changed, improved, or stabilized.

The end of psychotherapy is not the end of the psychotherapy's impact on your child, you, or your family. In fact, the end is the beginning of a new chapter. You may be surprised that we talk about endings at the beginning of this book. There are many different models of child psychotherapy, needing different time frames and time commitments, but what they all have in common is that there is an ending. Endings are an important part of the psychotherapy—maybe the most important part. They need planning and scheduling to make sure there is enough time to help your child retain the benefits of his or her psychotherapy experience. Think about this—a bad ending can shape the way that we remember a relationship forever.

We want you to enter this process of psychotherapy with your eyes open. We feel that being prepared gives you, your child, and your family the best chance for success. Understanding how psychotherapy works will help you feel more in charge of what you are doing. We want to acknowledge that after using this book, you may decide that psychotherapy is not for your child, and we hope that you find some relief for whatever caused you to seek help in the first place. Sometimes a parent's knowledge, combined with the basic resilience of a child, is enough to help move everyone forward in a positive way.

Our job as parents is to take care of our children. In many ways, seeking psychotherapy for your child is a loving and caring action to take if you believe your child is suffering. Children suffer when they cannot concentrate in school, are subject to consequences because they have trouble following the rules, are the center of tension or stress in their families, or are experiencing feelings they cannot put into words but only into behaviors that are unhealthy or dangerous. Working toward obtaining help for a struggling child can only be an act of love and caring, not an admission of failure in our role as parents.

When a child needs any form of medical treatment, the parents need to be aware of any changes in their child's condition, to make sure their child is taking the prescribed medicine, to follow the doctor's instructions and suggestions, and to develop a structure to ensure that their child makes all the doctor's appointments.

Similarly, when your child is struggling emotionally and needs psychotherapy, parents have the same roles. Addressing a child's needs in times of sickness or distress sometimes requires expertise. It is an act of good parenting to find outside help for our children if these situations occur.

CHAPTER 1

A Holistic Perspective of Child Psychotherapy

Making the best therapy decisions for your child (which psychotherapist, type of therapy, and focus of treatment) is as important as making the choice for your child to enter therapy in the first place. It is by no means an exact science, and it can include many factors. By many factors, we mean that there are many key elements to a successful therapy. This way of thinking about therapy is a holistic perspective. We like it because it spreads the responsibility for a successful outcome over a wide range of elements. In addition, looking at a problem from many different angles often gives us a clearer picture of what is happening. It is similar to seeing an image that has height, depth, weight, width, and length—as opposed to a flat, two-dimensional picture.

WHAT IS A CHILD? WHO IS MY CHILD?

The first and most important factor is your child. Knowing who your child is happens to be an essential component to identifying the "right" therapist, creating the appropriate treatment plan, and moving through the therapy process successfully. To this end, we think it is helpful to view your child as an exquisite yet complex combination of an intellect, a mind, a body, and a personality, all working together and contributing to how he or she functions. This view of your child is a multidimensional one.

We define these aspects or dimensions of your child as the following:

1. A child's mind—memories, feelings, dreams, fears, thoughts, and ideas;
2. A child's intelligence—judgment, decision-making, opinions, beliefs, and identification of choices;
3. A child's body—genetics, physical features, organ functioning, and conditions; and
4. A child's personality—temperament, self-awareness, ways of relating, and abilities to connect with others.

Some parents will find it helpful to be able to describe their thought processes about what is happening with their children in this multidimensional way. It may help parents understand why it is difficult to "solve" their child's issues on their own. Perhaps the actual complexity may relieve some of the frustration and guilt about their children's issues. Changes can only happen gradually—not magically overnight.

All of these aspects work together (or do not) within your child, affecting his or her ability to learn, adapt, and progress to independent adulthood. Although we will go into more depth regarding many of these aspects of your child later in the book, we think it is important at this point, early in the process, to acknowledge that something this complicated very well may take more than one expert to help navigate.

Max Blames Himself

Max, the parent of a Caleb, a young boy with severe behavioral issues at home, blamed himself on a regular basis for his son's struggles. Max worked tirelessly on altering his interactions with Caleb and changing their relationship for the better. Max learned how to view his son and his issues holistically:

1. *His son had very intense and at times highly emotional thoughts and feelings.*
2. *His son got along well with others and had many friends.*
3. *His son's intellect was developing appropriately.*
4. *His son was physically healthy.*

Taking into consideration all of these aspects, Max concluded that, overall, Caleb was functioning at a normal level. Because he was able to identify the many aspects of his son that were functioning "normally," Max was able to concentrate on the one area that seemed to be problematic: his son's intensity. It felt less overwhelming. Max acknowledged of all the thriving parts of his son, and his acknowledgment diluted the belief that he had "failed" his son.

WHAT IS A PSYCHOTHERAPIST?

Next, let us ask the question, What is a psychotherapist? You may already have a notion of what this word means, but this idea may be affected by television, movies, or novels and may not be quite accurate.

- *Psychotherapist* or *therapist* is a general term for a person practicing the "art" of helping and healing through a relationship with an individual seeking assistance (a client, a patient, or a consumer). A psychotherapist helps by listening and by providing empathy, problem-solving skills, affirmation, reality testing, witnessing, pacing, and interpretation. During the course of this book, we will examine the use of many of these elements. It is these elements, as well as others, that together create the process of psychotherapy (a mental health service).
- Each state has a licensing process for people permitted to provide mental health services within that state. The titles of the licensed mental health professionals vary by state and include, but are not limited to, marriage and family therapist, mental health counselor, psychoanalyst, psychiatric nurse, psychologist, and social worker. Professional membership organizations maintain membership listings that indicate the states and cities where their members work. We provide you with contact information for mental health resources in each state (see Appendix C).
- A psychotherapist or therapist is someone to whom you are going to pay a fee to help you, your child, and your family. Payment for services is another important component affecting the therapy, as it creates a consumer-provider type of interaction that sets it apart from getting advice from your friends and family.
- A psychotherapist can have different educational backgrounds in addition to the state licensure. He or she may often have additional postgraduate training in specialized areas of focus or specific theoretical models in the field of psychotherapy. These can include psychodynamic psychotherapy, psychoanalysis, behavior modification, play therapy, family therapy, hypnosis,

cognitive restructuring, and so on. As there are many different professional groups that practice psychotherapy, our book will simply define this person as the *therapist* as the clearest and least cumbersome way of talking about a psychotherapist. It is important that as you select a therapist and begin a working relationship, you ask about and understand the therapist's treatment or therapeutic philosophy.

- A therapist is a trained objective person who does not have a prior personal relationship with you or a member of your family. Since you will be talking about your child's problems, issues, struggles, and your concerns, and at times, about yourself, you need someone who is *objective* and can clearly assess the issues and develop a treatment plan. You will find that sharing personal information and feelings with a therapist feels very different from talking to a relative, friend, or coworker.

- A therapist is someone you will be seeing and spending time with each week in his or her office. Ironically, you may even see this person more often than you see friends or extended family. This relationship can become close and comforting when working well.

- A therapist is someone who is going to ask you and your child to consider looking at your family's situation differently. Your child's therapist will have his or her own view of the world, of child development, and of how to work with children, and will have opinions, viewpoints, and feelings. It is your therapist's job to include you in the exploration of new perspectives and new ideas concerning your child.

- Although this may seem obvious, a therapist is someone who has a gender. It is an important aspect of who your child's therapist is. Gender can have an effect on the relationships created in the therapy. There are several factors to consider:
  1. The gender of your child;
  2. Your child's developmental stage at the point you are considering therapy;
  3. The makeup and dynamics of your family system in terms of gender;
  4. If a specific parent is having an issue with the child, the gender of that parent; and
  5. The temperament or personality of the child.

You may have heard that boys should see male therapists and girls should see female therapists (especially during adolescence). This idea can be true because some children identify with adults of their own gender at certain ages and may feel that someone of the same gender will understand them better. That said, we would like you to consider that there are many gender-related factors that go into how a child will connect to a therapist. It is difficult to tell prior to meeting someone how your child will feel about the gender of a therapist. Having different options is always preferred.

This may be a good opportunity to discuss an important relationship aspect of therapy called **transference**. Transference has the word *transfer* as its root. Many psychotherapists believe that transference occurs as the patient (in this case your child) projects or transfers his or her feelings, thoughts, wishes, dreams, fears, and experiences with others onto the therapist. Many therapists consider this to be a natural and typical human aspect of therapy relationships and some would say of relationships in general. The gender of the therapist may seem important at first, but through transference, your child will project onto his or her therapist those characteristics that both help and thwart the therapy. Thus, transference can render the therapist's gender as unimportant.

The therapist is not a replacement for a missing parent or gender presence in your child's life. Nor is a therapist of a specific gender an "antidote" to negative experiences with adults of the same gender. Believing that your child may need to see a therapist because she or he is missing the influence of a person of a specific gender creates an expectation for both you and your child that no therapist could ever meet. Rather than concentrating on the therapist's gender and appearance, we prefer that you and your child focus on the therapist's manner, tone of voice, posture, and eye contact. These issues can reflect the therapist's personality. You can help your child to think about how the therapist's personality matches with her or his own.

- A therapist is someone who has a cultural and ethnic background. Not all communities have access to therapists of every cultural or ethnic group. Your choices may be limited in this regard, and once again, the therapist's personality is most likely the most important factor to consider. Nonetheless, similar to gender, cultural and ethnic difference or similarities play a role in the development of a therapeutic relationship. As we all have some biases based on our own experiences, we may feel that our children would prefer, or feel more comfortable with, a therapist who they feel is similar to them. This may be true, and it may not be. The developmental stage of your child will affect how he or she views these qualities of the therapist. Younger children do not perceive or use differences and similarities as adults typically do. Adolescents tend to need to have some connection to a person in order to feel comfortable. We feel that all aspects of your child's therapist will be important to discuss with your child.

Jane and Steve Look for a Therapist

Jane and Steve were looking for a therapist for their 7-year-old son, Louis. At the suggestion of his teacher, they had met with several highly recommended therapists and settled on one. The therapist they chose was the most experienced of all their referrals. He was a psychologist in private practice. It took two weeks for Jane and Steve to set up a session for Louis because their schedules were complicated and the therapist's office was quite a distance from their home. After meeting with the child and the parents, the therapist called the parents and stated that he did not feel that he was the appropriate therapist to do the work that their child would need for a successful therapy experience. He stated that, in terms of his available time, the coordination with school personnel and the other needs Louis might have during therapy were beyond his ability to provide at that time. The parents were understandably upset and angry. They felt frustrated that the therapist they had selected had said "no" to them. However, they also felt some relief because they had concerns that the therapist was older than they thought would be appropriate for their son. It was also logistically difficult to get to the therapist's office. They felt worried about the high fee arrangement and that a long-term therapy would be challenging to manage financially. They realized that they were both still struggling to understand Louis's exact needs and what the best way to help him would be. As a way of getting started, slowly, they contacted a mental health clinic close to their home to discuss options.

We share this case example to illustrate just some of the issues that make child therapy so complex and to point out that thinking about the *why*, the *who*, the *when*, and the *where* of therapy for our children is a good place to start.

A therapist could decide not to work with a child for practical, ethical, or professional reasons. The practical reasons can include not having a mutually convenient time to work together, or that your child's school is located too far from the therapist's office to enable visits there. Ethical issues concern therapists who have had a prior personal relationship with one of your relatives or friends. Professional reasons can be that your child needs a different kind of treatment than the therapist can provide.

Therapy for Louis had yet to begin, and his parents were grappling with many issues having to do with the therapeutic process. It is one thing to make the difficult decision to enter into psychotherapy when someone is an adult and is making the choice for him- or herself, factoring in money, timing, and his or her feelings about the therapist. It is a more complex choice to decide to enter one's child into psychotherapy and juggle these same issues.

Here are some helpful pointers:

- Finding a therapist for your child requires that you find a person who makes you comfortable. "Being comfortable" means someone who helps put you at ease, making it easier for you to begin to share personal feelings and private information about your family. Logistics (scheduling, travel, timing, etc.) can affect comfort.
- Trust of a therapist, for you and your child, is different from comfort. It grows over time. The development of trust is often a slow and gradual process with "ups and downs." The goal is that you feel understood, heard, listened to, not rushed, and supported. Remember, your child's therapist is your partner in working together to help your child.
- Consider accepting three referrals to three different therapists. We believe that having and making choices increases your sense of control over the process.
- Even if you interview the first therapist on your list and decide that this is the one, it is better to compare that person to at least one other therapist. Contrasting therapists during the selection period helps you to uncover more of your feelings of why you are comfortable with one rather than another.

CHAPTER SUMMARY

CHAPTER 1: A HOLISTIC PERSPECTIVE OF
CHILD PSYCHOTHERAPY

We think it is helpful to view your child as an exquisite yet complex combination of an intellect, a mind, a body, and a personality, all working together and contributing to how he or she functions. All of these aspects can work together or not within your child, affecting his or her ability to learn, adapt, and progress to independent adulthood:

- A child's mind—memories, feelings, dreams, fears, thoughts, and ideas;
- A child's intelligence—judgment, decision-making, opinions, beliefs, and identification of choices;
- A child's body—genetics, physical features, organ functioning, and conditions;
- A child's personality—temperament, self-awareness, ways of relating, and abilities to connect with others.

We believe that successful child psychotherapy requires a holistic approach that includes the many important players in your child's life. This especially includes you as the parent. In addition to you, other individuals also contribute to helping your child with his or her problems and issues.

A psychotherapist or therapist practices the "art" of helping and healing.

It is the therapist's desire to help that is the most essential aspect of the therapeutic relationship between your child, you, and the therapist.

Several factors can have an effect on the relationship:

1. The gender of your child;
2. Your child's developmental stage at the point you are considering therapy;
3. The makeup and dynamics of your family system in terms of gender;
4. If a specific parent is having an issue with the child, the gender of that parent;
5. The temperament or personality of the child;
6. The sustainability of managing the fee for the therapy.

CHAPTER 2

Systems-Based Approach to Child Psychotherapy

Working Together

A SYSTEMS-BASED APPROACH

In trying to think of a very general way to help parents understand the way that child therapy works and how the individuals involved in a child's therapy are organized, we use a systems perspective.

A systems-based approach helps us diminish the myth that psychotherapy for a child is a closed and exclusive relationship between the therapist and the child. We believe that successful child psychotherapy requires a holistic perspective that includes the many important players in your child's life. This especially includes you as the parent. In addition to you, other individuals also contribute to helping your child with his or her problems and issues.

Let us begin with a few basic definitions and examples. A **system** is an interrelated group of parts that work together to accomplish a task. For example, an engine is a system made up of machinery parts (hoses, gears, nuts, bolts, gasoline, water, etc.) that all work together to make a car move. We can look at each of these parts to assess how they are working, and if they need to be repaired, replaced, or augmented. The fact that few of us know exactly about all the parts of the car—what their function is, how to measure their functioning, and how to address problems when we encounter them—feels natural and normal. We would take the car to the garage and have an expert on that system, a mechanic, examine the car.

Systems can also be groups of people, like a church or a football team or a family. Your family system is a very important part of your child's therapy. Regardless of the makeup of your family, however it looks, the family system is always a critical part of the treatment of children.

This book will focus on three systems—your child, your family, and the group of people involved in your child's care, which we call the **treatment team.** If we can agree that children are more complex systems than cars, then it follows that a complicated and nuanced system like a child might have many "mechanics," all with a different understanding and knowledge of each of the many aspects of this vast system. You may have already discussed the issues that your child is having with family, friends, doctors, teachers, and so on. If you have, then what follows here will feel comfortable to you and will encourage you to continue in an organized and thoughtful fashion involving experts in your child's treatment. If you have not, we think that having a holistic strategy for your child's care that includes the people who have professional contact with your child is important, and this book will help you organize your thoughts to that end.

It is the nature of a system of people that there is often a hierarchy among those individuals. The hierarchy is determined by the specific role that each individual within the system has been designated. Armies have generals, lieutenants, and privates. Schools have principals, directors, teachers, and students. Hospitals have administrators, supervisors, and line staff. Teams have coaches, captains, and players. This hierarchy and the roles that are established for each of the individuals serve the important and necessary purpose of maintaining an organized process for decision-making, production, and execution. Without well-defined roles and a clear hierarchy, there is tendency toward disorganization. This confusion can slow or even derail the process of accomplishing the goals that we create (in this case, to help your child).

So let us begin by naming and defining your child's treatment team and giving roles to each of them. Then, we will look at their interconnectedness and the hierarchy necessary to make the treatment system work efficiently.

This is a comprehensive list of individuals who may have some impact on your child's treatment system. It is important for planning purposes that you at least consider and define the role of each individual, even if his or her role may be minimal.

1. *Patient, client, or consumer.* These are different terms that institutions and therapists use to describe the person or people who are the focus of therapy. In this book, our focus is on individual therapy. That said, a family or a couple might be the focus of therapy and, in that case, are labeled in the same fashion. A child can be a patient, or a family can be the patient.

   Typically, a medical-based setting will use the word "patient." Psychologists and psychiatrists use this term. Professionals who work in mental health institutes and clinics whose primary stance toward a patient is an analytic one will also use the term "patient." It stems from the idea that these institutions use a **medical model** of helping a person. Simply put, this is a view of therapy that includes an examination, diagnosis, and treatment, leading to an end of symptoms (a cure). The medical model points to idea that the knowledge for helping an individual is proprietary and resides with the "expert" helper. You go to a doctor because he or she knows how to help and will give you the material necessary for a change in symptoms.

   A social work–based setting will use the word "client." Social work was created as a community-based institution to help the poor and mentally ill, in which the workers themselves were often part of the communities. Social workers saw that many factors could contribute to a person's symptoms. Living in the communities created a foundation of **mutuality**—connection with shared responsibility—between the helper and the helped that has shaped social work. The word "client" speaks to the idea that everyone is working together, none more important or critical to the process of change than anyone else.

   The term "consumer" or "customer" is a relatively recent creation. This stems from the idea of **self-determination**—that individuals have power, free will, and the right to make their own decisions about their lives. Individuals who use mental health services are purchasing those services, as they would any type of service. In this model, the service provider, the mental health professional, has certain service-related "obligations" to the person seeking help. It's like a contract between the helper and the person being helped. It focuses on creating a sense of control and empowerment in those looking for mental health intervention.

We also want to mention here (we will talk about this more in Chapter 11 in the section entitled "Types of Contact") that during your child's treatment you may, at times, feel that you are being provided with information, support, and comfort that creates the feeling that you, yourself, are in therapy with this therapist. This is normal. We would like you to view this feeling in a positive light. The more you feel helped as a parent, the more you will be able to assist your child.

2. *Primary caregiver.* In the eyes of government, this is an adult-age person (or persons) who has custody of a child. He or she provides care for the child and has specific decision-making authority in the child's life. This is a formal definition. The two categories of custody are legal and physical. Legal custody centers on healthcare and overall welfare, and physical custody refers primarily to living arrangement. We are making a point to be very formal in our definition of primary caregiver because your family may have many people who care for your child during the day. All of these individuals are caregivers and will have some level of decision-making authority with your child at different times. Being the primary caregiver makes you the focus of your child's therapy.

3. *Other caregivers.* Individuals who have various levels of caregiving responsibility for your child.

   a. Kinship parent: A biological relative who has the same relationship structure to the child as a foster parent.

   b. Non-custodial parent: A biological parent who does not have primary physical or legal custody of his or her biological child by court order. (The level of connection and actual responsibility vary based on a variety of factors, including visitation arrangements, supervised or unsupervised).

   c. Foster parent: A parent who is the caretaking representative of an agency (a foster agency, child protective service agency, the court system). These individuals have day-to-day decision-making responsibilities for the child, but physical (medical, mental health) and legal decision-making remain with the agency.

   d. Relative: An individual who is biologically related to the child and is given various responsibilities with regard to the child by the primary caregiver.*

e. Babysitter/Nanny: A person with various responsibilities for the child selected by the primary caregiver.*

f. Family friend: A non-biologically related individual with various responsibilities for the child, as determined by the primary caregiver.*

* For these individuals, we suggest that you inform your child's therapist about the scope of the relationship if it is significant. Also, if any of these individuals are going to have contact with the therapist, it will be important to structure the contact. How much information does this person have about the treatment? What do you feel comfortable with this person knowing? How does your child feel about this person having contact with the therapist? Does information pass from therapist to parent through this person?

Talking to Paul's Babysitter

Paul, a pre-teen, was escorted to treatment by his "nanny." Paul had difficulty managing his anger, was often reluctant to end the session, and occasionally needed assistance to leave when it was over. During these times, the therapist (with permission from Paul's parent) discussed with the nanny a variety of relaxation techniques to assist Paul in feeling more in control so that he could go home safely. Over time, and as the nanny felt more and more a part of the treatment team, the nanny began to share her thoughts (and those of Paul's parents) directly with the therapist, either at the beginning of the session or at the end. Paul expressed frustration with this and felt "ganged-up" on. The therapist needed to restructure the way information was passed around the treatment team.

---

4. *Psychotherapist.* She or he is the individual whom you have selected. We have and will be discussing different aspects of your child's therapist throughout this book.

If your child takes psychotropic medication, your child's psychiatrist is the team member with the most information and experience regarding everything about the child's medication (the purpose, the type, the dosage, the duration, the frequency, and the side effects). This is not to say that other individuals on your child's treatment team will not have professional input and opinions regarding the choices about medication. General practitioners and therapists typically have had some experience with psychotropic medication and can give you their own feedback.

We encourage the professionals on your child's treatment team to speak to one another, and we recommend that you encourage them to do so. We feel that this process enhances treatment for several reasons.

a. It communicates a level of containment to your child that we see as beneficial. It says to your child that all the people that she or he knows are involved in her or his "care"—physical, emotional, academic, social, and legal—all know each other and talk to each other.

b. It decreases any sort of potential misunderstanding among team members.

c. It decreases the chance for a dynamic that is called **splitting**. You may call this playing one person off another. This can occur if a child provides one person on the team one piece of information and another person on the team a different piece of information, or if a child withholds a piece of information from one team member. It is a way that a child maintains a sense of control over the process of therapy and can create miscommunication and strain on the team.

d. It generates ideas that can be very helpful to the treatment process. As each of the individuals comes from a different discipline, and sees the child at different times, in different contexts, and with different purposes, speaking can create new ways of understanding the child.

5. *Medical professional.* We have used a generic description for this team member because your child may be involved with a variety of doctors. These individuals are important because your child's physical being is a key component to the child's overall emotional well-being. Typically, this person is your child's pediatrician, but other doctors may be seeing your child. Please do not leave any specialists off this list. Often your child's therapist will want to have some contact with your child's general practitioner if your child has a medical issue of note or a medical issue that can affect your child's functioning in some way.

6. *School mental health professional.* This is an individual with training (see Chapter 3) employed by the school to provide a variety of mental health services. It can be a counselor, a social worker, or a psychologist. While these individuals are employed by the school to provide mental health services to the students and the caregivers of students, we want to emphasize that they are school employees. Why is this important? We often hear from parents that their child is seeing a social worker at school or

that they attend a counseling group at school. We applaud these interventions because they are often very important and helpful. That said, from a systems perspective, the primary client of a school mental health professional is the school itself. These individuals wear multiple hats—they care for the integrity of the school, the student body as a whole, and each individual student. There are motivations other than the exclusive care for *your* child, and so conflicts of interest may develop (i.e., pressure from administration, other parents, etc.). That is not to say that these people will not be helpful to your child, only that we ask that you look critically at the scope of the assistance that your child needs and that school mental health professionals can realistically provide. The school mental health professional will be doing the same, which is why, if he or she feels that "your child needs something more," he or she may make a referral to an outside therapist.

7. *Teacher.* This individual is the professional educator tasked with teaching your child. In order to train new teachers, education programs typically include some foundational courses on psychology, human development, and learning. Teachers are not mental health professionals, and we encourage you not to see them in this way. Some will have taken a greater personal interest in the psychology of children than other course work. You may ask them about how your child is doing emotionally or socially, and they will give you answers that are based on their own understanding of how the psychology of your child is being exhibited in the classroom. We recommend that you view this input within the context of what the teacher's formal role is with your child. In addition, teachers are human beings with feelings and, unlike the mental health professional, are not specifically trained to be self-aware (although some are). This can shape the responses you receive with regard to your child. We also would like to note that teachers (and other school professionals like coaches, guidance counselors, previous teachers) also take on a more caregiver-like relationship with your child.

Anxious LaShawn and Her Teachers

LaShawn was a 5-year-old girl brought to treatment by her parents because of the problems she was having in school. She was getting upset, fighting, arguing, and generally having difficulties relating to most of the people at school, classmates and teachers alike. The feedback from the teachers was that LaShawn was disruptive, defiant, and probably not suited for their classroom. Their solution was to alter the rules for LaShawn, allowing her the space to feel more control and hopefully to reduce the frequency of her outbursts. This dynamic went on for some time, with little positive effect, as the teachers altered more and more rules for LaShawn. The unintentional message was "we cannot handle you," or worse, "we do not want to handle you." The misstep was unfortunate, but understandable. In attempting to manage a large class, the teachers and school officials responded to LaShawn by addressing only her problematic behavior. When a therapist began working with the family, the teachers, and the school mental health professionals, the discussion changed to center on understanding LaShawn's issues from a psychology and developmental perspective, that the more control she gained over the environment, in actuality, the more anxious she became because she felt less contained by that environment. Rules were re-established and new expectations discussed with LaShawn; she began to feel better, and her behavior changed.

---

8. *Sibling.* We want to include biological siblings, identical twins, fraternal twins, half-siblings (having one parent in common), step-siblings (having neither parent in common and being connected by some legal form, like marriage), or foster siblings (having a foster parent in common and no genetic connection) in our description. It is often unclear how a child sees his or her sibling and how to use the relationship with him or her. Are they close or distant, competitive or supportive? We want you to think about and shape what your child's sibling(s) know about the treatment. This includes your child's input, depending on his or her age. Some children will feel strongly about this one way or another. They may not want anyone to know—siblings or friends. If this is your child, you can call this a doctor's appointment or simply an appointment.

Issues of Disclosure

Disclosure is the sharing of what people might consider private or confidential information. As the parent, you may believe that your child's therapy is supposed to be private.

For some children, telling people will be important. We think it is important that you have a developmentally thoughtful conversation with your child about who can know, who should know, and what are some of the outcomes of telling people.

Preschool children typically do not have reactions to knowing that a friend or sibling is in therapy. They find it curious. They may ask questions in an attempt to understand, but seldom will they make a negative statement. "What do you talk about?" "What's a therapist?" The corollary to this is if they have an older sibling in treatment. Or possibly, they may have a parent who has been in treatment.

Elementary-age children may have reactions, but these reactions will typically be self-referential. They may respond by stating something they have heard, positive or negative. "My friend told me that only crazy people go to therapy." This is less a statement about your child and more a response based on the developmental need of children at this age to know things and feel a sense of control over their environment.

Adolescents can experience a sense of stigma when they feel different from their peers. Their reactions to finding out that their friend is in therapy can prompt a level of worry and concern about themselves that will shape their response. The nature of the response depends on the specific person and his or her relationship to your child. They could withdraw from your child—"What's wrong with you?"—creating distance as a way to feel more secure. They could become hostile toward your child—"You are crazy"—spreading rumors, saying or doing harmful things, as a way of feeling stronger and counteracting their own feelings of anxiety. They could become supportive of your child—"Are you okay?" as they identify with your child and gain a feeling of security by being closer.

One can use this understanding of responses for relative and friends alike. Close family relationships (siblings, aunts, uncles, cousins) could make disclosing easier for your teenager, but we recommend that you do not assume this and ask your teenager who, if anyone, he or she would like to tell.

9. *Law guardian.* This individual is a child's chosen legal decision-maker in any family court proceedings. Law guardians are hired by a family, can be a family friend, or can be appointed by the court. This is not the child's lawyer. He or she can be involved in all aspects of a child's life while a family is in family court. Typically, the law guardian is needed if the family system has broken down to the extent that the decision-making process has been compromised. For our purposes, the law guardian can be involved in carrying out a court directive to begin mental health treatment for a child, can

direct the choice of a mental health professional for a child, and can follow up on the progress. The law guardian would then receive periodic reports from a child's therapist. Like any professional who works with children, the law guardian will most likely have a working knowledge of the mental health issues facing your child. We recommend that you provide as much information as possible regarding any ongoing treatment to the law guardian and press for his or her contact with other members of the care team.

When we mentioned earlier a compromised decision-making process, we were referring to any situation that would bring parents and their children to family court. We are not making any distinction as to the reasons. We believe significant differences in opinion, whatever they may be, make it complicated for agreement or compromise. It is with this in mind that we are acknowledging that choosing a therapist for your child under these circumstances may not progress as we will describe in Chapters 3 and 4. That said, the principles are the same, and we hope that for this purpose you will set aside differences and think about the process of choosing the right therapist for your child. If you cannot, the court will instruct the law guardian do so without your input. We can assure you that having your involvement from the beginning is better for you and your child.

COORDINATION OF THE TREATMENT TEAM: A CONSUMER APPROACH

So who coordinates this group of people—this treatment team? By coordinate we mean the following:

1. Facilitates communication—ensures that the individuals are talking to each other and passing important information to one another. In some cases, the coordinator will need to pass the information from one individual to another, functioning as a liaison.
2. Establishes goals—ensures that the individuals have created realistic goals that address the issues and that there is some consensus on these goals.
3. Maintains focus on goals—ensures that the individuals are staying focused on the treatment goals, are achieving goals, and are revising goals as needed.
4. Updates composition of treatment team—ensures that the individuals who make up the treatment team are the appropriate people in order to reach goals and optimize communication.

Think of this system of individuals as a wheel—with spokes coming out from a central hub. Each individual involved in the treatment is a spoke, and the person who coordinates the treatment is the hub.

We wrote this book to create the opportunity for you to function as the hub—having the information, the knowledge, and the wherewithal to organize your child's treatment. That said, we understand that not all parents will feel that they are equipped to manage this function and that is fine, especially if they have no previous experience in treatment. This may change over time. You may begin by relying on a treatment team member to help you make organizational decisions as you become more familiar and comfortable with what is happening. As therapy continues, you may feel more competent and knowledgeable and may want to coordinate the therapy yourself.

We would like to stress that having information about what is happening with your child, why it is happening, and what your options are for your child is really the most critical point of this discussion. We want you to *know* what is going on and be able to discuss it with your child if you feel it is important or if your child chooses to talk to you about it.

CHAPTER SUMMARY

CHAPTER 2: SYSTEMS-BASED APPROACH TO CHILD
PSYCHOTHERAPY: WORKING TOGETHER

We believe that successful child psychotherapy requires a holistic approach that includes the many important players in your child's life. This especially includes you as the parent. In addition to you, other individuals also contribute to helping your child with his or her problems and issues.

We call this group the treatment team, and it can include any of the following individuals:

- Primary caregiver
- Additional caregivers
- Psychotherapist
- Psychiatrist
- Medical professionals
- Allied health professionals
- School-based mental health professionals
- Teachers

- Siblings
- Law guardians.

Think of this system of individuals as a wheel—with spokes coming out from a central hub. Each individual involved in the treatment is a spoke, and the person who coordinates the treatment is the hub. It can be you or someone you designate to coordinate the treatment. The coordinating functions are as follows:

- Facilitates communication—ensures that the individuals are talking to each other and passing important information to one another. In some cases the coordinator will need to pass the information from one individual to another, functioning as a liaison.
- Establishes goals—ensures that the individuals have created realistic goals that address the issues and that there is some consensus on these goals.
- Maintains focus on goals—ensures that the individuals are staying focused on the treatment goals, are achieving goals, and are revising goals as needed.
- Updates composition of treatment team—ensures that the individuals who make up the treatment team are the appropriate people in order to reach goals and optimize communication.

Seeking Out a Child Psychotherapist

REFERRAL SOURCES

Therapists become somewhat known entities if you have received the referral from a personal or professional contact—someone has worked with this person and can vouch for him or her. As we said before, choosing a therapist is a highly personal process, so even if you receive a personal or professional referral from someone, you will have to meet this person to see if you can work with him or her. You will be able to find referrals through many sources.

- *Personal referral.* This is a recommendation from someone you know. Perhaps this person's child is in therapy or knows of the therapist in some professional context.
- *Professional referral.* This is a recommendation from your pediatrician, clergy, or staff from your local hospital or school personnel.
- 1-800-LifeNet is a toll-free crisis telephone line that helps find referrals based on your stated issue and your local address. You would simply call this number and a customer service agent will ask you for your local address and your stated issue and will provide you with local agencies that can help you.
- *Community mental health clinics.* The names of these community mental health clinics or centers are available by searching the Internet or calling your state's office of mental health, bureau of behavioral health, or department of health and human services. We have compiled a list of contact

information (see Appendix C). The Substance Abuse and Mental Health Services Administration (SAMSHA) has service locator capabilities. In addition, hospitals with child psychiatry programs often have their own outpatient clinic programs. Because the clinic is located in a hospital, it is not technically a community mental health clinic, but in most states, the licensure and certification are the same.

- *Psychotherapy training programs.* Many cities have state approved and licensed postgraduate training programs to teach therapists the art of psychotherapy. These agencies provide both therapists in training and full-time therapists to individuals seeking psychotherapy. Again, we suggest that you contact your state's office of mental health, bureau of behavioral health, or department of health and human services to find this information.
- *Mental health professional Internet-based locators.* Websites such as *www.networktherapy.com, www.psychologytoday.com, www.therapistlocator.com,* and others have private therapist finder functions by zip code. You would go to the website, enter your zip code and the major issue you want to focus on, and the website will give you a list of therapists in your area, along with the expertise and focus of practice (i.e., children, couples, trauma, etc.), and statements about their philosophies.

CONTACTING CLINICS/AGENCIES/PROGRAMS/ HOSPITALS OR PRIVATE THERAPISTS

Once you have a name or names as referrals, you can call to make an appointment to meet with the therapist or the clinic/program. A first appointment with a private therapist is a consultation. A first appointment with an agency (whether it is a clinic or program) is an intake. Making a first call can be anxiety provoking. The telephone call is an interview in that you are trying to find out more about the therapist, and the therapist is trying to understand a bit about your child and your concerns. You may want to write some information on a sheet of paper to feel organized. Some information to prepare in advance includes the following:

- What you see as your child's main issues;
- How long you have been seeing these issues;
- Why you are calling now;

- Times that you would be available for an appointment;
- How you found out about the agency or therapist.

If you have to leave a message, keep your message brief and include your name, how you found out about the agency or therapist, your child's first name, and a brief statement of the issue. For example, a message may sound like this.

> *Hello, Ms. R., my name is Mr. K and I got your name from the school counselor at my son's school. My son's name is Ronald and he is having difficulty concentrating and is getting into lots of fights at school with his classmates. Please call me so we can discuss this further and possibly set up a time to meet.*

When you set up a first meeting, you may be setting up two appointments, one for you to meet the therapist and one for your child to meet the therapist. Depending on your availability and the time constraints of the therapist or intake therapist, you can schedule your appointment and your child's back to back or separately. Some parents feel more comfortable waiting before scheduling the child's appointment in order to see how they feel about the process and the therapist before introducing their child to therapy. This is completely reasonable. Typically, adolescents meet the therapist for this first appointment before their parents. This helps adolescents take more responsibility and ownership for their treatment. Adolescents can be concerned about how they are presented to new individuals and, consequently, typically want to provide the initial information to a therapist.

Sometimes parents struggle with finding the best age-appropriate words to explain a first meeting to their child. Parents can ask the therapist or agency intake coordinator for help in determining these words. It is important to know that the words are only one part of the communication; your child will also see the meaning of what you are saying by the emotions that he or she sees in your face. We will discuss different ways of talking to your child about the first meeting in Chapter 4.

THERAPIST SELECTION: CLINIC/AGENCY/PROGRAM/ HOSPITAL OR PRIVATE THERAPISTS

The ability to choose your child's therapist sometimes depends on where and with whom your child is in therapy. Choosing to work with a private therapist provides you with the most input and control over who works with your child.

Private therapists are individuals who have decided to work as independent practitioners. They often have their own office space in which they see patients, and they have the ability to choose the patients they see.

Community mental health clinics and psychotherapy training programs often designate the therapist whom their patients will see after an intake process. In these places, you can have some impact on the selecting a therapist for your child by expressing your thoughts, your wishes, and your concerns to the intake coordinator at the clinic or program. The final decision lies with the facility's admissions staff, but as a step to retaining some control over the process, you can ask the admissions staff for information, such as why this therapist was chosen to see your child. This can give you an idea about the way the staff sees your child's issues. Admission staff does have experience regarding matching patients with therapists.

If the therapist assigned to your child is not whom you expected, it is still possible that the match will work and that you may grow to feel comfortable with the therapist. Obviously, in the end, you as the parent can always decide that your child will not see the therapist selected. In these situations, clinics and programs have the ability to assign an alternate therapist but often will attempt to address the issues first.

WAITING LISTS

Clinics and programs may have waiting lists. There are a limited number of therapists, and this can create waiting lists when the demand for therapists outweighs the number of therapists on staff. Our suggestion is to place your child's name on any waiting lists you encounter. As we said before, having choices and options is a way of retaining some control over this process. Try not to get discouraged if you run into several waiting lists. The lists tend to move quickly. Speaking frankly, it is in the institutions' best interest financially to have your child as a client. August and early September tend to be good times to call for therapy to clinics and training programs, as September is the beginning of the school year and many trainees begin their learning cycles in these places at that time. Private therapists typically do not have waiting lists. If a private therapist cannot see you, you can ask him or her for a referral to another therapist. October and November tend to be months in which waiting lists grow as the identification of school-related issues begins. After November waiting lists decrease again.

EXPERIENCE

The experience levels of the therapists you may meet can vary greatly. Knowing how to understand the licenses, degrees, specialties, and areas of focus can be challenging. Making sense of whom to choose—and why—can be even more challenging. Do I want my child to work with a psychologist, a social worker, a counselor, or does it matter? How would it affect the therapy? How should I feel if my child works with a trainee or an intern? What we want you to remember is that most everyone you meet during this journey will want to help you and your child. It is the desire to help that is the most essential aspect of the therapeutic relationship between your child, you, and the therapist. That said, you should "select" the therapist whose experience and training you feel can best help your child.

You should know the reasons that you are choosing your child's therapist, for example, why this professional's particular degree makes more sense in your child's situation. There are many degrees and licenses that you may encounter when choosing a therapist. Let us begin by examining what the acronyms stand for and the types of training that go into acquiring these titles.

- Clinical/counseling psychologist (Ph.D/Psy.D) means that the therapist has a doctorate of philosophy in clinical psychology (Ph.D.) requiring four to seven years of training beyond a two-year master's degree, plus a dissertation that focuses on research and science. The therapist must have three years of practicums in patient care: one year of internship in patient care before graduating and two years of internship in patient care after graduating before becoming licensed. Similarly, a doctorate of psychology (Psy.D.) requires four to seven years of training beyond a two-year master's degree with at least one year of internship in a clinical setting. There is practical work and examinations rather than a research dissertation in some cases.
- Clinical social workers have a master's of social work degree that typically requires two years of training beyond a four-year bachelor's degree with two one-year internships in patient care settings that provide several different tracks of focus, including clinical social work. There are accelerated one-year programs as well for people with pre-master's experience. Doctorate of social work and doctorate of philosophy in social work require an additional five to seven years of graduate education beyond the master's degree.

- Mental health counselors have a master's degree in mental health counseling or a closely related mental health discipline and two years of clinical work, supervised by a mental health professional.
- Psychiatrist (MD) is a doctor of psychiatry with a medical degree with a psychiatric residency for approximately three to four years. The residency takes place in hospital-based psychiatric settings. Specialties in working with specific populations, such as children, require additional training, often as a one- to two-year fellowship in a psychiatric setting.
- Some states also license family therapists, marriage therapists, and addictions counselors.

Therapists with any of these degrees will be able to provide therapy for your child—in this there is very little difference between psychologists, social workers, psychiatrists, or mental health counselors. Additionally, a few specific areas of focus are important to know.

- Psychologists, based on their training, are also able to provide psychological testing for children. This is the testing used by schools and state Boards of Education to create Individualized Education Programs (IEP) for children in need of extra services at school.
- Any therapist can also receive additional training in the area of psychotherapy or psychoanalysis, based on his or her specific interest. For work with children, this can include different types of therapies such as anger management, filial therapy, cognitive behavioral therapy/rational emotive behavioral therapy, play therapy, relational psychotherapy, solution-focused therapy, or systems theory/therapy, among others.
- Several types of professionals write prescriptions for psychotropic medication. These individuals fall under the umbrella group of psycho-pharmacologists and have training in the working of psychotherapeutic drugs. They include psychiatrists, psychologists (in some states; see Chapter 14), doctors, nurse practitioners with specific psychopharmacology training, and other medical professionals with specific psychopharmacology training.

TRAINING PROGRAMS

All therapists go through a training period. During this time, therapists train at clinics, agencies, or hospitals for their internships. The internship will include seeing patients in treatment while under close weekly supervision. Senior therapists, who have already been through the program, teach the trainees and provide supervision for their work with patients.

You may feel that a therapist in training may be insufficiently prepared to address the needs of your child compared to a therapist who has completed his or her training. This is an understandable concern, so consider these other points. Your decisions about this issue need to take into account the concrete financial issues, which include the following:

- the cost of treatment as it compares to your income
- the contracts that have been negotiated with your insurance carrier
- the limitations of your insurance coverage.

You will also need to consider the clinician availability issues, which include these factors:

- The available alternatives to the training clinic in your community;
- The availability of senior staff therapists at the training clinic who work with children.

And you will need to consider the therapy-specific issues, which include the following:

- Trainees' positives (consistent supervision, eagerness and commitment, small caseload, fresh point of view);
- Trainees' negatives (inexperience).

Your comfort level is important, and these issues should be discussed with the therapist and with the training program or clinic's administration. Regardless of the cost of your child's therapy or the alternatives in your community, you as the parent should always feel able to voice your concerns and opinions, and should receive the information and feedback you need.

SUPERVISION

Supervision is the formalized verbal input, oversight, and instruction of one therapist on another therapist's work with a patient. This practice is very common in the profession and is a useful tool for therapists to receive support and perspective on their work with individuals; it reduces the chance for any problem situations in the therapy and maximizes the opportunities for success. In clinics, training programs, and larger agencies, therapists must have a supervisor by state law. Private therapists are not required to have supervisors, but many do. You may ask any therapist about their level of supervision.

THERAPY FEES

Private therapists typically offer a "sliding scale" of fees based on the patient's financial wherewithal. The therapist's fees are set at the start of therapy. Clinics and training programs typically use an insurance-based payment setup (see "Insurance," below). If the clinic or training programs do not take your insurance, you can work out a fee in a similar fashion that you would with a private therapist. Clinics and training programs may offer a sliding scale to patients in need. In the case of sliding scale negotiations, a private therapist will discuss your thoughts about the fee and will share his or her own ideas. Clinics and training programs will typically have you fill out income and expense documentation in order to set a "reasonable" fee.

INSURANCE

Both private therapists and clinics/training programs may accept your insurance, but they are not required to do so. In each case, you should ask when first making contact. Therapists who work in clinics or are part of training programs accept insurance as contracted by the clinics or training programs. It is up to each private therapist which insurance rosters or panels they join. He or she can also choose to be a therapist who does not take insurance at all.

You may decide, based on your finances or the rules of your insurance, that you would like to find a therapist within your insurance company's network. You will find a list of participating therapists on the company's website, or you may be given the names by phone. This list is a panel. For most insurance companies, "behavioral health" is the term used (not "mental health"). Therapists on an insurance company's panel take that insurance. They cannot charge you out-of-pocket if they are on the panel with your insurance company.

Tabitha Needs Her Insurance

Tabitha was a mother of a young boy who recently suffered a trauma. She decided that therapy would be helpful. She looked at her insurance company's website and called all the local therapists in the network. No one called her back. She called her insurance company's behavioral health program and shared with them her dilemma and her worries about the timing of getting her child help. The insurance company was helpful and called the therapists on her behalf. After several days, the insurance company called Tabitha back with an appointment time—at 10:00 AM on a Tuesday, 45 minutes from her home with traffic. Tabitha indicated that this was possible for a single appointment, but that her son needed ongoing help and that she worked and he was in school. The insurance company worker shared with her that of the 25 therapists in the network, this was the only one who returned her call.

We share this story for several reasons. It is an attempt to address the institutional discouragement that comes with interacting with insurance companies.

Insurance companies are required by law to help you and to provide services. Tabitha's insurance company had other options to help her son, but Tabitha had to stay the course in order to be informed about them. First, this happened to be a new insurance policy for Tabitha, and the insurance company had a policy called "transition of care" that allowed for three months of covered treatment for any therapist that Tabitha found. Second, when all searches were exhausted and a treating therapist was not found, the insurance company had another policy called a "single-case agreement" that allowed Tabitha to make a contract with the insurance company specifically to cover her son's therapy. They agreed to a fee and that Tabitha could go out of network to find a therapist. Clinics and training facilities can make requests for single-case agreement with insurance companies, but there is no guarantee that the insurance company will agree. That said, there is no downside to requesting this option; we just want you to be prepared.

Clinics and training programs typically accept most insurance policies, but it is still important to ask up front when calling for an intake. Most insurance providers are managed care programs, and a clinic may have service contracts with some types of insurance but not all. Insurance coverage for mental health needs is different from the coverage for medical needs. There is a strong movement in the United States to have mental health coverage follow the same formula as medical coverage, but to date there is not complete parity. Recent rule changes will extend coverage for mental health hospitalizations and will create parity for copayments (i.e., 80% for medical and mental health appointments).

Most insurance companies allot their participants a certain number of outpatient appointments (behavioral or mental health sessions) per year, regardless of diagnosis or the extent of the problems. They designate a set number of sessions to address an issue from start to finish.

Some insurance companies will approve only the intake at first and then will need to approve the balance of the sessions. Some will approve the first 10 sessions or so and will need to approve others as you go. Some will not need to approve sessions and you will simply be able to use your annual allotment until it is gone. If you are going to use your insurance to pay for therapy, it is important for you to know your specific coverage details at the start, because it can impact the duration and flow of therapy and needs to be part of the planning process of how best to help your child.

Insurance Weighs in on Jed's Therapy

Jed, a 16-year-old, was in therapy for several years with his therapist. His insurance denied a routine request to continue therapy. A representative from the insurance company indicated that he no longer felt the treatment was addressing Jed's issues. He reduced the number of sessions approved to a level that the therapist thought would not be helpful for Jed. Jed's parents could not pay out of pocket for sessions and so Jed's session frequency was reduced from once a week to twice a month, while his parents searched for new insurance. This situation created gaps in Jed's therapy, even though the therapist believed that Jed needed consistent sessions. His parents were able to secure new insurance at the next enrollment period.

This type of problem is more frequent than we would like to acknowledge. Insurance issues, such as this, do occur from time to time and require careful management. Because longer term psychotherapy is managed in this way, you may have to be creative in planning out vacations, school breaks, and start times with your child's therapist in order to maximize your child's therapy experience. For example, beginning your child's therapy near the end of the year allows you to use your annual allotment for this year and your annual allotment for the upcoming year back to back. This doubles the number of contiguous sessions that your child can receive and improves the chance for you and your child's therapist to complete work when addressing any issues.

PUBLIC OR GOVERNMENTAL MEDICAL INSURANCES

Community mental health clinics are obligated to provide services to people who have public types of insurance (Medicaid, Medi-Cal, and low-cost state-supported medical insurance for children when their parents have a specific income level). Most of these insurance providers follow the same managed care principles of private insurance, and in some states there are multiple insurance options. Clinics may have a contract with some but not all public insurance program vendors. All clinics will have at least one contract. Currently, this system typically works in the way that private insurance does in that the clinic would have a service contract with your public insurer. In addition, you do have the ability to switch public insurer vendors to one with whom the clinic does have a contract. At times, your child may be eligible for a program within the Social Security Administration that provides disability medical coverage and financial support for children and families who are eligible. Supplemental Security Income (SSI) provides Medicaid coverage for disabled children. This is currently separate from managed Medicaid and therefore all community mental health clinics are able to accept it.

THE AFFORDABLE CARE ACT (ACA): OBAMACARE

There has been much talk about the new healthcare coverage legislation passed in the past few years. Much of it is complicated and seems complex and difficult to understand. We have distilled helpful points for you, and how they pertain to getting and paying for therapy for your child. We think that the following points are important to know:

1. The legislation expands coverage to low-income families in the form of expanded Medicaid coverage.
2. The legislation requires insurance companies to describe coverage requirements in a brief (and hopefully) easier to understand format so that people will know what is covered and what is not.
3. The legislation calls for the creation of Accountable Care Organizations (ACO), which will be responsible for setting mental health treatment standards for both mental health professionals and for ways that certain mental illnesses are treated. These ACOs could make decisions affecting (a) who the available individuals are whom you can choose to treat your child;

(b) whether your child's problems are even defined as a mental illness and should be covered by insurance; and (c) whether certain types of treatment are deemed effective and should be covered by insurance. All these changes could remove from you some of the choices and decision-making elements about your child's treatment.

4. The legislation and how it is enacted will vary from state to state, and so it is important that, depending on which state you live in, you do as much research as possible into the details of coverage. We do not want you to be surprised during the course of your child's treatment by an insurance issue that can lead to prematurely ending the treatment or creating extra stress for you.

5. The legislation and the way it is going to be implemented in each state is still being developed and will continue to be rolled out in 2015 and beyond. Because of this, at the writing of book, some details are still unknown.

CHAPTER SUMMARY

CHAPTER 3: SEEKING OUT A CHILD PSYCHOTHERAPIST

Referral Sources

- *Personal referral*: a recommendation from someone you know.
- *Professional referral*: a recommendation from your pediatrician, clergy, or staff from your local hospital or school personnel.
- 1-800-LifeNet is a toll-free crisis telephone line that helps find referrals based on your stated issue and your local address.
- *Community mental health clinics*: There is a list of contact information in Appendix C. Also the Substance Abuse and Mental Health Services Administration (SAMSHA) has service locator capabilities. Hospitals with child psychiatry programs often have their own outpatient clinic programs.
- *Psychotherapy training programs*: state-approved and licensed postgraduate training programs to teach therapists the art of the psychotherapy.
- *Mental health professional Internet-based locators*: websites such as *www. networktherapy.com, www.psychologytoday.com,* and *www.therapistlocator.com.*

The experience levels of therapists can vary greatly. Understanding the licenses, degrees, specialties, and areas of focus can be challenging.

All the following professionals, listed in alphabetical order, can provide psychotherapy to your child.

- Clinical/counseling psychologist (Ph.D/Psy.D) has a doctorate of philosophy in clinical psychology (Ph.D.) or a doctorate of psychology (Psy.D).
- Clinical social worker has a master's of social work and a state license to practice as an independent practitioner.
- Mental health counselor has a master's degree in mental health counseling or a closely related mental health discipline, licensed by the state they practice in.
- Psychiatrist (MD) is a doctor of psychiatry and can have a subspecialty in treating children.
- Some states also license family therapists, marriage therapists, and addictions counselors and psychoanalysts.

CHAPTER 4

The First Session

Consultation and Intake Meetings

When you make your first appointment, it will be helpful if you give your-self some time to prepare. You may be surprised what it can take to get yourself and your child ready. We suggest that you allow at least a week between the day you call and the date that you set the appointment. You may feel some urgency about getting started. Giving yourself a short amount of time can be helpful—modeling a calm, step-by-step, prepared approach to tackling any issues. Once you have done this, your next step will be to prepare yourself and your child for these meeting(s) or session(s).

Make sure that you understand how the clinic or therapist orchestrates the first meetings. Often the first meeting is with you as the parents, and if you are comfortable with the therapist, then your child attends the second meeting. Some clinics and therapists want you and your child to come together for the first meeting, but you are seen first, then your child is seen. If your child is an adolescent, therapists often will see him or her first and then will meet with you second, or there is the possibility of a session together. Changing the order addresses the fact that children in their teen years wrestle with independence and privacy issues. The therapist should acknowledge this as a way to begin to develop a relationship based on trust.

First meetings can follow one of two basic structures: the consultation or the intake.

THE CONSULTATION

- The consultation is the first meeting structure used by private practitioners.
- It is usually the same length as a typical session. Therapists tend to prefer one of two session lengths: either 50 minutes or 45 minutes. The therapist will inform you about his or her preferred length for a session.
- The first consultation meeting is often with you. The second consultation meeting is with your child. This may be reversed for adolescents.
- The private therapist may have a list of questions for you to answer and at times a self-report questionnaire for you to complete, but this session will not be structured like an assessment interview. In general, the tenor or feel of a private therapist consultation tends to be somewhat informal and frequently reflects the therapists' typical way of interviewing new patients.
- It is also important to know that the private consultation serves as a time for you as the parent to interview and get information about the therapist.

    Here are some questions that you can ask the therapist:
    1. What type of training has the therapist had?
    2. How long has the therapist been working?
    3. What types of child problems has the therapist worked with in his or her practice?
    4. Has the therapist ever worked with a child who has issues like your child's?
    5. What is a typical length of psychotherapy for a child with issues like your child's?
    6. What is the therapist's psychotherapy philosophy, and what does it mean in plain language?
    7. How does the therapist see the role of the parents in psychotherapy?
    8. How does the therapist involve the parents? Are there parent collateral sessions? Are there child-parent joint sessions?
    9. How does the therapist share information with the parents?
    10. How does the therapist receive information from the parents?
    11. What are the therapist's ideas about non-participating parents? Custody issues? Divorced parents? Separated parents? How are these situations addressed as part of the psychotherapy structure if applicable?
    12. What type of contact does the therapist have with individuals outside the family unit? The school? Doctors? Extended family?
    13. What are the therapist's ideas about psychological testing?
    14. What are the therapist's ideas about medication?

15. What are the therapist's approach to record keeping?
16. What is the typical fee that the therapist charges? Is there a sliding scale?

- A consultation with a private therapist in many ways also functions as the first psychotherapy session, even though questions are being asked and perhaps recorded. Many times, the next appointment for psychotherapy is made before the end of the consultation.

- It is perfectly acceptable and advisable to "shop around" for a private therapist when your community or insurance offers you several alternatives. We recommend choosing from two or three therapists. Although this may be seen as extra work for you, we believe that having the perspective of seeing therapists with different styles, genders, or ages can be helpful in choosing the right one for your child.

THE INTAKE

- The intake is the first meeting structure used by clinics, agencies, and training programs.
- It frequently begins by completing an application/request for service, which is similar to the forms one fills out at medical/healthcare appointment.
- The intake is usually a longer type of meeting. It can be 45 minutes to 90 minutes, depending on the clinic, and is sometimes separated into parts. The intake may begin with you alone, then a session with your child, and perhaps a shorter session with both of you. As we stated earlier, if your child is an adolescent, he or she may be the first person seen by the therapist in the intake process.
- The intake therapist will ask you a specific set of questions (often in questionnaire format) in order to fill out the intake paperwork. This questioning process is often similar from clinic to clinic and program to program. This is in large part due to the state requirements for detailed documentation and record keeping for all mental health cases seen in these facilities. Your answers to the questions will lead to other questions as the intake therapist attempts to get a more detailed picture of your child and the issues.
- The person conducting the intake may not be your child's therapist.
- Your child's assessment is then reviewed, usually in a group setting with the clinic's/program's therapists, supervisors, and medical/psychiatry staff. This can cause a short delay in the actual start of psychotherapy.
- Once reviewed, a therapist who has been assigned to you and your child contacts you to arrange the first appointment with him or her. Be sure to ask about the amount of time between the intake and the start of your child's

psychotherapy when you make your intake appointments. On occasion, especially during the summer, clinics may schedule an intake and then assign a therapist to you once one is available. Waiting times vary, and you can ask for assignment to a therapist as soon as possible.

- Therapists take their vacations during the summer months when children are out of school, and many internship programs for new therapists begin in September. If this is the case for you and you want a more timely start to therapy, you can express your wish to accelerate the process, or you can look around for another clinic.

FOCUS OF THE FIRST MEETING

The focus of both of these types of meeting structures is to gather information in order to gain an understanding of your child. This can include the following:

- Demographic information, including your child's name, age, gender, living situation, and contact information
- The main issues that your child is struggling with in your own words (sometimes called the *presenting problem(s)* or the *chief complaint(s)*)
- Any important or pertinent history of the main issues (how long these problems have been going on, what in your opinion has contributed to these problems)
- Any pertinent life history (your child's health record, childhood illnesses, experiences that may be relevant, socialization dynamics, developmental milestones, school history, or family mental health history)
- A mental status examination (a structured interview with your child to assess his or her feelings and thoughts as well as behavioral and cognitive functioning).

There are specific ways of going about preparing yourself and your child for either session structure.

Here are some areas that you can take some notes on beforehand to prepare yourself for the consultation:

1. A description of what you think is the main problem or problems. Do not be concerned about whether this is "correct" or not. This can focus on observations that you have made about your child's
   a. Behaviors
   b. Feelings (described by your child)

c. Fears (described by your child)

d. Thoughts (described by your child)

e. Types of play

f. Drawings

g. Statements (made by your child)

h. Relationships

2. Observations that you have made about any of the above categories—the more detail the better

3. The duration of the problems

4. The frequency of the problems.

To this list it is important to add a description of your child's mood. Mood is a feeling state that describes how your child responds to daily activities, experiences, difficulties, and positive events emotionally. Here is a list of moods that may help you focus your thoughts:

> aggravated, angry, annoyed, anxious, apathetic, ashamed, blank, bored, calm, cheerful, confused, content, cranky, dark, depressed, determined, discontent, energetic, enraged, exhausted, frustrated, gloomy, grumpy, indifferent, irritated, lethargic, listless, moody, morose, relaxed, restless, rushed, sad, silly, stressed, tired, uncomfortable

We suggested a week to prepare for the first session because it can take some time to create this list of information. You can carry around a small note pad or put the information into your phone in order to keep the information accurate. The brain works by altering much of what we experience immediately after it happens, and the brain continues to change this information when we try to recall the experience. We call this distortion. Logging the information can limit this distortion.

MANIFEST AND LATENT CONTENT

At this time, we want to describe two new concepts to you that will be helpful in your understanding about how this first session works. The concepts describe the dual nature—the multiple levels—of the type of information that you are giving to the therapist in this session or sessions. The first concept is **manifest**

content. On its surface, the list of information that we have suggested that you prepare for the consultation is what we call manifest content. By manifest, we mean observable. Imagine a boat on the ocean. You are in the boat. All that you can see and perceive around you is manifest content—the clouds, the wind, the birds, the boat, and the water and waves. If you were to describe the scene to someone, you would describe these things because you can see them. If you describe what you see about your child, such as what your child is doing, what your child says, or what his or her emotions appear to be, you are describing manifest information about him or her.

The second concept is **latent content**. Imagine being back in the boat. If the manifest information is what you can actually observe outside the boat, then the latent information is what is under the water—the fish, the currents, the plant life, even the part of the boat that is beneath the surface. It is the information that we know is there, but cannot see with our eyes. We know that there is a whole world under the surface of the water. So, if our boat began sinking lower in the water, how would we understand the "behavior" of the boat? Is the boat too heavy? Is there a leak? We would have to infer the reasons because we cannot see them.

In terms of your child, the latent information is the underlying reasons and/or meanings behind the behaviors, the emotions, and the moods that you have been observing. As parents, we may not see the latent content, but we are aware of it instinctually at times. When our infant cries (manifest), we believe that she is hungry or has some other physical need that we cannot see (latent).

Another metaphor that may help us understand manifest and latent content is an iceberg. We only can see the very tip of an iceberg (manifest), but we know that the majority of it is beneath the surface, out of our view (latent).

At this moment in your child's therapy process, manifest content is, for the most part, the domain of the parents, and latent content is the domain of the therapist. As therapy moves forward, the therapist should help you become more and more aware of the latent communications and the meaning behind what you are experiencing with your child.

INCLUDING YOUR CHILD

When you have decided to schedule the intake or consultation appointment, it is time to talk to your child about the decision you have made and to bring him or her into the process in a more direct way. Every child needs preparation for new things in his or her life. Feeling prepared allows for an increased sense of control, which improves confidence and self-esteem. Therapy is no different. We know that for some, therapy is embarrassing or stigmatizing. Stigma is something that the individual or community believes damages your reputation or credibility. Recall the questions that you may have had yourself, and add a child's perspective. What is wrong with me? Can I tell anyone? What will my friends think? What will happen if my friends find out? Will they think I am crazy? Do my parents think I am crazy? Are my parents mad at me? Why can't I just talk to my parent about this? For how long will I have to go?

The idea of normalizing therapy is an important first step. Normalizing is the idea of making something viewed as not typical into something that is more typical and acceptable. The therapist will assist in this process once therapy begins, but you can lay some important groundwork. You can accomplish this by explaining your reasons for wanting to try therapy, clearly and lovingly. You can convey that going to therapy is similar to taking someone to a doctor if he or she is not feeling well. You can make it clear that this is a team effort and that you will participate and address any issues that you need to change also. Your accepting some responsibility allows your child to feel less like the one who is the problem.

You may be feeling angry, frustrated, or scared. These feelings are for you to explore and discuss with people other than your child. As important as these feelings are, demonstrating them to your child at this time could inadvertently give your child the message that therapy is a form of punishment. Feeling like the cause of all the problems can make a child feel separate from the rest of the family and may make him or her less likely to want to listen to or try your solutions.

COMPONENTS OF INFORMING YOUR CHILD ABOUT THERAPY

We can divide our discussion about this conversation into four parts. This is important because looking at the key elements of this conversation will help you make sure that you create an environment in which your concerns and your decision to start therapy can be best heard and understood by your child.

- *Timing*: This includes the timing of when you choose to discuss the issues with your child—how long prior to the session, how often, and so on. Are you going to talk to him in the morning, before school, at night, before bed? Are you going to tell him just after an argument?
- *Location*: This includes the environment in which you choose to discuss the upcoming therapy appointment with your child. How are you going to arrange to have the discussion? Are you going to take your child to dinner? Is it going to be both parents, one parent? Are siblings going to be around?
- *Purpose*: This includes the reason you will give your child for making the appointment. Why do I need therapy? Why do I need it now? Is anyone else in the family going to therapy? Is it a consequence or punishment?
- *Method*: This includes the way in which you convey the information about your reasoning. Do you feel angry or frustrated that you have to do this? Have you thought about all the questions your child may have? Have you considered that he or she may say no? What would you do? Have you considered that he or she may cry? How would you react? Do you feel in control, calm, and ready to have the discussion?

AGE-APPROPRIATE LANGUAGE AND DEVELOPMENTAL STAGES

All professionals who work with children recommend the use of age-appropriate language. We recommend that you use concepts and words that your child will be able to understand. These concepts and their related words are then called age-appropriate language.

When we use the term "age-appropriate," we mean taking into account your child's developmental level of thinking ability (cognitive/brain), maturity, and emotional growth. These factors of development evolve and change as children get older. These periods of growth are developmental stages. We can define this concept of a developmental stage as a combination of physical, mental, and emotional components that we can use to characterize a child at any given moment in his or her life. You may find different definitions or divisions of these stages. In general, they include infancy, toddlerhood, pre-latency, latency, early adolescence, late adolescence, and early adulthood. Your child's developmental stage becomes the guide for making decisions about the timing, location, purpose, and method that we mentioned earlier. There are many books on this topic.

Children at this stage have limited time perception (the "are we there yet" issue). It is important to inform your child of the appointment, but not more than a week or less than two days prior. We suggest that you remind him several times about the appointment. This will allow him enough time to feel prepared and ask questions if he chooses to (he may not, and this is fine), but not so much time that he forgets what you have said.

For a child who has not yet reached kindergarten, it may be enough to say that you are taking her to a feelings doctor to talk about what is happening at school, home, and so on. At this point in her development, your child is still looking to you to define her world, especially in times of difficulty. Being very concrete and talking about specifics like who, what, when, and where should alleviate any worry about the unknown that your child may have. Focusing your child on details increases her sense of control.

Children in this age range look at the world as if they are the center of it. They often feel responsible for events or situations that are under no one's control—not by choice, but because of their developmental stage. This is important to take into account when you describe the reasons you are bringing your child to therapy so as not to reinforce your child taking the blame.

When discussing the session, children this age need an environment in which they are comfortable. Choose one that has as few distractions as possible in order to help your child concentrate on what you are saying. If she or he fidgets, moves around, or plays with something, this is a latent communication of needing comfort during the conversation. It is typical.

Talking to Charlie (Age 5) About Therapy

Robert and Deborah were speaking to their 5-year-old son, Charlie about going to a therapist. Charlie was having terrible nightmares ever since his family was in a car accident three months earlier.

We are taking you to a talking doctor. He talks about feelings. He will ask mommy and daddy questions about your scary dreams. He will also ask you about the scary dreams and he will help us try to make them go away. It will be in an office. We will have to wait a little while so we will bring some of your toys or books. You can choose what we bring. Sometimes Mommy and Daddy might talk with the doctor and sometimes we might talk together as a family and sometimes the doctor might want to talk to you. You are probably going to play and draw and answer questions.

You know how doctors check your eyes, your nose, and your mouth . . . well, talking doctors check your feelings like happy, sad, and mad. Is this OK for you? Do you have any questions? If you have any questions later, you can ask either Mommy or Daddy. We want to know what you think.

LATENCY (AGE 7–11)

Once your child has reached elementary school, she or he may be able to give opinions about the situation and the ways you are thinking about addressing it. Time perception is better developed, and so for preparation we suggest at least a week and not more than three weeks in advance. Latency aged children are often attracted to orderliness. This is how they learn—through repetition and simple instructions. This makes basic logical decisions more easily understood by them. This makes the clarity of your explanation about therapy more important.

At this age, children many have developed deeper feelings of empathy. If you seem sad, frightened, or nervous about the process, your child may respond with anxiety. It is important to find the words that convey your sense that you are in control (of your feelings), that you are doing this so that things will feel better in your home, and that there is no blame placed on the need to address these issues.

Pride in her ideas and abilities is a major focus of your child's development at this moment, so it may also be helpful to solicit your child's feelings about your decision and let her make some choices about the process that could increase her sense of control and give her some ownership over the process. An example of this could be letting your child know that she will be able to share as much or as little as she wants with the therapist. It is her choice.

In addition, they have developed a sense of privacy and can feel embarrassed and disrespected. So we suggest choosing a time to have this discussion when you will be uninterrupted by others.

Shannon and Becky (Age 10) Talk About Therapy

Shannon was talking to her 10-year-old daughter, Becky, about going to therapy because of issues at school, including fighting, dropping grades, and lying about homework. Shannon and Becky's father recently separated and Becky was very upset.

I was thinking about what has been happening to us, all the fighting, arguing, and school problems, and I feel it needs to change. Your father and I have spoken and he agrees.

We love you and we feel that the problems are causing all of us pain, especially you. We don't want this to keep happening. We realize that there are a lot of reasons for what is happening, but we have not been able to change them ourselves. So we have decided that we are going to talk to a therapist who can help us. You may have heard of a therapist. He or she is like a talking doctor, someone who you talk to about your feelings and things that are bothering you, and who we can all talk to, so that we can help each other. You will do some talking and also answering questions. You may even do some drawing or playing. What do you think? Do you have any questions? Will you help us to choose a therapist?

EARLY ADOLESCENCE (AGE 12–15)

You will not necessarily know how your early adolescent child will respond to you about therapy until you bring it up with him or her. The growing sense of independence and autonomy and the, at times, hostile stance against being told what do will make this conversation both difficult and very important.

Remember that at this age, friends' opinions can be crucial to adolescents. Since young teenagers want to be the same as their peer group, they are highly sensitive about feeling different, weird, ill, or crazy. Frequently, young teenagers have these insecurities and fears without therapy even being a part of their lives. When therapy is introduced, it can often be viewed as stigmatizing and un-cool. In addition, an adolescent has a vested interest in feeling older. In fact, he or she spends a great deal of their time trying not to feel young. Admitting that he needs help can often make a child feel younger. Facing these conflicts may cause your young teenager a great deal of angst.

Your early teenager will need support and patience from you as you discuss the option of therapy. You will want to strike a balance between your child's developmental needs and his therapy needs. Finding a way to acknowledge the conflicts that we mentioned will help to make this conversation easier. This can be accomplished by instilling a sense of control and structure within your reasons for therapy and how therapy can fit your child and your family. Adolescents can have feelings about many of the details of the therapy that we have discussed earlier, such as how confidential it is, the gender and age of the therapist, the location, and so on. Involving them in the decision-making in these areas will assist in increasing their support of the therapeutic process by increasing their sense of control and ownership over it. It is also important to remember that if your child rejects the idea of therapy, simply taking him or her will typically not get the result that you are looking for.

Jonathan (Age 15) and His Mother Discuss Beginning Therapy

Jonathan was a 15-year-old Chinese American boy, whose grandmother recently came to stay with the family and displaced Jonathan from his room. Jonathan was angry and was getting into arguments with his parents. When he threatened to hurt himself, Thea, his mother, decided to take him to a therapist.

Jonathan, your father and I have decided that, because of everything that has been going on for the past few months, we need some help. We are worried about you. We have decided to talk to a therapist to see if getting that kind of help will change things for all of us. We want you to know that we think that this is no one's fault, but if things keep going this way, we think our problems are just going to get worse. We don't want that to happen to you or the family. We think that talking to a therapist is a good idea. It is important that we know how you feel about this. We want your help in picking the therapist and the place for therapy. We want you to try it and we will try it with you. What do you say about all of this?

LATE ADOLESCENCE (AGE 15–17)

To develop a plan to talk to your late adolescent child, you should be aware that your child is striving for a sense of being an adult. She has ideas about adulthood and its privileges. At the same time, she is struggling with the increasing responsibilities and complexity of young adulthood. Late adolescents want to be adults without completely grasping what this means. They may be having difficulty managing new adult ideas such as compromise, uncertainty, and not knowing all the answers.

The most important concept to convey to your late adolescent is that your wish to have him or her try psychotherapy is rooted in the concern that you feel for someone who is struggling, especially when that someone is important to you. This idea places your child on slightly more equal footing with you and may appeal to the young adult in her.

Threats and ultimatums used to affect agreement are doomed to fail and often may make the situation worse by further isolating your child. Children in late adolescence often believe that needing help is an indication of being young or weak or a failure. The idea of getting help from therapy may create a fear of never becoming a functioning adult. The notion that recognizing and accepting help is a function of healthy adulthood is an important one to explain. The process of helping your late adolescent child is one based on well-worded explanations that speak to her at her highest and most mature level of thinking. It is to help her see therapy as a step in the forward direction, not back.

Reggie Presents Therapy Options to Rebecca (Age 17)

Rebecca was a 17-year-old high school senior who was depressed and anxious about having to go to college. She was struggling with what was going to happen with her and her boyfriend. She had panic attacks and refused to go on any trips to visit colleges. She was smoking increasing amounts of marijuana to keep herself calm. She was arguing frequently with both of her parents. Reggie, her father, decided that therapy should be an option.

I love you very much and I am very worried about you. I imagine that you do not want me to worry about you so much, but that is just me. It is upsetting seeing you so sad, lost, and nervous. Please let me help you. I think getting some professional help could make a big difference. As we get older, sometimes we need help. If you do this, I will be with you every step of the way if you want me to be. If it makes sense, your mother and I will go and get professional help, too. We can work on this together. I am going to call and make appointments for us. I know that making you go will not help you, so I hope you will at least try this first appointment and see how it goes. I can imagine you have some thoughts about this. I want to listen.

YOUNG ADULTHOOD (AGE 18–MID-20S)

When an individual, in this case your child, reaches 18 years old, talking to him about therapy takes on new dynamics. Your role shifts from organizer to supporter. In legal terms, clinics and private practitioners will view your child as an adult. Even if a clinic or a private therapist sees your child as an adult, your young adult child will still need your support to make his or her own decision about whether or not to enter therapy. Depending on how he is feeling or to what extent he is struggling, you can help him find a therapist or clinic, and can assist him in making his own calls and setting up his own appointments. This will be practice for how the clinicians with whom he will be working will interact with him. Remember, even though he is moving into adulthood, he will always be your child and will need support when he asks for it. You would not go on a job interview with your adult child, but you can still help him prepare so that his chance of success is increased.

Clarence (Age 22) Listens to His Grandmother Betty

Clarence was a 22-year-old young adult who lived in his college dorm. He was failing all of his subjects, was losing a great deal of weight, was no longer seeing his friends, and was not bathing. Clarence was not making much sense when his grandmother Betty, who raised him, visited him at college.

Clarence, I have always taken care of you and I have always loved taking care of you. I was very worried after our last telephone conversation. I came to college not to baby you but to see if you are all right. I am afraid things are not going well for you, and you do not look well or healthy. Please let me help you as I always have when you are not feeling well. I would appreciate it if you would talk things over with a therapist, sort of like a checkup with no commitments. We can do this back home because, Clarence, I want to take you home with me to help you get better. Will you let me do these things for you?

Obviously, in each of these cases you would find your own words and your own tone—so use the above statements as a guide. You are looking to create a sense of inclusion and teamwork. A group effort stands a better chance of success than creating a sense that your child has to work on these issues, whatever they may be, on his or her own.

Children of any age or developmental stage may not be able to respond to your explanation in the moment. Children need time to think about the information, and the meaning to them. Try to build in time for your child to think about what you have said. If you give you and your child time, you can repeat variations of this conversation multiple times before your appointment.

EMERGENCIES

No matter which developmental stage your child is in, there are situations that involve dangerous behaviors that could seriously harm your child or others. These situations may need quick action because they are emergencies. This is a time when your child urgently needs protection, and you may not have the opportunity to explain things to your child. We feel that sometimes as parents you must act quickly to ensure the well-being of your children and then play catch-up to explain once they are safe. Obviously, if possible, acting early before problems become unsafe is the best for you and your child.

GETTING READY

To help you think through how to prepare for the first meeting with the therapist, there are a few "helpful hints" that can increase your abilities to manage the beginning in the best way possible.

- Wear comfortable clothing. Being comfortable will help you be better able to tolerate minor frustrations, delays, or small annoyances.
- Bring a drink like coffee, juice, or water. For many people, their mouth becomes dry when having to talk in certain types of meetings.
- Bring your list of questions for the therapist that we discussed earlier. Even if you do not get to ask them, having them will reduce your anxiety by helping you feel more prepared. This is an opportunity for you to talk about your worries and concerns about your child. Other questions could relate to fees and scheduling.
- Bring your observations and thoughts about your child's behaviors, thoughts, moods, and so on, which we discussed earlier.
- Bring a notebook and a pen to take notes and write down information from the session that you find helpful.
- Bring a recent photograph of your child if she or he is not accompanying you to the session.
- Bring any important reports from your child's school or teacher.
- Have the contact information of your child's school and medical doctor available for you to share with the therapist.
- Ask the therapist for advice on how to explain a first session to your child in ways that make sense to her or him and that do not add to any concerns your child may have.

Some therapists will be comfortable if you want to record your meeting with them. It is polite for you to ask permission before recording. Some therapists may prefer that you not record the meeting, but this does not necessarily mean that this is the "wrong" therapist for your child. Some therapists may be concerned that your child or another unintended listener will overhear the recording of a private and confidential meeting.

Preparation involves your child as well.

- You may want to bring a non-sugar snack or drink. Hunger and thirst can cause restlessness and fatigue.
- Allow your child to decide what he will wear to the first meeting. Clothing choice is a form of nonverbal communication (latent communication).
- Agree that your child can bring a book, toy, game, or anything else he would like to have handy (within reason). Sometimes children bring things with them to help them feel less nervous. This can have a specific meaning for your child, a way of showing the therapist something about himself—like an "ice-breaker."
- Tell your child about having to wait when you arrive at the appointment. With all the conversations and setup work, your child may demonstrate problematic or concerning behaviors in the waiting area. This is a communication (usually of being nervous). It will help you to not see this as a way of embarrassing you or not following your instructions.

THE OFFICE/CLINIC ENVIRONMENT

You may want to arrive early for your appointment so that you and your child can have time to relax prior to meeting the therapist. This also gives you and your child time to look around and to get used to the office space. Looking around and exploring is your child's way of increasing feelings of mastery (control).

As we mentioned earlier, the clinic admissions process requires that you fill out paperwork at the intake. The intake coordinator will have a specific suggestion about how early you should arrive. Clinic waiting rooms will have a reception area to check in, along with couches, chairs, tables, and a bathroom.

Private therapists' offices will most likely have a waiting area. In private offices without receptionists, you will not have anyone to check in with or to announce your arrival. The therapist's office door is closed. At first, it seems awkward or uncomfortable to wait for the therapist you have never met to appear. If the therapist practices alone, the waiting room will be small and may or may not have a bathroom. Private therapists who practice within a group will have a larger waiting room and a bathroom (although the bathroom may or may not connect with the office). It is common for private therapists to have their office within their apartment or home. The private therapist will let you know this prior to the first session. There should still be an area to wait, and the space will be private. It is important to think about how you and your child feel in the office space. An office space with no privacy may not feel secure. An office space with a waiting room that is too small may be too constricting for your child.

Regardless of the office setup, clinic or private, a therapist will come to greet you and your child when it is time for your appointment.

SAMPLE QUESTIONS

To continue the preparation for the initial meetings with the therapist, it helps to understand the topic areas that are usually covered and their formulation as questions. Below are listed some but not all of the types of questions you may be asked:

- *Demographic questions* are a way for the therapist to understand your family size, who lives with you, and your lifestyle, neighborhood, ethnicity/culture, and religion/faith system.
  Q: What is your child's name?
  Q: How did you happen to choose this name?
  Q: How old is your child?
  Q: Does she have any brothers or sisters?
  Q: How old is her brother?
  Q: What is your child's race or ethnicity?
  Q: Do you work, and if so, what do you do?
  Q: Who lives in your home with your child?
  Q: What are the sleeping arrangements?
- *Education* is an essential part of your child's healthy development. School records and reports, even those you disagree with, are very helpful to the therapist in assessing the difficulties and issues.
  Q: Where does she go to school?
  Q: How far is the school from your house?
  Q: How does she get to school?

Q: What grade is she in?

Q: What is her favorite subject? What is her least favorite?

Q: Is she in special education or does she receive any education assistance?

Q: Has she ever been suspended or expelled?

Q: How does she get along with her classmates?

Q: How did your child transition into school?

- The *presenting problem* is your idea, thoughts, or fears of what your child's difficulty or problem is. Often, an incident or series of incidents have contributed to you taking the steps to involve a therapist.

Q: Why are you bringing your child to therapy today?

Q: What are the specific issues that you are noticing?

Q: Can you explain this issue in further detail?

Q: Can you tell me how long you believe your child has been having these difficulties?

Q: Have the school/other family members/neighbors/doctor brought some of these difficulties to your attention?

- Your child's *friendships and play activities* can be a barometer of your child's feelings about herself and the world. Play is one of the key ways in which children relax, ventilate unspoken feelings/thoughts, and connect with peers (to read more about how children use play, see Chapter 6).

Q: What kinds of play have you seen your child engage in?

Q: Has your child's play changed in any way recently?

Q: Does your child have friends? What gender are they?

- Your child's *developmental and medical history* is important as it can relate to developmental delays and/or trauma.

For biological parents:

Q: Did you have difficulties becoming pregnant?

Q: Did you have any miscarriages or stillbirths prior to the birth of this child?

Q: How was your pregnancy? Full-term? Complications?

Q: How was the birth? Vaginal? C-Section?

For non-biological parents:

Q: When did you begin caring for the child?

Q: What were the circumstances by which you came to care for the child?

Q: How does your child understand the caregiver-child relationship at this time (i.e., adoption, kinship care, foster care, etc.)?

For all parents:

Q: Were there any issues with the baby after the birth?

Q: When did your child start crawling? Walking? Talking?

Q: When was your child toilet trained? Issues?

Q: Has your child had any injuries or accidents?

Q: Does your child have any health problems?

Q: Does your child take any medications, both prescribed and over the counter, on a regular basis?

Q: Was your child ever medically or psychiatrically hospitalized?

Q: Is this the first time you have sought counseling for your child?

- Your child's *traumatic experiences* can have a strong impact on your child's feelings and emotional state. Death of a loved one is one of the most traumatizing of losses. In addition, other important situations can affect your child.

Q: Has a close relative of yours, or your child's, died recently?

Q: Has your family added a new child, or did any member of the family move out or move away recently?

Q: Have you recently married, separated, or divorced from a partner?

Q: Has a pet been added to your household, or has a pet died recently?

Q: Have you changed homes/apartments or moved into a new neighborhood recently?

Q: Has your child ever been physically abused? Sexually abused? Emotionally or psychologically abused? Neglected?

Q: Has your child ever suffered a traumatic experience of any kind?

- The *mental status* part of the first meetings is structured to evaluate if there are any serious psychiatric symptoms that need to be addressed. It is likely that you will be asked challenging and intense questions.

Q: Does your child have any nightmares or night terrors?

Q: Does your child have any intense fears?

Q: Have you seen any dramatic, maybe disturbing changes in your child's behavior?

Q: What is child's predominant mood? How does your child express anger?

Q: Does your child ever describe hearing voices or sounds that other people cannot?

Q: Does your child get into fights?

Q: Does your child appear anxious? When? What are the symptoms that you see?

The therapist will ask your child similar or related questions about school, friends, his likes and dislikes, and specifics about his feelings and thoughts. How the therapist collects this information depends on your child's age and how your child is feeling at the time of the appointment. In some cases, this will be a structured interview. In others, your child will be encouraged to play or will be asked to draw pictures while some of these topic areas are discussed.

Beginning therapy is an uncharted journey for most parents and most children. Just as you try to pack the right clothes, arrange transportation, find places to stay in advance of any journey, so too do you need to prepare both you and your child for psychotherapy in straightforward ways. Preparation will make it easier for you to create a relationship with a therapist as well as with clinics or other programs.

THE SESSION

Once you have prepared, your first session should be straightforward and unsurprising. It is like a conversation with a purpose. It moves in a direction that is noticeable. You can expect there to be moments when you may be upset, confused, sad, nervous, or even angry. All these emotions are typical for a first session. The session will be comprehensive, and you will probably not spend too much time on any one topic. This may feel at times like you are not spending enough time on important aspects of your child, but it is all part of getting a complete picture of your child. We can recommend a few rules of thumb:

- Notice your surroundings. Look at the setup of the room, the furniture, the space. Feeling grounded in the environment can help you feel safer and more secure.
- Take your time. Do not rush through material. The therapist can pace the session, but if you feel like it is moving too quickly and you are missing things, ask to slow it down.
- Say what you feel. Try not to over-think your answers. The best responses are the ones that pop into your head first, even if they feel too difficult to say at times.
- Ask questions. Feel free to ask questions of the therapist. This is an opportunity for you to begin to feel more in control about your child's issues.
- Relax and breathe. If you feel upset, take a moment to collect yourself. Do not worry if you run out of time or leave something out. You can always have time to go back to it in later sessions.

- Stay present. If you feel that your mind is wandering, ask for a moment and take a break from the session. You are the most important source of information about your child, so it is important that you take care of yourself in this session.

We will address the workings of a typical therapy session more extensively in later chapters.

CHAPTER SUMMARY

CHAPTER 4: THE FIRST SESSION: CONSULATION AND INTAKE MEETINGS

Give yourself some time to prepare. Allow at least a week between the day you call and the date that you set the appointment.

Some clinics and therapists want you and your child to come together for the first meeting, but you are seen first, then your child is seen. If your child is an adolescent, therapists often will see him or her first and then will meet with you second. There is also the possibility of a session together.

First meetings can follow one of two basic structures: the consultation or the intake.

- The consultation is the first meeting structure used by private practitioners.
- The intake is the first meeting structure that is typical of clinics, agencies, and training programs.
- Both of these types of sessions can vary in time from 45 minutes to 90 minutes.

The focus of both of these types of meeting structures is to gather information in order to gain an understanding of your child and includes the following:

- Demographic information (your child's name, age, gender, living situation, and contact information)
- The main issues that your child is struggling with, in your own words (sometimes called the *presenting problem(s)* or the *chief complaint(s)*)
- Any important or pertinent history of the main issues (how long these problems have been going on, what, in your opinion, has contributed to these problems)

- Any pertinent life history (your child's health record, childhood illnesses, experiences that may be relevant, socialization dynamics, developmental milestones, school history, or family mental health history)
- A mental status examination (a structured interview with your child to assess his or her feelings and thoughts as well as behavioral and cognitive functioning).

Prepare yourself for the consultation/intake. Focus on observations that you made about your child's

a. Behaviors
b. Feelings, fears, and thoughts (described by your child)
c. Types of play
d. Drawings
e. Statements (made by your child)
f. Relationships.

Use concepts and words that your child will be able to understand when discussing the idea of therapy. These concepts and their related words are called age-appropriate language.

Taking the Next Steps

Moving Forward

So at this point, we would recommend that you ask yourself some questions:

- Did I like the therapist?
- Did I feel comfortable with him or her?
- Was I at ease enough to imagine eventually forming a relationship with this person?
- Do I understand how the therapist plans to help my child?
- Do I agree with the therapist's therapeutic philosophy?
- Is the setting right?
- Is the fee reasonable?
- Does my insurance cover the costs of therapy?

Your answers are important because your child's therapist is a person

1. with whom you may feel sad, angry, or frightened at times;
2. who may ask you questions that you may find hard to answer, that seem too personal or too private to answer; and
3. who may ask you to think in ways that you have not thought before.

Your answers to these questions are important because your commitment to your child's therapy and its progress depends on how you feel about therapy and the therapist. Let us look at both external (outside) and internal (inside) factors that can affect a caregiver's motivation for therapy.

THE CHOICE OF THERAPIST (EXTERNAL)

You have considered the points from the previous chapters including training, setting, fee, gender, and background, and it is now time to choose. The idea of depending on your instincts may seem unscientific, but choosing a therapist is based in part on instinct. Sometimes a therapist just feels like the correct choice. Try to take all the information that you have and then figure out whom you liked the best, who made you the most comfortable, whom you could talk to, who seemed to connect to your child, whom you could see your child interacting with, whom you want to work with. These all may seem very subjective, but research has shown that the therapeutic relationship and its resulting successes are based on simply liking our therapist—not his or her training, ideology, philosophy, degree, or place of work. It may be difficult to put your finger on exactly why or what you like about this person (although it is important to ponder this feeling). If your child is older and has met more than one therapist, then the balancing of your thoughts and your child's thoughts is an important step in this process. Ask your child, Who did you like the best? Who do you want to see again? What did you specifically like about this therapist or the other? Although he may say that he does not know, it is asking the question that is important, not necessarily the answer. We want you to model the importance of discussing therapy and its different aspects for your child.

Think about the language to use and follow the model that you began when you originally discussed the idea of therapy with your child. Until your child is 18 years of age, the decision of whom your child sees in therapy is still ultimately yours. Prior to becoming a young adult, your child can have quite a bit of control of different aspects of therapy (content, pacing, etc.), and we think it is important that you are aware of your responsibilities with regard to your child's therapy as they change depending on your child's age.

YOUR CHILD'S AGE (EXTERNAL) AND YOUR EXPECTATIONS (INTERNAL)

Using a child's age as a determining factor for your expectations is using a developmental approach. A developmental approach is based on stages that are a summary of many years of study about how children function during various times in their lives. What your child needs emotionally may not necessarily coincide with how old she is or acts, but a developmental approach gives you some way of understanding what is expected and what is typical for most children in a specific age group.

Our expectations of our children are a very complicated mixture of our own dreams, fantasies, wishes, successes, failures, triumphs, disappointments, and many other elements of our own lives. Basing our expectations on these aspects of ourselves is measuring our children against our own limited experiences. This is a subjective measurement because it is specifically about us—our opinions. Using a developmental approach helps us to have a more independent and less personal way of responding to our child. It is objective.

For children, the idea of therapy can be very different from the reality of therapy. If you have not participated in child therapy yourself, it can be very different from adult therapy. Books are a great way of connecting parents to children in the early stages of figuring out the process.

For young children, age 3 to 7 or so, we like the book *A Child's First Book About Play Therapy* by Nemiroff and Annunziata. This is a picture book. A 7-year-old may find this book a bit immature, but we feel that anxiety about therapy (anything new) can often make a child feel younger, so we feel comfortable recommending this. That said, if you feel that the book is too "young," feel free to try our next suggestion.

For children a bit older, latency age, we like the book *Feeling Better: A Kid's Book About Therapy* by Rashkin. We would recommend reading this book to early elementary school-age children even if they have the ability to read themselves. If they want to read it themselves afterward, that would be appropriate. Also, the book is divided into journal entries and can be read in a way that parallels the beginning of your child's own therapy process.

For teenagers, we like the book *Analyze This?* edited by Longhine. Written by teenagers about their own therapy experiences, it can be an effective tool for helping therapy feel "normal" for adolescents. The fact that it was written by teenagers makes it more acceptable to this age group. That said, as with the previous books, reading this book with your child is fine (especially with younger teens), but we would recommend that you leave that choice up to your teenager.

TODDLERHOOD THROUGH PRE-LATENCY OR
EARLY CHILDHOOD (AGE 3–7)

Your feelings about and comfort with the therapist are critical and should always be the paramount consideration in the final selection of a therapist for your child at this age. It will help your child more if you like the therapist and communicate your approval and support of the relationship. It will help him or her to connect to a new therapist by seeing your commitment. Equally important is your child (at the older end of the age range) having some perceived control over the process. This can include a choice between therapists (of whom you approve), the times (which need to work for your schedule), the day (which also needs to work for your schedule), how you travel to therapy, or what snack you take. If you commit to a schedule that creates difficulty in your life, the therapy becomes much more susceptible to ambivalence.

LATENCY OR CHILDHOOD (AGE 7–11)

With this age group, the decision to move your child's therapy forward relates to what you think about each therapist and how you convey your thoughts and decisions to your child. What do you like about each therapist? What do you not like? What you are unsure about each therapist? As we stated before, self-efficacy and pride are important aspects of your child's development at this time. It will help your child if you ask for his or her feedback and thoughts about your choice and address in an open way any concerns that he or she may have about your decision. If your child does not approve of your choice, we do not necessarily think that you should change it. It would be important to understand exactly why and to weigh that against your reasoning, as this can identify any ambivalence. It is helpful for the therapist to know of your child's concerns.

EARLY ADOLESCENCE (AGE 12–15)

For children this age and older, the more say they have in choosing their own therapist, the more ownership they will take over the therapy process as a whole. Teenagers want to be big. While they show this desire in many ways, they, simultaneously, often to parents' consternation, still want to be small.

It is a strange developmental push-and-pull dynamic that leaves parents (and the child, mind you) confused and exhausted. Exhaustion comes from teenage ambivalence about maturation. We see a fight between the forces of forward growth (**progression**) and maturing and the backward pull (**regression**) to remain young and carefree. We see the early adolescent demanding more independence (autonomy) and then having difficulty managing his or her responsibilities. This is why early teenagers often struggle with parents being in charge—it reminds them that they are still young—and obligates them to fight back against the "young" feelings. Because the therapist is an individual with whom your child will share a great deal (translate: be vulnerable with), and because vulnerability can create regression, an important way to balance this is with choice. Giving your early adolescent child some choices regarding whom she will see provides your child with a participating role and some responsibility for her own therapy. This is helping your child have a sense of ownership of her therapy.

LATE ADOLESCENCE/TEEN YEARS (AGE 15–17)

Your teenager needs increasingly more ownership over the decision about the therapist and his or her therapy in general. Your teen may travel to therapy on his or her own and may schedule and reschedule sessions with the therapist. This potential for more independent responsibility within the therapeutic relationship requires your teen's serious intention (commitment) to participate in his or her therapy. At least at the beginning, that commitment to therapy comes in large part from having the choice of therapist. At this age, after their parents' initial work of introducing the idea and developing the process of therapy, teenagers increasingly engage in therapy and stay in therapy by choice. None of this is to say that you will not have input into whom your child sees in therapy. It is important that you do. Giving him options and helping him be thoughtful about his choices with regard to therapists is an important teaching moment about the healthy and productive use of independence in self-care.

YOUNG ADULTHOOD (AGE 18–MID-20S)

Your young adult child can feel different from moment to moment. Sometimes she feels like an adult, sometimes like a teenager, and sometimes maybe even like a younger child, depending on the stress and difficulties of the moment. Decision-making for this age group is full of conscious doubt and nervousness. For your young adult child, this doubt ends up being managed by the impulsive nature that is characteristic of this developmental stage. The idea behind this coping style is to move quickly through the feelings of uncertainty. Your young adult child makes the choice of therapist based on an indescribable feeling level, rather than anything highly specific or concrete. This is called a visceral response, one based on "feeling right" without knowing specifically why. Even though there is considerable research about what types of psychotherapy may work best with specific types of patients, the basis of success in therapy is the relationship (relational bond) between the patient and the therapist. The social world of a young adult that includes many of the "firsts" of being an adult is critical, and the choice of therapist is an extension of this. We feel that the choice of therapist lies with your adult child only. If he or she cannot choose or will not choose, you can see if he or she will choose the most preferable therapist for a test period. This can be one or two sessions. This is a version of selecting without committing. It is a middle step. It addresses your adult child's ambivalence about treatment and about getting help, and possible feelings of loss of control. It addresses this by creating a sense of control, the same one we feel when we put a toe in the water.

A BIG AND IMPORTANT STEP: LEAVING THE FAMILIAR BEHIND (INTERNAL)

It is important for you to trust yourself and your instincts. You have collected quite a bit of information through this process so far, both direct (things you have been told) and indirect (things you have felt and noticed). Your child's therapy must go forward with you. Indeed, your child's therapy is very unlikely to be helpful without you.

You now have met with a therapist or, as we suggested, more than one. You have had consultations or intakes, depending on the setting that you have chosen. This was a lot of work. Do not underestimate the effort it takes to push us out of our familiar thoughts and feelings about these problems. This is because our issues in a strange way are familiar, expected, and known to us. We call this our uncomfortable "comfort zone." We may feel angry, nervous, or sad in our uncomfortable "comfort zone," but we know it well and it is familiar.

Think of a seesaw. The issues that we are referring to are on one side of the seesaw and we are on the other. We adjust our position on the seesaw in order to stay in balance. This adjustment happens every day, and the process of adjusting becomes second nature to us, and is something that we hardly notice. This is the "comfort" part of comfort zone. When the issue on the other side of the seesaw becomes too big and the process of adjusting no longer creates the balance that we need to function on a daily basis, the discomfort becomes too great and we must change. This is what you are doing now.

It is a significant step to push oneself out of that uncomfortable "comfort zone" and one that should be applauded. That said, because of the often and understandable difficulty about starting therapy for our child, there is a tendency to take a moment after an intake or consultation in order to gather ourselves. It is like climbing to the top of a long staircase. We need to take a deep breath and wait before we take another step. You can think about what you have experienced so far in this process—talking about the problems, meeting new people, and so on. This time is important. We believe in pacing yourself and your child's therapy. By pacing, we mean adjusting the speed of the therapy so that it works best and helps you and your child feel comfortable with the changes that are occurring.

You may also feel an urgency to solve or fix the problems facing your child and the family as soon as possible. This is typical and normal. It is very important to discuss these feelings of urgency with the therapist. From our perspective, speed in this process is a complicated factor. Figuring out what pace is optimal for a given therapy must take into account the child's needs (emotional and developmental), the parents' needs, the issues being addressed, and the other individuals and institutions involved. Going fast does not create change any quicker.

WHEN MY CHILD REFUSES TO EVEN START THERAPY (EXTERNAL)

"What if my child says he does not want to go to therapy after the intake or consultation?"

This is a typical problem confronting parents. If your child remains reluctant to engage in therapy, the choice becomes secondary to working with his struggle about getting help at all. We are going to revisit this theme many times throughout this book. How or whether to start therapy, how or whether to continue, and how and when to end are all complex decisions. At the beginning, we are typically dealing with fear and anxiety about the unknown. What is this thing? What is it going to feel like? How long do I have to go? These are difficult questions to answer until there has been at least some consistent contact between the therapist and your child. We think that about four sessions is sufficient for a therapist to begin to formulate a good idea of what the therapy may look like and how long it may last. Sometimes this takes longer, sometimes shorter, depending on the nature of the difficulties, how quickly your child is comfortable opening up, and the information at hand. Remember, sometimes issues have been brewing for extended periods, and reworking them cannot happen quickly.

For your child, the reality of child therapy is that because the decision to start therapy does not typically come from the child, there very well may be some persuading that needs to take place to start. What we recommend is that you take the "try it and see what you think" approach with your child: "Let's try it for a few weeks and see how it goes." This gives children who are anxious, who are feeling uncomfortable or vulnerable, more perceived control over the situation. It is the light at the end of the tunnel. Knowing that there *can be* an end, not necessarily that there is one right now, can be helpful. You might even indicate that if the child does not like it, you can talk about alternatives (after a few sessions). This give you time to bring the therapist into the equation. Including the therapist in these discussions can dilute or decrease your feelings of having a power struggle with your child. We caution against conveying the idea that if your child does not like it, then he or she does not have to go. Often this is a reflection of our own ambivalence about the therapy and can lead to our child's question: "Does my mom/dad/parent really want me to go or not?"

If you experience discomfort at the start of your child's therapy, our suggestion is to go month to month—commit yourself to four weeks of sessions (four sessions for your child, two sessions for you).

AMBIVALENCE (INTERNAL)

Ambivalence is the concept of feeling two opposing ways about something at the same time—also known as "mixed feelings." Ambivalence is ever-present in our lives and is obvious when we begin to look for it. It is the feeling of being torn. Sometimes it is demonstrated in the feeling of being stuck (I just cannot decide where to go). Other times we see it when we know that something is good for us (i.e., we should be doing it) and we still do not pursue it. Some examples of topics we might have ambivalent feelings about are going to the gym, having dessert, changing jobs, going to the doctor, or making that difficult phone call.

Ambivalence may be seen in connection with something going on in your child's therapy, or during or after one of your meetings with your child's therapist. An example of this may be remembering something you wanted to tell the therapist, but only after your collateral session ends. Another example could be "forgetting" a session that was scheduled. The presence of our ambivalence is not always obvious.

One of the complexities of ambivalence is that we can often justify following either course of action. We can do or not do. In a situation about which we just *do not* know how to feel or think, we can come up with completely valid reasons not to do something. Why should we make this decision instead of that one?

The purpose of ambivalence in our lives may also not be obvious. Ambivalence allows us to maintain a sense of control over our lives during moments of uncertainty. It is a communication to ourselves that something about a given situation is complicated for us emotionally. It requires us to view multiple sides of the same situation by communicating that something feels off, possibly wrong.

One of the most common examples of ambivalence is procrastination. When we cannot complete an assignment, we can be sure that something about that assignment is bothering us. What that something is can vary. It can hide from our awareness and is often quite complex.

We like to think of ambivalence as one foot in, one foot out. The foot that is in is making us feel like we are moving forward—but very slowly, like a glacier. The foot that is out gives us a sense of control by indicating that we can stop—pulling the other foot out if we want. Being able to manage and cope with the feelings and thoughts of "not feeling certain" is called being able to tolerate ambivalence.

Tolerating ambivalence is a crucial element of a successful treatment. There will absolutely be times during treatment when you and your child feel ambivalence. We recommend that you do not try to manage these feelings and thoughts on your own. Talk to your child's therapist about these ideas. Your child's therapist should be encouraging of ambivalence because it serves such an important purpose.

Parents who ultimately bring their children into the therapy process can "think" about it for quite sometime, can have that phone number in their pocket for months but not make an appointment with the therapist or take any other type of action. These are forms of ambivalence. We want to stress that there is nothing wrong with feeling ambivalent. It is completely normal and can often be very useful as a way of pacing the therapy.

Ambivalence shows up in many other ways. Sometimes clues that ambivalence is at work in your child's therapy can be seen in the "not" doing (or avoiding)—to "not" want to continue, to "not" want to discuss, to "not" remember to go. Ambivalence about your child's therapy can show up in several ways.

- You have researched and interviewed more than three therapists but have not found one for your child.
- You may not share all the information asked by the therapist.
- You may find that taking the child to therapy is too complicated to do regularly.
- Your child says he or she "doesn't want to go" to therapy and you give in.
- "Things are better" so therapy is no longer needed and can just stop immediately.

Parents' and children's ambivalence about a therapist or the issues being discussed in therapy always affects the development of a helpful, trusting, and successful relationship with the therapist. Although we are saying that ambivalence is common, expected, and typical, we are also saying that when parents consistently act on their ambivalence (or their child's) instead of sharing it with the therapist, it can have a negative effect on their child's therapy.

Pedro, His Mother, and Ambivalence

When Pedro entered therapy, his mother identified the main issue as the fact that Pedro was very shy at school and often did not talk. His mother was very concerned about what this meant and spent the intake detailing all the many traumatic events in Pedro's life as possible causes of his withdrawn behavior in school. As the intake ended, his mother requested that the therapist not talk to Pedro about his unwillingness to speak in school, indicating that he felt very embarrassed about talking about this problem. The therapist was concerned that not discussing Pedro's problems would lead to the therapy becoming stuck (lack of trust, honesty, real treatment goals, etc.). The therapist also believed that Pedro's mother's request was a sign of her ambivalence about getting her son help. The ambivalence, if acted upon in the way Pedro's mother requested, could create a situation in which no one was discussing Pedro's main issue. Ultimately, the therapist discussed the issues with Pedro and helped his mother with her own ambivalence about dealing with her feelings about her child.

Your child may be confused if your ambivalence creates a wait that is too long between intake and first session. He or she may determine that this has to do with your lack of commitment to or interest in this process. Any time that parents can convey their clear commitment to therapy, the therapy invariably has better results.

Sick Anthony Misses His Appointments

Anthony was a very anxious 12-year-old boy whose parents were very active in his care. They attended parent sessions regularly and tried all the therapist's recommendations. A main issue with the treatment was that Anthony often was "sick" on the days of therapy. He would come down with a "low grade" fever, or a stomachache, or a nauseous feeling. His parents would keep him home, often from school also, on those days. This occurred frequently, at least once or twice a month. The parents indicated that it was just too difficult to get him moving on those days. Because of this dynamic, it became very difficult to achieve any kind of consistency in his therapy. The therapist noticed that when Anthony was challenged in session, the following week he would be "sick." Without an acknowledgment by his parents that Anthony's "illness" might be his ambivalence, there was no way of addressing the reasons behind his ambivalence. The lack of acknowledgment was also a sign of the parents' ambivalence about Anthony's therapy.

FLIGHT INTO HEALTH (INTERNAL)

You may notice that after the intake, the situation at home may improve suddenly. You may find that saying you are going to find help for your child and visiting a therapist for a consultation has altered the dynamics at home already. This is hardly ever a sign that there is no need for further intervention. We would like you to view this "doing better" dynamic with some skepticism. Harsh as it may sound, the issues that your child is struggling with have been building over time and do not just get better overnight, although we very much want them to. They need time to be undone and redone.

In fact, the idea that things have suddenly gotten better is such a common occurrence that it has a name—the "flight into health." We do not want to characterize the flight into health as a negative. There is nothing wrong with feeling that we are better, that we do not need much help.

In reality, children getting better or situations improving swiftly is a very important detail in the therapy and can be a very encouraging sign. The underlying communication from your child (if things have improved soon after beginning this process) is that you have found the correct response to his or her issues. It is a communication that your child feels heard—that by looking for a therapist you are a caring and loving parent. The "getting better" is a message to continue—sort of like a cat purring. We do not stop petting a cat when it begins to purr; we take it as a message that the cat wants us to continue doing what we are doing.

INCREASING (ESCALATION OF) SYMPTOMS (INTERNAL)

There is an opposite side to the flight into health coin. In this, the dynamics and symptoms addressed in your child's therapy—the behavior or the emotion—intensify and appear worse as treatment gets underway. Therapy can be confusing at times. You bring your child to therapy to help him or her feel better or to help the family get along better. Yet often the problems seem to increase. This unfortunate dynamic is a reality that occurs in many therapies and is always difficult to endure and manage for everyone involved. Even though your child and your family are having difficulties when therapy begins, they are difficulties that you know (remember the uncomfortable "comfort zone"). They are familiar, even if they are problematic.

The initial sessions, discussions, and interactions with a therapist can create basic changes in your family system. You may be asking questions for the first time, or your child may be getting a new message from you. Old feelings expressed for the first time or new thoughts may be articulated. Perceptions are changing. These changes may initially be felt as big, unfamiliar shifts and may, just by the very nature of being new, cause distress.

It is important to remember that these are positive shifts, even if they do not feel like it. Change is uncomfortable because it is new. Just like a pair of shoes needs to be "broken-in" to feel "right," so does therapy. Initially, change seems like a loss of control.

Just as a flight into health can be a typical reaction for your child to the start of her treatment, the escalation and intensification of symptoms can also understood as a normal reaction to beginning the process of healing.

Another way of think about this is noticing the pressure you feel if you hold your breath for a long period. The first breath you take, the one that fills your lungs for the first time, includes intensity and emotion. Try it. Beginning to address problems holds the same potential for release. It is the combination of relief and struggle, released simultaneously. This intensity will slow as you continue breathing and get used to breathing again. It will also slow as your child gets into the flow of therapy.

Jen's Feelings Get More Intense

Jen was a very angry and anxious 5-year-old girl whose parents were going through a very hostile divorce and custody battle for over a year. Her school reported aggressive behavior toward other children. Jen's father brought her to therapy for her problems at school as well as to increase his understanding of how the hostility between his ex-wife and himself was affecting Jen. After the therapist's second session with Jen, her father reported to the therapist that Jen had spent over an hour shaking, crying, and screaming that she was afraid to lose him. Her father was terribly worried that Jen's emotions were suddenly worse because she had never exhibited any outbursts such as this. The therapist theorized that by starting her in therapy, the father gave Jen "permission" to let these scary feelings out.

There is no exact timetable for these dynamics. They can come and go throughout the therapy. Like the unsettled dust after spring cleaning, or the sore leg after a workout, this issue is an aspect of the newness of the process. There can be "newness" in every change or improvement. As you and your child move through the therapy experience, each step has its growing "pains." Keep in mind that therapy is not a straight-line process. There will be further periods of discomfort as you, your child, and your family adjust to the growth that the psychotherapy can generate.

CHAPTER SUMMARY

CHAPTER 5: TAKING THE NEXT STEPS: MOVING FORWARD

Take all the information that you have about the therapist and evaluate:

- Whom did you like the best?
- Who made you the most comfortable?
- Whom could you talk with comfortably?
- Who seemed connected to your child?
- Whom could you see your child interacting with comfortably?
- Whom do you want to work with?

Research has shown that the basis of the therapeutic relationship's success is the client liking and feeling cared for by the therapist—not his or her training, ideology, philosophy, degree, or place of work.

Tolerating ambivalence is a crucial element of a successful treatment.

When we start therapy, we are typically dealing with fear and anxiety about the unknown.

- What is this thing?
- What is it going to feel like?
- How long do I have to go?

We recommend that you do not try to manage these feelings and thoughts on your own; rather, talk to your child's therapist about these ideas.

We think that about four sessions is sufficient for a therapist to begin to formulate a good idea of what the therapy may look like and how long it may last.

You may notice that after the intake, the situation at home may change.

- The idea that things have suddenly gotten better is such a common occurrence that it has a name—the "flight into health."
- Typically, this is not a sign that further intervention is unneeded.
- The issues that your child is struggling with have been building over time and do not just get better overnight.
- They need time to be undone and redone.

- There is an opposite side to the flight into health when behaviors or emotions intensify and appear worse as treatment gets underway.
- The problems may seem to increase.
- Change is uncomfortable because it is new—just like a pair of shoes needs to be "broken-in" to feel "right."

CHAPTER 6

Types and Forms of Child Psychotherapy

There comes a time in every pregnancy that the relationship between the mother—and maybe even the father—and the fetus begins to take on the form and structure that will exist after the baby is born. The parent(s) begin to "listen" to the communications of the unborn child—is he moving, is she kicking, how does he respond when I do this, how does she or he act when I eat that? The parent(s) begin to have feelings about these communications and begin to respond to them in a variety of ways.

Once your child is born, your infant is pre-verbal (meaning not developmentally ready/able to use spoken language). Communication between the infant and the parents enters a new stage that is primarily the communication of feelings without words. Many parents can distinguish various ways that their infants cry. Each type of cry communicates a different message and feeling from the infant to the parents. As your child begins to communicate using words, his or her feelings are part of the communication. Your infant's various cries become a child's tones of voice (still accompanied by tears) that are now more easily distinguished as anger, frustration, fear, pain, or fatigue.

This process—the communication between two people—becomes the crux of any child therapy. Communication of all kinds is the information that therapists and parents use to understand what is happening with a child and is a key component of how therapists develop a plan to address a child's issues.

Before we continue, we want to develop a foundation for understanding child communication. First, we want you to recall when we talked about the concepts of manifest and latent content. Within this framework, we think of communication in these two ways: verbal (what we hear-words and sounds-from the communicator), and nonverbal (what we see—facial expressions, body movements; what we can smell, touch, and taste). These make up the manifest content of a child's presentation. The latent content is the underlying meaning related to these manifest communications.

Let us further define these two major types of communication:

- **Verbal communication** is communication that uses words and sounds to convey meaning or messages. Words in this case are symbols—they represent an idea. The word "happy" represents an idea—positive, pleased feelings—communicated by saying the word "happy." The word "happy" is a symbol of the idea of "happy."

  A confusing aspect of verbal communication is that sometimes symbols and feelings may not match what one would expect. The meaning of the symbol is completely dependent on what the communicator's ideas are about that symbol. So, although it may seem strange, one can say they are "happy" while experiencing a sad, angry, or anxious feeling state because "happy" is the symbol they have learned coincides with these other feeling states.

- **Nonverbal communication** is a communication type in which information is conveyed through a mode other than words. Body language, facial expressions, body movements, scent, timeliness, and attire are examples of nonverbal communication. The idea of "being happy" can be communicated by smiling or jumping for joy. We know someone is happy when he or she shows us this, even without saying anything.

  It should be noted that sometimes nonverbal communication and verbal communication do not match. An individual can look sad and say that they are not sad.

As caregivers, we are always interpreting the manifest communication (what is visible and audible) of a child and trying to discover its latent meaning (what is hidden, underlying). Understanding helps us feel more in control and increases our ability to make choices in the care of our children. But as we know, the actual meaning is often difficult to know definitively—it is usually a matter of trying many things until something works. Does a cry (manifest content) mean that infant Silvia is hungry (latent content) or tired (latent) or in pain (latent)? Does 10-year-old Pedro's inability to make friends (manifest) mean that he has a developmental delay (latent) or is depressed (latent) or is shy (latent)? Do poor grades (manifest) mean that teenaged Chen is depressed (latent) or not comprehending the material (latent) or unfocused (latent)? Does Kelly's fear of bees (manifest) mean that she has worries about losing control (latent) or that she has been stung before (latent) or that she has a typical age-appropriate worry (latent)?

What can make this effort more complicated is that each child uses his or her own combination of forms of communication to let the outside world know what is happening. No two children communicate in the same way. It is our job to optimize the child's ability to communicate, to figure out what is her most comfortable way of communicating and what form of communication helps her tell us or show us what she needs and/or what is happening with her.

Essentially, child therapy's centerpiece is its effort to interpret the latent meaning of what we are seeing, hearing, and experiencing with a child.

When deciding what type of therapy to use with a child, a therapist will consider several related elements of communication.

1. The form by which a child communicates (based on age, developmental stage, and/or cultural norms);
2. The content that a child is communicating (both manifest and latent);
3. The effort that a child undertakes when communicating (based on issues not related to age or developmental stage such as health, culture, language, developmental problem);
4. The intensity of the child's presentation of her or his feelings during and following communication (based on age or developmental stage, cultural norms, and situational/historical issues specific to that child's life and experiences).

FORMS OF COMMUNICATION

The following are the four forms of communication that children utilize:

1. **Affective (feelings/emotions)**—children can communicate with their emotional expression. These are typically nonverbal communications. They "show" how they feel. They can feel angry, sad, happy, or afraid and can display these various *affective* states by smiling, looking grumpy,

cringing, crying, screaming, laughing, or being silent. They can be quiet or boisterous. They can seem down or active. They can be highly emotional or withdrawn. They can use body language or facial expressions or physical appearance.

The Importance of Devon's Father

Devon sat with his therapist and answered questions during an intake. Devon became very angry at times, and at other times he was quiet and subdued, with his arms crossed. The therapist noticed that Devon's emotions (affect) changed when questions were asked about his relationship with his father. Devon's affective communication highlighted this relationship and helped the therapist to know going forward that special care must be taken in how material regarding Devon's father was discussed.

The word "affect" is one of those psychology words that you may hear used during an intake, so we want it to be familiar. For our purposes, "affect" means emotions, but it can also be used to describe how a person conveys emotions. You may hear other words associated with affect—blunted (displaying a lack of emotional reaction), constricted (having limited range of emotion, not too high or low), flat (having no emotion), or full (showing a full range of emotion). In this case, Devon showed full affect, and his affective communication gave the therapist insight into the specific issues at hand (namely, problems with his relationship with his father). If Devon had indicated that there was conflict between him and his father, but had shown very little emotion when describing the relationship, this would have provided a different understanding to the therapist, possibly anxiety or fear.

Affective communication is important because there are times in which one cannot effectively communicate how one is feeling with words. Depression can be effectively identified through affect—a sense of sadness, being tired, bored, or run down. Anxiety can also be identified via affective communication—highly active, edgy, keyed up. In fact, many disorders have affective components. Feel free to ask your child's therapist what your child's affective communication appears to indicate. Remember, while not an exact science, it can provide important information.

All children use affect as communication, but some more than others. Infants use this form of communication as their primary way of letting people know what they need and what is going on with them. Crying, fussing, cooing—parents are constantly interpreting these communications. In fact, if a parent seeks therapy for an infant or a child who is pre-verbal, the therapist will most often see both the infant/young child and the parent together because the infant/young child's life is almost completely centered on affective communication with the parent. The therapy then centers on helping the parent respond to these communications from the child.

2. **Symbolic**—children can communicate with their play. They tell stories. Play is made up of both nonverbal and verbal communications. We call it *symbolic* because it is the beginning of a child being able to construct and communicate ideas (symbols) that are in their heads in an organized way. A child's play is the stories of a child's life and a necessary part of a child's healthy development. It is the middle step for a child—one foot on each side of the developmental fence between pre-verbal and verbal. Play allows a child to communicate a complex world before he or she is equipped with enough words to sufficiently describe this world and while he or she is still figuring it out. The play is made of two parts: the **conscious** (intentional and under control) and the **subconscious** (level just below a level of intentional control).

   - *Conscious play material*—content that a child is aware that he or she is communicating. This is the planned and thoughtful aspect of the play. Therapists sometimes call this the "metaphor of the play." The concept of metaphor describes the child's use of play instead of conversation to express her or his thoughts and feelings. The therapist responds in the child's language, using the play as determined by the child as a mode of communication.

     The actions of a child building a tower with blocks, playing house, chasing after a friend, and playing a game of checkers are all examples of a child's conscious play material.

   - *Subconscious play material*—content that a child is unaware that he or she is communicating. It is the window into a child's real life. It is often made up of imagery, ideas, and meanings that a child cannot yet comprehend and integrate because they are too
     a. complex (beyond the child's intellectual capacity), or
     b. overwhelming (overpowering to the child's current coping level).

Using our previous examples, a child's subconscious play is (in parentheses):

- (*trying to feel powerful by*) building a tower with blocks,
- (*recreating a difficult situation about a new baby sister by*) playing house,
- (*searching for a connection by*) chasing after a friend,
- (*attempting to control the rules by*) playing a game of checkers.

Very Active Natalie

Natalie was 5 years old and came to her therapist's office to play. Her play consisted of jumping off the chairs and the couch, running back and forth, trying to climb dangerously up on the top of cabinets, opening drawers that she was told not to, throwing toys over her head, and eventually needing to be gently restrained physically by her therapist. The metaphor of the play was the activity and rules that govern the activity—Natalie was active, energetic, brave, and risk-taking. Natalie also tried to break rules, break things, and "break" herself. The underlying meaning of the play had to do with Natalie's home life, her parents' separation, divorce, and past and ongoing hostility. Everything in Natalie's life was broken. This part of the play was about how unprotected and unsafe she felt in the past when her family was breaking apart and how unstructured she felt in the present as problems continued.

In this example, Natalie was trying to **master** (understand and have control over) her surroundings and herself using both types of play—the conscious and the subconscious. She attempted to gain mastery, as all children do, over feelings and situations that she was encountering. Getting back to the metaphor concept, Natalie manages all of this by "burying" the subconscious material (the family difficulties and her feelings about it) within her conscious and, very active, play. At age 5, Natalie could not understand everything that had happened to her family or to her parents or what it all meant for her future. She had seen the pain and the anger and the fear. It was all too overwhelming and too complex to comprehend, and so, at her developmental stage, symbolic play in therapy (and elsewhere) provided Natalie a medium to communicate and work through her feelings about all of this.

3. **Kinetic (movement, action, behavior)**—children can communicate through their actions and their behavior. For our purposes, action is a single

instance of activity (i.e., the action of not waking up) while behavior is a pattern of actions, the way in which someone acts (i.e., noisy behavior). This form of communication has both verbal and nonverbal components and centers on a child's activity and energy. We can see children using kinetic communication as soon as they are born to let people know how they feel and what they want or need.

At very young ages, this form of communication is fairly uncontained, as rules around actions and behavior are still being learned. Parents are constantly asking children, "Why did you do that?" or "What were you thinking?" Although these questions are important, the action is the communication. The children think and/or feel, and then they act (communicate). These communications are actions and behaviors that parents often see early in their child's life: having a tantrum, throwing, biting, hitting, ignoring, touching, and walking away, to name some examples. As children learn about the rules governing certain behaviors, their kinetic options become more limited, and they look for new ones (testing limits).

As children get older, engaging in kinetic communication seems to become more volitional (an aspect of choice). They are more in control of their physical selves, and their physical options are more nuanced and extensive. That said, they also have words now, and so not using their words is an important component of kinetic communication in older children and adolescents. They can slam doors, fight, skip classes, remove eye contact, miss appointments, wear provocative clothing, engage in sex, and so on. Please note that older children are not more conscious of the meaning of behaving in a certain way or acting in a certain way just because they are older. Self-awareness is not necessarily a function of age.

Victor Visits the Teacher's Lounge

Victor was a very bright 14-year-old who was having problems at school. He was failing most of his classes, was hostile to many of his teachers, was skipping classes, and was acting out in the classroom. His teachers were exasperated, his parents were overwhelmed, and Victor could not (would not?) stop this problematic behavior. He also had a habit of going to the teachers' lounge of his high school. He was not allowed in the teachers' lounge, but he went there often after one of his classroom altercations and sat until a teacher spoke with him about leaving or called for the school social worker.

Victor's kinetic communication told the story of an adolescent boy in deep conflict and suffering. Two levels were apparent—the oppositional/rejecting side (that got him in trouble and kept him isolated) and the reaching out/connecting side (that could not figure out how to ask for help appropriately). He had great difficulty talking about his feelings or the reasons behind his behaviors without become overcome with anger. The behaviors ended up being the most secure way to "tell" how he was feeling and what he needed.

4. **Verbal**—children can also communicate with their words. With the ability to create words (also a type of symbol), a child can form his or her ideas in a new way.

Remember earlier when we discussed symbolic communication—children putting form to their abstract ideas. We focused on play as a visual and concrete formation of their ideas. For example, hugging a doll may represent the connection to a caregiver. Two matchbox cars crashing into each other may represent the conflict of two parents fighting. A chaotic drawing with black and gray crayons may represent the fear of nighttime.

Now, children can describe these ideas with words. Hugging a doll is "mom" or "love" or "happy." Crashing the cars is "hit" or "hurt" or "mad." Bedtime is "lonely" or "scary" or "sad." These words develop over time, starting with monosyllabic words that children put their own meanings to. It typically starts with "mom," "dad," "cat," "sad," "no"—words that each child makes important by learning and using them. This is the reason that the words "mom" and "dad" are often the first words that children use.

The more words a child learns, the more complex and nuanced the verbal communication can be. That said, some children learn to use words and use verbal communication earlier than other children. The number of words and the use of these words do not necessarily indicate maturity or advanced development, only a comfort with this form of communication. A 4-year-old may know many words and use them to share with others her ideas and feelings, but she still has only been alive and developing for 4 years.

In terms of therapy, especially at the start, it is far more important to assess which form of communication your child is comfortable with using. Developmentally, children will eventually move toward a verbal form of communication and so treatment may begin focused on one type of communication and move toward others as the therapy progresses.

Randall Begins to Describe His Feelings

Randall, a 12-year-old boy, was very anxious when he saw his therapist for the first time. He had difficulties interacting with his sister. His mother described his behavior as odd. She said he would cover his face with his hands and run from the room. During the early stages of therapy, when the therapist asked him about this, he shook his head and looked down. He would say, "I can't talk about it." As Randall began to feel more comfortable, he began to respond to the therapist's prompts regarding the ideas that were being conveyed by Randall's face covering and running. You seem "scared." You seem "angry" when you run from her. Eventually, Randall began to put his own words to his feelings and ideas about his sister. It began simply, "I hate her" and "she is mean" and grew from there.

Randall was old enough by societal standards to be able to use words to communicate, but he was not doing so. He was intelligent enough and he had the words, he just chose to share his feelings using another mode of communication. In fact, his choice actually conveyed quite a bit of information about his problem. The way he communicated, covering his face, is typical of a small child—maybe 2 or 3 years old—and most likely indicated when the problems with his sister had begun.

Note: A child who does not speak, speaks infrequently, cries a lot, throws tantrums, or runs around is still communicating. As we have said, there are many ways that a child communicates. It is our job to listen to and try to understand any and all of these forms.

COMMUNICATION OF CONTENT

When children are young, they may be able to communicate verbally, yet because they are still in the process of learning their spoken language, they will often use their affective communication as a more familiar and comfortable way of communicating to others.

The developmentally younger a child is, the more likely it is that she or he will communicate affectively more than verbally. As the child matures developmentally, he or she communicates verbally, with decreasing emphasis on communicating affectively. We use the developmental concept rather than a chronological age because children's communication abilities are based on cognitive (brain) rather than physical (body) maturation.

Changes in a child's sense of **autonomy** (ability to think and act independently) can intensify kinetic communication. Within a typical lifespan of a child, we see some of the most dramatic changes to autonomy centered on a process called **separation**. Separation is a child's emotional, cognitive, and developmental move toward more independent thought and action. Although separation is occurring constantly in some fashion during a child's development, there are two significant moments when the separation process is the singular defining structure in a child's life. Clinicians describe these as the first (1½ to 3 or 4 years old) and second (10 years old and on) **separations**. Caregivers call these the terrible twos and teenage rebellion, respectively.

A child's developmental ability to communicate, as well as the type of difficulties the child experiences during his or her daily life, affects the therapist's choice of type of therapy. Even though a child is verbal, the nature of the child's difficulties may be too frightening to the child for him or her to verbalize. Some examples are a child's fear about his or her parent's health, being sick, hearing voices, having disturbing fantasies, being bullied, or abused. In these instances, the therapist might select a play therapy rather than a verbal therapy for this child because the play creates some space between the real and the make-believe. The play is a metaphor for reality—a stand-in, like an actor who uses a stunt double for a dangerous scene. It represents reality, but with enough differences to help the child keep reality out of his consciousness at a safe distance.

José Hits Home Runs and Wins

José's parents were getting divorced and he felt powerless. He was very upset and wanted them to stay together, to both live together in his home. He did not initially say this to his therapist, although the therapist asked about it. He did not say this to his mother or his father. Instead, he played baseball in the small office. The couch was first base, the shelves were second base, the door was third base, and the desk was home base. José began by hitting the therapist with the ball and requiring the therapist to discuss the concept of safety. Session after session, José and his therapist played game after game. José often altered the score, changed the rules, and controlled the therapist's actions (which the therapist commented on, but did not alter). He hit home run after home run; he never lost. The therapist praised José's performance, enjoyed his victories, and expressed frustration at his own defeats (losses).

One day, José abruptly changed the game. He created an obstacle course, and the therapist asked about the sudden change in the routine. As they climbed around the room in the new game, the therapist asked again about José's father leaving, and José for the first time told the therapist that he was angry and that he did not like talking about the divorce. The therapist acknowledged that changes in family were often very difficult to talk about.

There are many different types of play therapy that share many elements, but they differ in terms of how the therapist uses the play therapeutically. Sometimes, depending on the needs of the child, a therapist will use various types of play therapy within the same therapy.

The following are some of the more common play therapy techniques. Therapists may select among these techniques rather than use one type exclusively.

- **Analytic play therapy** is based on the concepts first developed by Sigmund Freud for adults and focuses on the individual's subconsious (below awareness) ideas and feelings. Other therapists, such as Anna Freud, Melanie Klien, Carl Rogers, and Virginia Axline, to name a few, adapted his concepts to help children. In this type of play therapy, the therapist closely observes and follows the child's play. The therapist communicates to the child both verbally and nonverbally about the child's play. This type of play therapy often uses non-commercial dolls, puppets, blocks, action figures, expressive arts, and so on.

Ned and the Dollhouse

Ned played with a dollhouse. He began using small figures of a dad and a mom and a little baby to act out a typical family scene. Soon the play changed as Ned picked up the house and began to shake it, toss it around, and flip it upside down. The therapist spoke to Ned, in a concerned voice, saying things such as, "the house is crashing, everyone is getting thrown, and the baby fell on his head."

The therapist believed that Ned was communicating information about the destructive nature of his home life. The therapist did not interpret this reality for Ned, but instead helped Ned to work toward expressing his anger, fears, and hostility through the metaphor of the destruction of a dollhouse and some figurines. For Ned, hearing another person acknowledge his feelings (often subconscious ones) helped him feel understood, more secure, and less alone. Also, he began to hear and learn the words (symbols) that were connected to his feelings.

- **Psychodynamic play therapy** is based on a number of concepts that focus on the relationship—the connection and growing trust—between the child and the therapist as the primary structure through which problems are addressed. The play is the vehicle of shared communication, using the same types of toys described above. The therapist often participates in the child's play as directed by the child. The therapist comments and asks questions, as well as observes the play.

Valerie, the Lion, Holds on for Dear Life

Valerie played with a variety of animals in her sessions. She talked about each and gave each a set of characteristics—one was tricky, one was angry, one was scared, and so on. There were approximately 10 animals that she played with, and they were always getting into some sort of trouble. The "trouble" usually took place on a small table in the corner of the therapist's office, with all the animals falling to their deaths—except for the Lion. Valerie commanded the therapist to enact the demise of all the animals except the Lion. The Lion was the animal that Valerie always saved. The Lion clung to the edge of the table until Valerie told the therapist to choose another animal and save the Lion. Sometimes the Lion then ate the other animals, and sometimes the Lion saved the other animals.

The therapist believed that Valerie, like Ned, was communicating information about the her home life and how fragile and precarious it was. In this case, the therapist commented on the Lion's bravery and asked Valerie why the Lion sometimes helped and other times hurt the other animals. Sometimes the therapist gave voice to some of the animals as a way of eliciting a response from Valerie's Lion. In this way, Valerie was now engaging in a metaphoric play about her life with another actor (the therapist) having his or her own part and lines.

- **Cognitive behavioral play therapy** uses concepts developed by Susan M. Knell. The core belief and focus is on the connection between a child's thoughts or cognitions and his or her behaviors. It follows that if we change a child's thoughts, this can lead to behavior change, and visa versa. The therapist uses the same types of toys as the other two play therapies. The therapist models alternative ways to problem solve, relate to others, ask for and use the help of others, accept comfort and support, resolve conflicts, and express feelings. The therapist models these alternatives through and while participating in the play selected by the child.

Zachary's Puma Warning System

Whenever Zachary entered the therapists office, he asked, "Where is the puma?" The puma was a large hand puppet that Zachary would have the therapist put on during the sessions. This puppet accompanied Zachary and the therapist throughout the session and periodically Zachary used a toy he was playing with to punch and "kill" the puma. As the therapy progressed, the therapist voiced the puma's sadness at getting hit and soon began to talk to Zachary about his feelings prior to punching the puma. Because the puma did not like to get hit, the therapist and Zachary worked out a warning system to notify the puma when Zachary had the impulse to hit.

Zachary needed this warning system. The ideas helped him at school and at home to manage his own angry moments and those of people around him. Having these new ideas about preparation and thought before action helped Zachary gain more control over his behaviors.

We would like to make the point that this play therapy technique relies less on the underlying relationship between the therapist and the child and more on the manifest communications between the two (although trust of the therapist is always important). It can be experienced by a child as more instructional and authoritarian.

It is our belief that the success of all therapy, but especially therapy with children, is dependent on the work that takes place within the relationship between the therapist and the child. Because of this, we feel that cognitive behavioral play therapy should be combined with a second play therapy technique (such a psychodynamic or activity play therapy).

- **Activity play therapy** uses the concepts of refocusing and distraction as a means to aid the connection between child and therapist. A good comparison is how we help children manage an injection at the doctor's office—we might read a book, sing a song, blow up a balloon, pulling their attention away from the scary thing that is about to occur. The therapist uses the play as a way of helping the child feel safe enough to share verbally. This type of play therapy uses basketball and other sports that can be easily and safely adapted to an office setting, commercial board games, checkers/chess, and so on.

Louie's Map

Louie was an 11-year-old boy who tried to hurt himself. He willingly spoke to his therapist about most things, but not his feelings. The therapist asked Louie what he wanted to do in session. Louie wanted to draw a map, something he did frequently in order to comfort himself. Louie decided to copy the map of Finland, a country with an irregular coastline and many lakes, requiring great detail. As Louie drew the map over several weeks, his therapist was able to explore his self-destructive feelings. Louie felt safer sharing his feelings while drawing the detailed map than he did just talking.

This type of play therapy helped Louie feel more comfortable sharing frightening feelings. While there are symbolic aspects of all play, Louie's therapist chose not to interpret Louie's choice of a difficult, intricate map, for example, but rather to allow the map drawing to remain a comforting device for Louie. When asked by his parents what he did in therapy, Louie spoke of drawing the map but not about any of the conversations with his therapist. This was difficult for his parents to understand until they talked directly with the therapist about the technique she used to help Louie.

- **Therapeutic play** is educational, instructional, and preparatory. Therapists choose toys that assist with these goals to prepare a child for a situation, experience, or event that the child may find difficult to emotionally cope with and productively understand.

Eloise Sees Her Mother Sick

Eloise came to see a therapist after her mother's stroke. Her mother had survived but with severely deteriorated capacity. She no longer talked, had trouble eating, had significantly less energy, and was struggling with her basic self-care. Before her mother came home from the hospital, Eloise's therapist began to work with her using a doll. The therapist informed Eloise that the doll could not speak and was very tired because she had been sick. Eloise and the therapist took care of the doll, helping her eat, talking to her, writing notes, and helping her to bed.

This type of therapy helped prepare Eloise to cope with her mother's condition. She practiced, learned skills and ideas, and was introduced to possible feelings that she and "the doll" may feel when interacting. It provided an element of mastery over a situation that Eloise would otherwise be experiencing without any level of control. Therapeutic play allows for processing difficult information and feelings while keeping a somewhat safe distance from the actual material. It is also easily duplicated by parents, thus helping to move the skills learned in therapy from the office to the home.

There are other play therapies that therapists use with children. We have provided what we view as the foundational ones and believe that the others are offshoots and variations. Some of the names are attachment therapy, expressive therapy (art, dance and movement, drama, psychodrama, music, writing), and filial therapy.

There are also a number of talk therapy techniques used to help children. There are more, but we find that some types of talk therapy are not child-friendly. We feel that children need more empathy than what some of the talk therapies structurally provide. We do include cognitive behavioral therapy (CBT) and behavior therapy categories below and want to reiterate that we strongly feel that some psychodynamic-based interaction must also be available to provide the holistic treatment model that we feel is most effective.

1. **Analytic psychodynamic therapy** is based on the establishment of a therapeutic relationship between the child and the therapist; it uses this relationship to work through any difficulties that the child may be having. A depressed child is asked to talk about his feelings related to his depression and the related behaviors (i.e., arriving at school consistently late, not spending time with friends, etc.). With great difficulty, vulnerability, and slowness, a child may open up to a therapist. In doing so, the child will experience and confront the same forces that are contributing to his isolation, low self-esteem, and so on. Using the structure of the therapy

and the relationship—testing limits, feeling vulnerable, disclosing, being responded to—the therapist and the child create a foundation to discuss and confront complex issues. This therapist is typically somewhat reserved, encouraging more contribution from your child.

2. **Relational psychodynamic therapy** is also based on the establishment of a therapeutic relationship between the child and the therapist and uses this relationship to work through any difficulties that the child may be having. The functional difference between relational and analytic psychodynamic therapy is how the therapist uses himself or herself within the treatment relationship. The relational therapist will be far more active—sharing thoughts, disclosing opinions, questioning, giving feedback, and so on.

3. **Cognitive behavior therapy** is a therapy that focuses on the connection between a child's thoughts and ideas (also called cognitions) and his or her behaviors. It was developed by Aaron Beck. If a child is coming late to school, he can be exposed to the idea that "late" or "early" are choices. This attempts to reorganize the thought process around the behavior. Late is described as a choice *against* the child, and early is described as a choice *for* the child. If a change can be made to a child's thoughts, this can lead to behavior change, and visa versa. This is a therapy often used with children who have been diagnosed with behavioral disorders such as attention-deficit/hyperactivity disorder or oppositional defiant disorder.

4. **Behavioral therapy** is a precursor to CBT and is a therapy that focuses on behavior change as the primary goal. Going under another name, operant conditioning, it was developed by B. F. Skinner. This type of therapy uses positive reinforcements, negative reinforcements, and structured track-ing of behaviors as the mode for change. If a child is coming late to school, he can be offered a reward for repeatedly coming to school on time for a week. If the behavior changes and the reward is received, the idea is that the child will feel strengthened and will continue to behave in a positive way. This therapy is not typically reliant on a strong therapist-child relation-ship, as much of the work is done between the parent and the child, with the therapist giving guidance. We sometimes call these interventions a token economy. This type of therapy is used in residential treatment settings and therapeutic schools. Another therapy that falls under the umbrella of behavior therapy is desensitization therapy, which is used to address some phobias. This is a therapy also used with children who have been diagnosed with behavioral disorders such as attention-deficit/hyperactivity disorder or oppositional defiant disorder.

CHAPTER SUMMARY

CHAPTER 6: TYPES AND FORMS OF CHILD PSYCHOTHERAPY

When deciding what type of therapy to use with a child, a therapist will consider several related elements of communication.

- The form by which a child communicates;
- The content that a child is communicating;
- The effort that a child undertakes when communicating;
- The intensity of the child's presentation of her or his feelings during and following communication.

The following are the four forms of communication that children utilize:

- **Affective (feelings/emotions)**—emotional expression. They "show" how they feel. They can use body language or facial expressions or physical appearance.
- **Symbolic**—play. It is the beginning of a child being able to construct and communicate ideas (symbols) and allows a child to communicate a complex world before he or she is equipped with enough words to describe this world.
- **Kinetic (movement, action, behavior)**—actions and behavior. Action is a single instance of activity (i.e., the action of not waking up), while behavior is a pattern of actions, the way in which someone acts (i.e., noisy behavior).
- **Verbal**—words. The ability to create words to form and express their ideas.

The following are some of the more common play therapy techniques:

- **Analytic play therapy**—the therapist closely observes and follows the child's play. This type uses dolls, puppets, blocks, action figures, expressive arts, and so on.
- **Psychodynamic play therapy**—focuses on the relationship—the connection and growing trust—between the child and the therapist as the primary structure through which problems are addressed. The therapist

often participates in the child's play as directed by the child and asks questions and gives feedback.

- **Cognitive behavioral play therapy**—focuses on the connection between a child's thoughts or cognitions and his/her behaviors. It follows that if we change a child's thoughts, as demonstrated in the child's play, this can lead to behavior change, and visa versa.
- **Activity play therapy**—uses refocusing and distraction as a means to aiding the connection between child and therapist. The therapist uses the play as a way of helping the child feel safe enough to share verbally.
- **Therapeutic play**—uses toys that assist with the goal of preparing a child for a situation or experience that may overwhelm the child's typical healthy coping abilities.

A number of talk therapy techniques developed to help adults are also used to help children are:

- **Analytic psychodynamic therapy**—focuses on how past history and events affect current feelings and behaviors
- **Relational psychodynamic therapy**—focuses on the relationship between the client and therapist, the client and others, and the client's view of the world
- **Cognitive behavior therapy** (CBT)—uses the behavioral concepts together with a focus on how thoughts create problematic behaviors and seeks to modify thinking and actions
- **Behavioral therapy**—focuses on problematic behavioral reactions to thoughts and feelings, and seeks to modify behaviors as a way of altering thoughts and feelings

CHAPTER 7
Child Diagnosis

As we begin this chapter, we want parents to remember one crucial fact about a diagnosis. Your child is the focus of the treatment; the diagnosis is not.

When it comes to a diagnosis, parents have many different reactions, concerns, and needs. Some of them may be:

- I am nervous about knowing the name for my child's problem.
- I am comforted by knowing that there is a name for my child's problem.
- I believe that if there is a name for my child's problems, then there is a solution.
- I want a name for my child's problem and I want to consume every piece of information I can find.
- I like having a name for my child's problem, but that is enough information for me.
- I am not satisfied that my child's problems are just typical problems of childhood.
- I prefer not having a name for my child's problem, but I would like to know the underlying details.
- I am worried that giving a name to my child's problem may stigmatize him or her.
- I am worried that if my child's problem has a name, then it is more serious.

Diagnosing your child's issues is a necessary part of the psychotherapeutic process. Your child's therapist should be able to provide a working diagnosis—when and if you ask—but that diagnosis is an opinion and is subject to change. It has meaning, importance, and value. It affects the plan that the therapist uses to help your child. It helps organize the therapist's thoughts and his or her understanding of your child and your child's problems. At times, it will help determine if your child needs more help in addition to psychotherapy (see Chapter 14). It will also be important if insurance is covering your child's therapy.

A diagnosis is also necessary for insurance companies to facilitate the reimbursement process (either to you or to your child's therapist/clinic). We recommend that you discuss the relationship between (1) your child's symptoms, (2) the working diagnosis, and (3) the diagnostic information (diagnosis codes and procedure codes) that is provided to insurance companies for billing purposes. Each of these categories has a specific purpose with regard to your child's treatment, and it is important to clarify and understand the differences.

SYMPTOMS

Symptoms tend to be manifest. There are visible parts of a problem similar to the tip of the iceberg that we mentioned before; the majority of the problem, the bulk of the iceberg, is left unseen. Symptoms function as clues to a person's underlying issues, concerns, anger, and fears. Symptoms may also have a purpose. Symptoms may be a form of communication to the self and to others. To the self, the symptom communicates an adaptation to a life problem that is ineffective, unsuccessful, or no longer matches the person's current life situation. To others, the symptom may communicate a need for protection, connection, or containment. Symptoms may be a way that a person *protects* him- or herself from potentially overwhelming thoughts, feelings, memories, fears, and unanswered wishes. Some believe that psychiatric symptoms, like psychosis or severe anxiety, are protection against feelings that are even worse. They contend that these severe symptoms push people to seek help.

Symptoms can be categorized in terms of the areas of everyday functioning that they may disrupt or impair. The symptoms within each of these areas vary for each child and are based on a child's ability to **manage** (cope with, adjust to, and balance) their daily life experiences. When we say that a child has problems with functioning, we are saying that there are symptoms present that do *not* respond to typical support and comforting. In terms of mental health, children may have symptoms in more than one category. These categories are the following:

1. Emotions
2. Behavior
3. Relationships.

Managing emotions refers to being able to express feelings about external events as well as maintaining an overall balance when presented with difficulties, crises, or obstacles in life. Children are able to accomplish certain aspects of emotional balance on their own, but they also need supportive relationships and environments to bolster their natural abilities. Inner emotional turmoil is often related to thoughts, worries, concerns, and fears that are connected to outside events that for various reasons produce a response with a greater level of intensity than these events might typically evoke. Some examples of these responses include excessive crying, explosive anger or aggression, agitation, anxiety, fearfulness, and/or somatic (physical) symptoms such as stomachaches, headaches, and nausea.

Managing behaviors refers to being able to control one's actions and impulses and perform necessary tasks within the structures of everyday life—home, school, and so on. Children are able to engage in certain behaviors on their own, but they also rely on helpful relationships, clear rules, and secure environments to shape their natural instincts. Behaviors can be viewed as the physical aspect of feelings, as often children will "act out" feelings through a disruption or impairment in day-to-day functioning. Some examples of acting out include inattention, forgetfulness, head banging, impulsivity, and disruptions in eating, sleeping, toileting, and bathing.

Managing relationships refers to being able to develop and maintain secure, stable, and effective age-appropriate emotional and physical connections with family members, friends, and other important people in children's lives (teachers, coaches, mentors, doctors, clergy, and other adults). Children are born with a drive to connect to others (called **attachment**), but they need guidance, structure, and caring environments to navigate the complexity of human interactions. A child's inner turmoil and/or external pressures and concerns can affect these human connections. The types of symptoms that disrupt relationships are sometimes referred to as the "acting in" of feelings. Intimacy, sharing, and comforting are typically diminished by these symptoms. Some examples of these symptoms include yelling, lying, fighting, biting, social isolation or withdrawal, and bullying or being bullied.

DIAGNOSES

From Greek, "diagnosis" means to know something by examining its parts. We take things apart, look at the pieces, and try to make sense of what we are seeing by looking at the separate elements. Psychiatry has grouped symptoms together to create a sense of a person's overall problem. The overall or central problem is called a diagnosis. Therefore, diagnoses are descriptive labels given to sets of symptoms. In order to provide some level of consistency in the diagnosing of psychiatric problems, the field of psychiatry developed the *Diagnostic and Statistical Manual of Mental Disorders*, or *DSM*. The *DSM* is the creation of psychiatric experts, theorists, clinicians, and researchers who meet from time to time to discuss, debate, and update diagnostic criteria. Even so, when we follow the history of the various *DSM* versions in practice, there has been inconsistency in the categorization and application of diagnoses. This does not mean that the *DSM* is wrong or that psychological diagnosing is flawed. It does mean, though, that a psychological diagnosis does not have the same factual scientific basis as a diagnosis of heart disease, kidney failure, diabetes, and cancer.

The field of mental health is currently using the fifth version of the *DSM*. Some information available on the Internet may not be updated yet, as the *DSM-5* was released in May 2013. We have decided to include information pertaining to diagnosis from both the *DSM-IV-TR* (the fourth version) and the *DSM-5*.

Similar to how we categorized symptoms, diagnoses can be grouped around specific areas of focus. They include disruption in one's ability to think, perceive reality, manage moods, remain calm under pressure/stress, and/or recover following a trauma.

In our culture, most treatment for a symptom or set of symptoms is based on a diagnosis and is set forth in order to achieve a cure—*an end to the symptoms.* This process is called the **medical model** of treatment and is the model of treatment used by medical doctors (which includes psychiatrists) and many professionals within the mental health field. Please feel free to ask your child's therapist what treatment model they use. The steps of the medical model look like this.

1. Examination
2. Symptom identification

3. Diagnosis
4. Treatment
5. Cure.

As a *medical* concept, a diagnosis is the result of a history of the individual and a physical examination of the individual's body, which is augmented by the results of medical tests. Based on the results of these examinations, the finding of certain symptoms or the absence of others, the doctor will make a diagnosis and then determine the course of treatment. For medical problems, this process makes sense. It is model that can address concrete and tangible problems, things we can see and quantify—cells, bumps, injuries, and so on. It is a method that is clear and easy to follow. Think about it this way: if someone has elbow pain, he may have a variety of issues. Using the process of elimination, a doctor can work through possible problems. If we wanted to know for certain, a physical examination of the elbow or a medical test, like an MRI, should do the trick. And that is how it should be for these types of problems because what is causing the elbow pain is a tangible problem.

If your child receives a diagnosis of "oppositional defiant disorder" (ODD), he or she will have "often" displayed at least some of following symptoms based on the *DSM-5*:

- Loses temper
- Argues with adults
- Actively defies or refuses to comply with adults' requests or rules
- Deliberately annoys people
- Blames others for his or her mistakes or misbehavior
- Is touchy or easily annoyed by others
- Is angry and resentful
- Is spiteful or vindictive.

Your child will be placed in one of three categories:

- Angry/irritable mood
- Argumentative/defiant behavior
- Vindictiveness.

If your child's therapist is using the medical model, he or she can make a diagnosis of ODD with just the above information.

Why are we bringing up a treatment model used by medical doctors in a book about psychotherapy for children? There are two reasons: first, as stated earlier, many individuals treating children's mental health problems use this model, and so we want you know about it. Second, although it is often used, we find it to be a model that is incompatible with the treatment of children's mental health problems in three critical ways. It is

1. too concrete (rigid);
2. not holistic; and
3. misrepresents the end goal of treatment.

The Defiant Little Leo

A 9-year-old named Leo was recently referred to a therapist with a diagnosis of ODD based on a psychological evaluation. The evaluator did not include the marital problems the parents were having, the parents' psychiatric problems, or the problematic and ongoing issues with child's school structure. The diagnosis was technically "accurate" based on this limited way of examining the problems. Leo was defiant at school, broke rules, did not listen to teachers, and got into fights and arguments with classmates. The parents reported that these behaviors were not seen in the home. Leo's behaviors were examined in a vacuum and were seen as problematic behaviors, rather than a communication of an overwhelming and frustrating dynamic at home. Using the medical model, the therapy would be based on stopping the behaviors at school. Without addressing the broader issues within his life, the behaviors would likely continue or would progress into more severe issues.

The process of diagnosing children's psychiatric problems is often inexact, subjective, and flexible. Some would disagree, saying that we have very reliable tests for many childhood mental health problems—depression, anxiety, ADHD—and that we have the responsibility to make the diagnosis tangible, defined, and solid. We disagree with what we see as a rigid and concrete way of seeing these problems.

Children and their problems are complex and multifaceted. They include many factors, including experience, development, temperament, culture, environment, relationships, organicity, strengths, limitations, awareness, and physical state. All these factors have an impact on what happens to a child and, obviously, no two children can have the same exact combinations of these categories. As we undertake the process of diagnosing a problem in a child, it is our objective to use an examination process that takes into consideration all these aspects of a child's world.

The previous diagnostic manual, the *DSM-IV*, used a clever way of looking a problems that, although no longer in active use, retains merits that are important for parents to know. It was a diagnosis broken down into multiple parts that looked something like this:

1. Pervasive disorder (a psychiatric or neurological condition affecting all aspects of a person's life and functioning, e.g., depression, anxiety, autism, etc.)
2. Personality disorder (usually confined to relationships with other people, not given to children because personality is still developing, e.g., paranoid, dependent, etc.)
3. Medical problems
4. Social and environmental life stressors.

The significance of this type of diagnostic structure was that it required a holistic approach to understanding a child. The 6-year-old may have continued to have a primary diagnosis of ODD, but the therapist saw the stressors from the home within the diagnosis and factored these into the treatment plan and the treatment goals, by making the parents' difficulties part of the treatment plan and goals.

In the current version of the *DSM*, the *DSM-5*, changes in the definitions of diagnoses and the symptoms that make up these diagnoses have resulted in diminishing the importance of the multiple parts of a person's life. These and other changes (in fact, much of the information that appears in the *DSM-5*) are the result of a compromise—meaning that there were mental health professionals who agreed and others who disagreed with the legitimacy and presentation of that information in the *DSM-5*. The *DSM-5* was formed through debate, discussion, agreement, and occasional resignations within the group charged with the task of updating the publication. This is no different from any of the previous iterations of the *DSM*. What follows from the realities of its creation, however, should be an acknowledgment that as a compromise-derived document, the definitive nature of the information in the *DSM-5* must be critically examined and questioned. This is the reason that we consider its contents to be professional opinions rather than scientific facts.

We also want to address the concept of a "cure." Children are dynamic, and their mental health has an open-ended component to it. Issues of autonomy, separation, attachment, control, loss, self-esteem, and trauma occur within the context of a child's ever-changing and fluid development.

The medical model's concentration on a mental health "cure" creates false and limiting expectations. We may very well be able to address a problem and relieve a symptom *in the moment*. But that is only *part* of the goal, not the entirety of the goal. Supporting long-lasting psychological growth and strength is the key to helping your child, with any issue, as he or she continues to develop, change, and grow. The medical model simply lacks the scale to encompass a truly successful psychotherapeutic child treatment.

A DIFFERENT WAY OF THINKING

Taking all this into account, we want parents to become comfortable with the idea that a psychiatric diagnosis for your child is a *professional opinion*, not a fact. A fact requires a level of certainty that, with regard to the complexity of children, we do not have at this time.

We say this for a couple of reasons. First, we live in a culture that has always told us that our doctors are right and that they know more than us. The latter may be true, but it has led to a reluctance to ask questions and to expect understandable answers. We want you to be an active participant in every part of your child's treatment, even the parts that historically have been the exclusive purview of the professional. Second, because of actual subjectivity when diagnosing mental health issues, you will often find that different professionals can view the same set of symptoms and problems in very different ways. It can lead to confusion and consternation in parents, who just want to help their children and who are searching for answers that they can rely on.

As an alternative to the medical model, we suggest looking at all the components of a child's life and development as a way of discovering, identifying, and understanding a child's abilities, talents, and resources, in addition to his or her problems. This results in a diagnosis and treatment based on the "entire" individual. This is often called a **strength-based model**. Some also call it a **holistic** or **person-in-environment model** of treatment. It shares the pattern (although the details differ) with the medical model, but from a very different perspective, and includes these elements:

1. Assessment (instead of examination)
2. Strengths and symptoms (instead of only symptoms)

3. Possible causes (instead of diagnosis)
4. Treatment plan
5. Relief and resolution (instead of cure).

STRENGTH-BASED MODEL LEADS TO SUCCESSFUL TREATMENT PLAN

So let us take a more detailed look at first three steps of the process of diagnosing a child from a strength-based (holistic) model of treatment. The last two steps will be covered in subsequent chapters.

Assessment

The initial assessment and first few sessions should be sufficient for your child's therapist to have collected enough information. This process has no exact time frame, although we feel that you can expect it to be well underway within a month of starting therapy. The information that he or she is looking for should be focused on mapping out the current symptoms. That said, the more complex the situation, the more time a therapist typically needs.

The assessment may include interviews with the child, the parents, school officials, doctors, and any other individual with input on the child's health picture. You want the assessment to be thorough, but it is important to remember that unlike a physical exam, a mental health assessment should be paced based on the needs of the client. In light of that, your child could experience an interview or session that goes for more than 45 minutes as too overwhelming. In addition, based on the material that is being discussed, an interview with a child may need to be paced slowly and/or divided into separate sessions to decrease the intensity of the experience.

Also, new and different symptoms can manifest as therapy begins to move forward. This is a normal occurrence within the process of therapy, and it can be upsetting to both parents and children. Your concerns about this are important to discuss with your child's therapist should this occur. Simply because this is a normal occurrence does not mean that new symptoms are an acceptable part of the process. Rather, they need to be addressed with the same attention as any of your child's original symptoms, as they may be new communications about your child's thoughts and feelings.

You may have already had testing done with your child. Therapists and school officials often recommend this type of information gathering as a way of augmenting their own understanding of what is happening within your child. There is no exact time when this is helpful or necessary. You can always bring up testing with your child's therapist. Not all therapists are able to do testing themselves, so if you move forward with having psychological tests done with your child, you may be required to contract with an outside individual or agency. Even if your child's therapist is able to do testing, there are advantages to involving someone else for this purpose. A different professional may have more objectivity when analyzing the test results, in light of the connection that already exists between your child and his/her therapist.

We believe that the two most critical groups of testing are the Neurological battery and the Psychological/Emotional battery (also called Projective Testing). Most psychiatric issues can be identified and covered sufficiently within these tests. We want to emphasize two points here: (1) Many evaluators do not want to give Projective tests (House-Tree-Person, Inkblot, etc.) because they see them as too subjective. We feel that without them the evaluation is without a sense of the child's emotional world and is therefore incomplete. (2) Evaluators seem to give more weight to behavioral assessments than other assessments. As we have stated earlier and will continue to state throughout this book, behaviors are simply outward communications of internal states. Without additional testing to support it, a behavioral assessment is of limited value.

The categories of testing are as follows. There are many types of tests under each subheading; some are specific to a diagnosis and others are more general ways of collecting information.

- **Achievement**—measures academic achievement, typically for the purpose of school admissions
- **Autism Spectrum Disorders**—measures extent of autistic symptomatology and other developmental delays
- **Behavior**—measures behavior and executive functioning (impulse control, judgment, decision-making, planning, prioritization) as it relates to behavior
- **Cognitive/Intelligence**—measures Intelligence Quotient (IQ) and learning processes

- **Neuropsychological**—measures wide range of brain functioning including reasoning, concentration, problem-solving, memory, executive functioning, language processing (verbal, written, and reading), sensory processing, attention, language, and so on
- **Psychological/Emotional**—measures emotional state, perceptions, projective (latent) view of people and situations, mood, anxiety, and so on
- **Adaptive Behavior**—measures actual personal and social skills in the areas of communication, daily functioning, socialization, motor skills, and maladaptive behaviors.

For the rest of this book we are going to group of all of these tests under one heading—**psychological testing or assessment**. It is important for you as the parent to do your research. An agency, based on its founders' or financial backers' clinical viewpoint, may lean heavily toward diagnosing specific problems. This should be taken into consideration when you receive psychological testing results about your child. Do not be reticent to question what you are told. We will repeat this throughout the book—testing is based on research but is not an exact medical science. In addition, some tests have cultural and gender-based biases.

Psychological tests are assessed in the following way. These tests have been given many times to many children. The accumulation of results from a large number of tests helps determine the most typical response. On either side of the typical response (higher and lower, more extreme and less extreme) are the results that are not typical.

Psychological tests and their respective grading keys are commercial products, copyrighted and sold to people evaluated as appropriately trained by the American Psychological Association. Currently, the psychological testing industry and psychologists who rely on these tests determine that the typical is normal. Those results that do not reflect the typical, according to the grading key, are abnormal. In this manner of thinking, different or not typical results mean that your child is either not as good as or better than normal. These are value judgments that we believe present black-and-white thinking about a person's abilities, strengths, and potential. That said, the evaluators' interpretation of your child's answers would be based on this type of analysis.

We want you to know this because psychological assessments are often used to determine diagnoses. These diagnoses are based on the notion of the typical being normal and the atypical being abnormal. The notion that your child has a label of "abnormal" can be upsetting because it is based on a negative value judgment. It is more meaningful to focus on what your child needs in order to enjoy life and to thrive.

Nick Does Not Do His Homework

Nick is a 14-year-old boy seen in treatment for depression and anxiety. His issues (low self-esteem, anxiety about being alone, lack of focus, poor organization) became more problematic in terms of his school and social functioning as he moved from middle school to high school with the increase in academic and social expectations and pressures. The therapist suggested an extensive psychological examination and requested a battery of tests, including emotional/psychological tests and neurological tests. The therapist sensed that Nick's poor grades and difficulties with his schoolwork were related to problems at home, organic changes to his brain related to puberty, ongoing depression and anxiety, and possibly an underlying neurological problem as yet undiagnosed. The evaluator who worked with Nick provided cognitive/intelligence testing, neurological testing, and behavioral assessments, and determined that Nick had attention-deficit hyperactivity disorder (ADHD). Nick's depression symptoms were seen as a consequence of the ADHD.

Nick's psychological testing centered on emphasizing the fact that Nick's home and school behavior, study habits, and grades were his main problems. Without psychological/emotional testing to measure how Nick sees his environment and himself, the evaluation was limited to only seeing the manifest behaviors as the issue and not the underlying psychological distress that Nick was also encountering. Based on the manifest results of the testing, the recommendations were designed to focus on altering Nick's behaviors by altering his routines. The hope was that he would feel better if he were able to study and succeed in school.

What was not observable through this type of testing was that these problematic routines may have been serving an important (latent) purpose, such as preventing a more rapid deterioration of Nick's psychological state. For the sake of argument, what if Nick was struggling with an increase in paranoid thinking that he was embarrassed to speak about? How would altering his study habits have addressed this problem? Under these circumstances, could we not see these school-related symptoms as something other than "bad" behavior? Maybe we could see this as a helpful communication (a brave one at that) of something important and unspoken to those people in charge of taking care of Nick?

Strengths and Symptoms

We have spent a great deal of time discussing symptoms and identifying symptoms in this chapter. It is obviously a layered process. We can view them in a variety of ways—emotional, behavioral, developmental, physiological, or cognitive—and from both manifest and latent perspectives. We feel that all this is important to the understanding of symptoms.

We also can try to understand symptoms from a multicultural perspective. Every culture, society, ethnicity, and/or race has customs and norms that have developed over the generations. These make up instinctive aspects of family structure, behavior, ways of communicating, relationships, ideas about asking for help, rituals, and ideas about illness, privacy and disclosure, and so on. Identifying and incorporating these features of a child into the description of symptoms is a critical component to the holistic examination of a child. An example of the complexity of the multicultural perspective is a child displaying a lack of eye contact. There are cultures in the world that see this behavior as deferential to adults, which is an important aspect of respecting authority figures. It is also a symptom of certain developmental delay diagnoses and depression. It can also be viewed as an age-appropriate behavior for certain age groups.

In addition, we want to add the concept of **strengths** to this discussion. In this context, a strength is not physical strength and not necessarily emotional strength. It is a quality, ability, tangible skill, or an aspect of the person that he or she can rely on for support and assistance during day-to-day trials and tribulations, as well as during extraordinary events. It can be the individual's intelligence, resilience, sensitivity, unique perspective, faith/spirituality, artistic talent, innate courage, comfort with vulnerability, attachment to a cause, the love of a friend, or a family member's support. Your child's innate strengths are a crucial aspect of her or his mental health and therefore, we believe, need to be given at least the same recognition and attention as your child's limitations or problems.

Shelly Is Very Active

Shelly was 8 years old. She was a very active child. At home, she ran around the room playing all kinds of physical games, jumping, and dancing. She also banged her head against the wall. She told the therapist that she could run through walls and demonstrated this by crashing into walls. She was afraid to fall asleep alone. She was afraid to bathe alone. She needed the door open and one of her parents present. At school, Shelly was a poor student and often needed redirection. She talked during class, made jokes with friends, and was disruptive. She did not do her homework, typically did not bring it home and lied that she lost it.

SNAP-IV rating scale, which is commonly used to diagnose attention deficit/hyperactivity disorder (ADHD), includes 90 observations, of which approximately 15 focus on emotions. The other 75 observations are behaviors—often negatively worded—all related to control, autonomy, and testing limits, for example:

- Fails to give close attention to detail
- Makes careless mistakes
- Does not seem to listen
- Often loses things
- Often argues with adults
- Often is spiteful
- Often blurts out answers.

The above observations are designed to characterize these behaviors as pathology. If a child has a high number of these behaviors, then she can often be diagnosed with ADHD. Shelly presents with nearly all of these symptoms. The problem with this analysis is that it is decidedly manifest.

Manifest	Latent
Fails to give close attention to detail	Anxious
Makes careless mistakes	Depressed
Does not seem to listen	Anxious/Angry
Often loses things	Depressed
Often argues with adults	Depressed/Angry
Often is spiteful	Angry
Often blurts out answers	Anxious/Angry

Would it surprise you to learn that Shelly was abused as a small child, suffered from several significant family losses, and was struggling with a chronic illness? Could this affect a diagnosis?

What if, knowing what we know about her history, we rewrote these symptoms in a way that made these same behaviors look like strengths? What would the diagnosis look like then? Would the treatment be different?

- Has a very active mind
- Thinks about many things at once
- Likes to talk
- Likes to offer differing opinions
- Like to stand up for herself
- Wants to share ideas immediately.

What if we went further and stated that these behaviors, although being problematic in terms of Shelly's home and school functioning, were protecting her from terrible feelings (from her abuse) that she had on a daily basis and would overwhelm her if she thought about them too often. Could we, then, possibly see her behaviors as strengths, as coping strategies? They need to be cultivated and modified, but still are strengths and coping strategies—instead of problems or pathology associated with poor executive functioning (i.e., judgment, inattention, or poor problem-solving).

Possible Causes

The diagnostic approach that we espouse examines all symptoms through the lens of a "component" approach. Each component represents a different, yet interrelated, aspect of a child's world, both internal and external. What comes out of this process is a number of possibilities, or working hypotheses (educated guesses, rather than facts), regarding what is happening with your child. The following is a framework for understanding children from different angles.

Components

> *Personality component*—this refers to the child's innate nature and to the disposition that he or she develops during adolescence and into young adulthood. **Temperament** for younger children is the term given to the nature a child has at birth—feisty or difficult, flexible or easy, cautious or shy. As children mature, their personalities become a manifestation of how they relate to and experience other

people and the world around them—paranoid, dependent, avoidant, and so on.

Relationship/Attachment component—this refers to the nature of a child's close relationships and the ways he or she interacts with these individuals. The concept of **attachment** describes the parent/child connection—secure, ambivalent, avoidant, or disorganized. How or if the parent and child fit together affects their overall connection/ attachment. **Separation and individuation** are the terms given to the developmental process of children becoming more independent, emotionally separating from their primary caregivers. The concept of **fit** signifies the level of harmony between a parent and child—based on the parent's expectations of her or his child and the effect these expectations have on the parent's reactions to their child's actual personality. The **goodness of the fit** refers to how well the parent's personality and the child's personality work together to form a successful relationship.

Bio-Developmental component—this refers to the child's psychosocial developmental stage, his or her physical development, and the inter-relationship between the two. Children go through a variety of psychological and social developmental stages from birth to young adulthood—building trust, growing autonomy, trying new activities, expanding creativity, separating from family, establishing identities, and so on. These developmental stages are influenced by each child's unique biological growth and progress—brain, body, motor skills, and so on.

Cognitive component—this refers to the child's thought processes. **Cognitive** theories of development focus on the idea that children learn to think about and understand the world around them at different rates and in their own unique ways. Although each child progresses at a different speed, children move through steps from concrete to abstract, from unsymbolized to symbolized, from basic to advanced. These steps are influenced by each child's unique **neurological** (brain/nervous system) makeup, growth, and development.

Environmental component—this refers to the child's family system and living situation on a micro level (home, school, culture) and on a macro level (town, country, cultural norms). Family systems (and other systems, for that matter) have many different components, from the unique structure of family members (single parent, extended family, etc.) to the **boundaries** and type of connection that a family displays (enmeshed, disengaged, connected, separated), to how a family communicates (open, closed, positive, negative), to how a family manages change (rigid, flexible, chaotic, etc.). Children are affected by the rules and the composition of the systems in which they live and grow and the events/situations that they experience within these systems—changes, losses, and milestones.

Behavioral component—this refers to the child's actions and conduct within a system. Children display actions—running, jumping, climbing, tickling, wrestling, grappling, restraining, boxing, swinging, play fighting, kicking, chasing, tumbling, pushing, and knocking down. They present with a variety of physical reactions: anger (yelling, pushing, sleeping), anxiety (movement, inattention), and sadness (crying, withdrawal).

A Comparison of Models

For the purpose of diagnosing, let's look at the tantrums of a 4-year-old girl using both models. These are intense and repeating tantrums that seem to have no connection to what is happening at that moment. They happen several times a week and have been going on since she was 2 years old. The tantrums are the most severe at home, but they cause problems in the home and outside the home at preschool. This affects the way the child functions, the way the caregivers function, and the way the family functions. This happens regularly and causes concern to everyone involved.

Medical Model

1. Examination—Interview with parents, child, history and details related to the tantrums, behavior assessment, other tests.
2. Symptom identification and interpretation—The child presents with excessive, frequent tantrums, crying, yelling, and so on.
3. Diagnosis—Age-typical behavior, possibility of disruptive mood dysregulation disorder, possibility of physiological/behavioral causes.

Strength-Based Model

1. Assessment—Interview with parents, child, history and details related to tantrums, relationship history, birth history, family structure, medical history, cultural norms.
2. Strengths and symptoms—The child is fascinated by colors, enjoys creating things, is very responsive to music, and has several favorite toys that she uses in pretend play. The parents love her and know that what is happening is not helpful to their daughter and have a willingness to ask for help. Her parents use both calm and intense communication and physical control to address the tantrums. The child presents with excessive, frequent tantrums, crying, yelling, and so on.
3. Hypothesis of possible causes—
   a. Personality component—the child may be willful and strong-minded, feisty
   b. Relationship component—the child may be separating from her primary caregiver, parent may be exhausted and be having personal difficulty managing child's anger, intensity.
   c. Bio-Developmental component—the child may be confronting destabilizing (lack of control) feelings related to a changing body (toileting, etc.) or another as yet unidentified physiological process.
   d. Cognitive component—the child may be learning new ways of communicating and managing feelings/impulses in terms of her executive (organized thinking) functioning. To this we can add the possibility that this child is best able to express feelings and thoughts artistically through color, crafts, play-acting. The reliance on purely verbal communication may not be the most natural pathway for this particular child.
   e. Environmental component—changes in family, the child may be perceiving/encountering something around her that is causing a level of distress.
   f. Behavioral component—age-typical behavior, protective behavior, a communication of loss of control, lack of another more helpful form of communication.

Examining *all* the components is essential to making a diagnosis—a comprehensive understanding of this child and her tantrums. The medical model provides a different kind of diagnosis—a label solely based on manifest symptoms. Without this holistic viewpoint, important material may be disregarded, leaving us with an incomplete picture. This girl is more than a girl who has tantrums.

It is common that there may be disagreements among professionals regarding your child's diagnosis. Different theoretical backgrounds, disciplines, and training regimens produce mental health professionals with wide-ranging points of view. Using this type of information-gathering process allows for these differing perspectives and merges them into a more comprehensive picture. Having this holistic view can have far-reaching effects by creating an effective and tailored therapy to each individual child.

DISCUSSING DIAGNOSIS BY AGE GROUP

We want to touch on the concept of diagnosis and its meaning during therapy to children of different age groups.

Toddlerhood through Pre-latency or Early Childhood (Age 3–7)

Children of this age are not connected to the meaning of a diagnosis. The older children in this category may be somewhat aware of their symptoms in a manifest and concrete fashion—feelings they are experiencing, fears they have, behaviors they engage in that create negative responses in others. In this age group, children will not ask about their diagnoses and, typically, will not even want to know their symptoms.

Latency or Childhood (Age 7–11)

Children of this age may want to know their diagnosis label and symptoms, or they may not. These children can understand the manifest details of their symptoms and may even be able to comprehend the abstract ideas of diagnosis. In addition, we suggest that you identify their strengths for them. They are beginning to have the cognitive ability to understand the way the components fit together into a diagnostic picture. We feel that parents and therapists should allow this age group to take the lead in exploring the details of symptoms and naming a diagnosis. As these children get older, they will want to understand the meaning of their time in therapy and why they are different from their peers.

Early Adolescence (Age 12–15)

Because of the onset of puberty, this age group includes children who fall all along the continuum of maturity level, cognitive and physical development, and identity formation. This variability requires the discussion of symptoms and diagnosis to be managed with thoughtfulness and empathy. We suggest that you present holistic concepts such as the "hypothesis of causes" rather than (or in addition to, if you think it is necessary) the diagnostic label of the medical model. Some children will find the process stigmatizing and disorganizing, while others will find it empowering and grounding. For the reticent group, it may be helpful to allow the children to provide their own names and ideas to the symptoms that they are experiencing

> "When my brain gets messy"—instead of disordered thinking
> "I am sad and mad"—instead of depression and agitation
> "The trap door is back"—instead of anxiety

Late Adolescence/Teen Years (Age 15–17)

Although they are technically children, depending on their maturity level, nearly all teenagers in this group should be discussing symptoms and the diagnostic process as part of the engagement phase and treatment planning process.

Young Adulthood (Age 18–Mid-20s)

Symptoms and diagnostic process can be discussed with this age group as part of the engagement phase and treatment planning process.

CHAPTER SUMMARY

CHAPTER 7: CHILD DIAGNOSIS

Diagnosing your child's issues is a necessary part of the psychotherapeutic process.

- Your child's therapist should be able to provide a working diagnosis— when and if you ask—but that diagnosis is an opinion and is subject to change.

- A diagnosis is based on a collection of what is considered a typical grouping of symptoms for people with problems in daily functioning.
- Symptoms are visible parts of a problem, similar to the tip of the iceberg—the majority of the problem, the bulk of the iceberg—is left unseen.
- Symptoms function as clues to a person's underlying issues, concerns, anger, and fears.
- Symptoms can be categorized in terms of the areas of everyday functioning that they may disrupt or impair.
- The symptoms within each of these areas vary for each child and are based on a child's ability to **manage** (cope with, adjust to, and balance) their daily life experiences.

The components of a child's life examined for their contribution to symptoms are the following:

- **Personality component**—refers to the child's innate nature and to the disposition that he or she develops during adolescence and into young adulthood. **Temperament** (for younger children) is the term given to the nature a child has a birth.
- **Relationship/Attachment component**—refers to the nature of a child's close relationships and the ways he or she interacts with these individuals. The concept of **attachment** describes the parent/child connection. How or if the parent and child fit together affects their overall connection/attachment. The concept of **goodness of fit** refers to how well the parent's personality and the child's personality work together to form a successful relationship. **Separation and individuation** is the term given to the developmental process of children becoming more independent.
- **Bio-Developmental component**—refers to the child's psychosocial developmental stage, his or her physical development, and the inter-relationship between the two.
- **Cognitive (thought/thinking) component**—refers to the child's thought processes. Each child learns to think about and understand the world around him at different rates and in his own unique way. These are influenced by each child's unique **neurological** (brain/nervous system) makeup, growth, and development.
- **Environmental component**—refers to the child's family system and living situation on a micro level (home, school, culture) and on a macro

level (town, country, cultural norms). The different components include the structure of family, the type of connection a family displays, how a family communicates, and how a family manages change.

- **Behavioral component**—refers to the child's actions and conduct within a system.

Problems with functioning refer to symptoms that do *not* respond to typical support and comforting. In terms of mental health, children may have symptoms in more than one category.

These categories are the following:

- Emotions
- Behaviors
- Relationships.

A **strength-based model** of the treatment process is also called a **holistic** or **person-in-environment model**:

- Develop an assessment
- Identify specific strengths
- Interpret symptoms
- Identify possible causes
- Develop and engage in treatment
- Move toward relief and resolution.

CHAPTER 8

Engagement

The Framing of Child Psychotherapy

When your child enters treatment and goes for the first time (post-intake or post-consultation), he or she is beginning a new process. This chapter is dedicated to the start of therapy, which is called the **engagement phase**. The engagement phase describes the creation of the therapeutic relationship between your child and the therapist. We want to make a distinction between the intake or consultation and the start of therapy. The intake/consultation will feel different to both your child and you. It includes more questions and is handled in a much more directive way than therapy will be conducted going forward. By directive, we mean that the therapist is more active and talkative in the session and is focused on specific topics and issues that assist with assessment.

Any information (or the resulting assessment) that comes from the first session is cursory and incomplete due to the time-limited nature of the meeting. Because of this we counsel patience (which can be understandably difficult at moments of crisis or stress) until the therapist can more extensively assess what is happening with your child. The main purpose of the whole first part of therapy is to get a handle on what is happening and to create the relationship that will be needed to address the problems.

The use of the word "engagement" is interesting because it is the same word used to describe the phase when people publicly declare their intention to marry, prior at actually marrying. In this case, engagement means connecting.

Like a marital relationship, engagement is the start of a formal relationship in which individuals indicate to each other and the world that they are making a commitment. Getting engaged has its origins in a ritual of moving from informal connection to legal connection. It is a time to get to know someone and decide whether a legal (or, for therapy purposes, one that is more involved and deeper) connection is appropriate.

The engagement phase in treatment has no set time limit, and like marital engagements, can be short or long in duration. It is more important that the work of the engagement phase be complete, because moving on to the work phase (where the changes take place) is dependent on successfully establishing the core needs of the therapeutic relationship.

Think of therapy as a house. The engagement phase functions as the foundation of your child's therapy. It needs to be strong and secure in order to hold up to the weight of the subsequent layers of the house. During this initial phase in therapy, the therapist focuses on

1. establishing communication (ways of interacting and responding),
2. creating rapport (connection and empathy), and
3. building **trust** (openness to another person).

Carlos Finally Speaks About His Feelings

Carlos was an 8-year-old boy who was angry and depressed because of his mother's rapid deterioration due to lung cancer. He came to sessions every week. His aunt, with his mother's permission, arranged the sessions. His aunt was living with them while his mother was ill and would become Carlos's guardian in the event of his mother's death. He was doing poorly in school, was sleeping poorly, and was losing weight. Carlos refused to talk in session, to play with any of the toys, or to draw. His therapist read storybooks in the session while Carlos pretended to sleep. The storybooks were about feelings and emotions that mentioned loss (lost toys, friends moving away, etc.), but not death. In the ninth session, Carlos spoke and told therapist that the boy in the story who cried when his best friend moved away was "a baby." His therapist responded, "Baby?" Carlos continued: "Yeah, it's not like his friend died or anything like that."

Carlos took his time choosing whether to trust his new therapist or not. It made sense for him to do so, considering that his relationship with his mother had changed so much during the time that she had been sick. So many of the ways that they had interacted before her diagnosis had been altered, and Carlos's ability to trust grown-ups understandably had been compromised. When Carlos chose not to engage, in light of the problems in the family, the therapist established a form of communication that harkened back to early childhood of being read a storybook. Often, having an adult read to you is an activity that children associate with comfort and support. It presented Carlos with an opportunity to learn to trust his therapist.

To establish trust in any relationship, there needs to be some basic ground rules, elements of the relationships that each individual can depend upon. If these elements are absent or change suddenly or inconsistently, then fully committing to the relationship becomes difficult. Early therapy discussions focus on setting up and defining rules, routines, and responsibilities. It focuses on the way that a therapist and a child and the parent(s) will work with each other.

All relationships are defined by their rules, routines, and responsibilities that govern interactions between the individuals involved, and therapy relationships are no different. In fact, therapy relationships depend greatly on these details and really cannot be successful without specific awareness of how all the parts fit together. Whereas the rules and responsibilities of your personal relationships may be informal and are often unspoken, the rules and responsibilities in therapy need to be clear, formal, and discussed openly. You can come to rely on them for making decisions, asking and answering questions, and problem-solving.

We call these rules, routines, and responsibilities that shape the therapy structure **the frame**. If we continue with the house metaphor that we used in explaining the engagement phase of treatment, the frame of therapy is much like framing out a house before building a solid structure. You may or may not hear the therapist use this word, but if you do, this is what he or she means. To use another metaphoric image, think of it like a picture frame—anything on the canvas belongs within the structure of the therapy or the therapeutic relationship with the therapist. "Outside the frame" means that something may be beyond the scope of therapy. The picture frame makes up the boundaries of the therapy relationship—boundaries that create limits and expectations within a structure of therapist, child, and parent.

Engagement establishes the trust needed by a patient and his or her parents to accept and be comfortable with the management of information. Creating the rules of the frame sets the atmosphere of mutual respect and trust among all the participants. This is a process expressed throughout therapy, beginning with engagement.

Helen Makes a Birthday Invitation

Helen, who worked with her therapist for years, was having her very important 10th birthday party. She wanted the therapist to come to her birthday, to meet her friends and to celebrate with her. The therapist explained that she could not, that she met with Helen in the room that they always met and that she could not meet with her outside. The rules of their "relationship" were to meet each other in a specific place. Her teachers taught her at school, her doctors treated her at the doctors' offices. In addition, birthday parties were for family and friends, and although her therapist felt like a friend, and maybe even understood her differently than her friends did, there were important differences. She saw her friends and family whenever she wanted, she lived with them, and went to school with them.

It was important that Helen began to understand that this relationship had limits. By asking the question, she was beginning to compare and contrast the different relationships in her life. It is sometimes difficult for children to understand the concept of the frame. Children can blur the boundaries. They will test the structure, push it and pull it, but they rely on it, so therapists typically will be thoughtful and methodical regarding any fundamental change to the frame.

THE FRAME

D. W. Winnicott wrote extensively on a concept called "the holding environment." We like this concept because it neatly describes the idea of the frame of child therapy within a context of the most important developmental need of a child—trust. Winnicott held that a trusting relationship between a caregiver and a child depended on the caregiver holding the child well enough to allow the child to grow. He did not just mean physically hold the child, but also emotionally hold the child. When we hold a child physically we do not drop him, we do not let him fall, and we provide security and safety and structure for his physical being. A child should feel safe when a caregiver holds him. In the same way that a caregiver can physically "hold" a child, a caregiver can also hold a child emotionally by consistently listening, understanding, empathizing, and not rejecting or abandoning. The physical and emotional containment of a child by a caregiver was what Winnicott called the holding environment, and the therapy frame needs to be able to provide this same type of structure. To understand and use Winnicott's concept in connection to child therapy, let us define the frame in the following ways:

a. *Day and time*—The day of the week and the time of the day of the session. This should be chosen to allow for consistency and repetition. We know that children need consistency and repetition to be able to integrate ideas. Therapy flows and our brains get ready for the act of therapy, often preparing us beforehand. A consistent time and day helps a child engage in the treatment process by knowing, planning, and making decisions about his or her upcoming session. Imagine if a child did not know when the next session was; her thoughts would most likely be spent thinking about "when" the session was and not "what" she was going to do.

Whether your child is at an age that you bring him to the sessions or a child attends the sessions on his own, the time of day and the day need to work for you and your child in terms of the schedule. This is an important decision because if you choose a time or a day that does fit in your life and schedule, it may add to the difficulties and place undue pressure on the frame. Things to think about when you are figuring out a time and day include the following:

Geographic issues
- Where the office is in relation to home
- Where the office is in relation to school
- How long it takes to get to the therapist's office from school
- How long it takes to get to therapist's office from home
- The methods of transportation.

Daily routines issues
- What time school ends
- Day and time of after-school activities
- Volume of homework
- Bedtime and dinnertime.

Maximizing support issues

- Session at the beginning of week or end of the week in terms of child's needs, focus, problems
- Session coming out of the weekend or going into the weekend.

b. *Frequency*—The number of times per week or month that a session takes place. This is dependent on the nature of the problems being addressed and how urgent these problems are at the moment of starting treatment. Most often, child therapy begins at once a week. This is standard and will typically not be altered unless the therapist is concerned that your child needs more structure and support (more contact with the therapist). Children can benefit by going to therapy more than once a week, but financial constraints, including insurance, have standardized the once a week frequency.

The idea that the more frequently sessions occur the faster the therapy goes seems logical, but is not accurate. True, some individuals may be able to learn and understand new concepts and skills very quickly (external changes). A person typically needs time to actually integrate new material, gain insight, and allow the changes to become a true part of one's self (internal changes). In reality, the more frequent the sessions, the deeper the therapy goes and the more a child remembers and integrates information from the therapy.

Think about it like this. After each session, a child walks away thinking about the session in some way. After an hour, those thoughts decrease. After a day, those thoughts decrease even more. After a week, a child may remember only highlights of the previous session. The recall of the previous session's experience links sessions together and creates continuity and a flow over the therapy. If a child has therapy twice a week, the links between the sessions—the memories of what happened in the previous sessions—are clearer and can be used more readily.

We are not saying that once a week therapy is better or not as good as twice a week therapy for children, but we want you to know the impact of session frequency. The natural pace your child has in terms of growth and change is the important factor. At times, more frequent sessions can overwhelm your child's current coping skills. And sometimes a child is struggling to such an extent that multiple sessions a week become a helpful therapeutic intervention that focuses on increasing structure as a way of helping your child to develop stronger coping skills.

c. *Fee*—The amount of money that a session costs. For those parents paying for their child's therapy out of pocket, this amount is typically determined during the intake process. We wanted to include it in this section because the fee can have an impact on other parts of the frame, including overall session attendance, session frequency, and forms of communication. Mixing issues of payment and attendance (reducing your child's session frequency or altering your parent collateral sessions) is completely understandable and logical. Parents often make these types of decisions, such as canceling a session or choosing to use a telephone call—instead of a session—to update the therapist, without discussion with the therapist or the child. Talking to your child's therapist about all your thoughts related to fee is important. It happens to be an area that creates a significant amount of tension for many people.

We want you to consider that the fee can change over time—like all other elements of the frame, it does not have to be static. Based on a variety of factors, therapists can raise their fees, and parents can request reduction in fees. Just as we suggest with any other part of your child's therapy, there are many possible options regarding fee if it can be discussed on an ongoing basis with the therapist.

d. *Confidentiality*—The rules that govern who knows what and what can be disclosed to whom. These rules focus on the privacy afforded to the different individuals involved in your child's therapy. This privacy serves different purposes, depending on what information is being kept private and from whom it is being kept private.

Your child's privacy extends to all material communicated by your child to the therapist in the session *with some exceptions*. This is a matter of building trust. The idea that a child can share something that may be difficult (children often call them "secrets") with a therapist, and that that information will be protected if the child wishes it so, is a critical component to building a secure connection with a therapist. It is one of those first layers of the foundation of the therapy. This is not to say that your child will share secrets with his or her therapist and not you, but it is having the option that counts.

Children often test this boundary (frame) by sharing information with a therapist to see if a therapist will share it with their parents. Children may also share information with their parent(s) to see if parents will forward this information on to the therapist. This is all about mapping out the rules and attaining a sense of control over the new therapy dynamic. Openness about who discusses what with whom is an important aspect of the frame. If you have questions about what you or your child can say to the therapist, the therapist is the initial resource for those answers. It keeps the system contained.

There are also safety and security-related communications that therapists may share with parents. Depending on your child's age, developmental stage, and mental health issues, a therapist will consider if it is helpful to disclose certain types of information to the child's parents. This could include

- communication that is confusing and needs parents' assistance in clarifying or interpreting;
- communication that conveys an issue that, although not dangerous yet, creates a level of concern in the therapist; or
- communication that provides an incomplete picture of an issue that requires time-sensitive resolution.

Jacob Struggles in the Bathroom

Jacob was a 4-year-old boy who came to see a therapist because his parents were having marital conflict and because Jacob was exhibiting behaviors (significant sleep difficulties, excessive tantrums) that his mother felt were out of the ordinary. Jacob spent the first several sessions building Lego houses and then tearing them down. While he did this he said, "House is broken." During the fourth session, Jacob told the therapist that he had to go to the bathroom. The bathroom was just across the hall from the therapist's office and he showed Jacob how to get into and out of the bathroom. The therapist informed Jacob that because this was his first time using this toilet that the therapist would stand outside, just in case Jacob needed help. Jacob went into the bathroom and was still in the bathroom five minutes later. The therapist opened the door slightly and asked if Jacob was okay. Jacob said yes. Five minutes later Jacob was still in the bathroom and the therapist repeated his question. When Jacob responded with a yes, the therapist followed up with asking Jacob if he could come in. Jacob responded affirmatively and the therapist entered the bathroom. Jacob was standing outside the stall with no pants on. His pants and underwear were in the stall, clean and dry. Jacob could not answer the therapist's questions about whether he was having difficulty. The therapist helped him dress and they left the bathroom together.

The therapist thought that this situation (although not completely out of the ordinary for a 4-year-old) required a discussion with Jacob's parents. Why had he not asked for help when offered? Had the parents seen this before? The parents had not mentioned an issue with toileting or potty training. The therapist was confused about the multiple possible meanings of what had happened and had concerns about the latent communications underlying the bathroom experience. The therapist chose to disclose the bathroom occurrence to the parents.

Therapists are people with their own experiences and viewpoints. Disclosure of material that your child has communicated can vary, depending on the therapist. You can ask your child's therapist about his or her views on confidentiality. You can ask if you have a question about something happening in the therapy.

Safety Concerns

There are limitations on confidentiality that center on matters of safety and security impacting your child. Some of these limitations come from a code of professional ethics that the psychotherapist must adhere to related to his or her license to practice. Others are required by the laws of the state where the therapist practices and focus on the need to report to specific agencies or organizations. The extreme scenarios concerning safety are the following:

- If your child is in danger from another individual;
- If your child is presenting a danger to himself or herself;
- If your child is communicating that he or she wants to harm another individual.

Mandated reporting is a legal requirement to help protect children suspected of being in danger. All mental health professionals are mandated reporters of child maltreatment. Maltreatment is defined as emotional, psychological, physical, or sexual abuse and neglect of various kinds (i.e., medical, educational, etc.).

Health Insurance Portability and Accountability Act (HIPAA) is a federal law that protects you and your child's privacy. Written "release of information forms" signed by you give the therapist your permission to share information with other professionals, service providers, and organizations. Some therapists will accept e-mailed permission (but we want to remind you of privacy issues concerning electronic documentation such as e-mail and a lack of security). Excluded from this law are mandated reporting requirements to protect your child.

e. *Forms of communication*

The ways we communicate with one another in treatment (child to therapist, therapist to child, parent to therapist, or therapist to parent) are different from the ways we communicate in our everyday lives. In our therapeutic communications, it is important to consider each method in terms of quality, purpose and meaning. Choosing a specific method of communication affects how information is conveyed and received. Because of its actual and potential effects on the frame, we encourage therapists, parents, and older children to discuss all these forms of communication and to set up rules regarding each of them. As people turn increasingly to electronic forms of communication as their preferred method of maintaining contact with one another, it is useful to reach a mutual understanding regarding these methods of communicating. A therapist preferring not to speak on the telephone, to text, or to video chat with a client should be understood within a therapeutic context. The following are different methods of communication that the individuals in treatment can consider:

- **In-person contact**—this is the typical method of communication in treatment. This contact typically takes place in an office, but can take place anywhere—a playground, a hospital room, a basketball court, or a waiting room, and so on. This type of communication is useful because it allows for multiple levels of communication—verbal, nonverbal, physical proximity, olfactory, and so on. It also creates a shared experience due to the fact that the participants are in the same environment.
- **Telephone contact**—this is a common method of communication between parents and therapists. It is often the first contact between parents and therapist, as the participants can use it for brief updates and scheduling. **Telephone sessions** can be used if a child (or parent) is physically not able to make the session. This is *not advisable* for some children because without the nonverbal cues (smiles, nods, eye contact) that constantly take place between therapist and child, communications can be misinterpreted, misunderstood, and misconstrued. Parents can use telephone sessions, but for the same reasons, we advise against it. Discussing potentially difficult and complex information without the nonverbal cues

can lead a client to experience a lack of empathy. In addition, without the touchstone of the shared experience, there is an increased possibility of one or both of the participants becoming distracted by what is happening around them.

- **E-mail communication**—this refers to any information passed from therapist to client or visa versa over electronic mail. Aside from the inherent confidentiality issues (we recommend that you do not use your child's full name in any e-mail; an initial will do), e-mail lacks nonverbal aspects of communication, voice intonation, and volume that help us understand the mood, intensity, and quality of what someone is saying. Although we agree that people can communicate a great deal of important information in written form, we suggest that you use this for one-way communications (and do not expect the same level of reciprocity). A response of more than an acknowledgment of receipt has the potential to be misinterpreted or misunderstood.

- **Texting**—this is an electronic method of written communication that conveys information in a rapid fashion directly to the recipient's telephone. Therapists typically do not use this type of communication except to convey small amounts of factual information, addresses, times, and so on. If a child or a parent chooses to use this form of communication, again, we suggest that you use this for one-way communications. Concerns that we have about this type of communication from a therapeutic perspective include privacy, lack of nonverbal cues, lack of intonation, usage of unknown abbreviations (i.e., LOL, etc.), and lack of timely reciprocity. All these concerns affect the therapeutic relationship in potentially negative ways.

- **Video chat** (FaceTime, Skype)—this type of communication combines the electronic component (smart phones and computers) with a version of in-person contact. Although this can be an effective form of communication, without the touchstone of the shared experience, there is an increased possibility of one or both of the participants becoming distracted by what is happening around them. In addition, the potential for loss of online connectivity runs the risk of prematurely ending contact.

- **Social networks**—(SnapChat/What's App/Twitter/Facebook/Instagram)—these are communications that are sent to the recipient's online account (via a smart phone application ["app"] or a computer), but they are not necessarily direct communications to the recipient. The recipient may choose to have these communications "pushed" to them (receive a message on their smart phones that someone has made contact). We suggest that these types of contact are avoided within the therapeutic process. They create the sense of continuous contact, a relationship with fewer boundaries that is much more reminiscent of a friendship than a professional helping relationship. They are typically used for personal use and so potentially provide extraneous information about those involved. If they are used for professional use, then it is beyond the scope of this specific therapist-child therapeutic relationship. Personal information, like that accessible within these accounts, may be shared in the process of treatment, but the sharing of personal information needs to be discussed and processed by therapist and child. Twitter, SnapChat, and What's App allow for a client to establish ongoing contact with therapist's account (and visa versa) without some initial contact requesting permission for ongoing contact. Facebook requires an initial request for ongoing contact (called a Friend request). Instagram provides the option of approving those with whom you are in contact (called "followers").

What seems to be clear regarding changes to forms of communication in this age of technology is that they are creating an increasingly connected population. Based on this ubiquitous technology, children are expected to have ongoing, rapid contact with the people who are important to them. Far from debating the long-term effects of these changes and expectations, we feel it is important to acknowledge them and accept them. The process of healing is often slow and methodical and may be a counterpoint to the speed of technology. Therapist and parents can provide empathy to children regarding the inherent tension and frustration regarding this dichotomy.

YOUR CONTRIBUTION TO THE FRAME

These are the main features that govern foundation of the therapy—the structural limits that all participants can use as guidelines for how to engage and interact with one another. With the goal of forming long-lasting trust, they are by no means set in stone, and can evolve and change as the relationships within each *unique* therapy grow and as external factors impact the therapy.

This is an important aspect of the frame—that therapists do not have a monopoly on the creation or preservation of the therapeutic frame. Parents have a major impact on the frame, both in maintaining it and in altering it.

Changes to the frame always need to be addressed and integrated into the therapy, including the following:

- An illness
- The time
- The day
- How parent and therapist communicate
- A vacation
- The fee.

For every change to the frame, there is some adjustment period for all those involved in the therapy. It is greater for some, less for others. When a change is planned and there is sufficient preparation time, the adjustment period is typically shorter; when it is sudden or unplanned, the adjustment time will usually be longer. Obviously, we know that not all frame alterations can be planned for, but when possible, it is recommended to discuss changes with the therapist.

The choices that parents make regarding the frame and any changes to the frame they make as the therapy moves forward create ripples throughout the workings of the therapy. How exactly the moment-to-moment choices influence the therapy is not always known, but we do know that it can affect the therapy's basic foundation elements—communication, flow, and, ultimately, trust.

CHAPTER SUMMARY

CHAPTER 8: ENGAGEMENT: THE FRAMING OF
CHILD PSYCHOTHERAPY

The engagement phase describes the creation of the therapeutic relationship between your child and the therapist. The engagement phase has no set time limit.

During this initial phase in therapy, the therapist focuses on the following:

- Establishing communication (ways of interacting and responding)
- Creating rapport (connection and empathy)
- Building **trust** (openness to another person)

- Creating the frame of the therapy (rules, routines, and responsibilities)
- Initial thoughts regarding goals of treatment.

The frame includes the following:

- Day and time
- Frequency of sessions
- Confidentiality rules
- Forms of communication (in-person, telephone, text, etc.).

It is important that the work of the engagement phase be complete, because moving on to the next phase of therapy (where the changes take place) is dependent on successfully establishing the solid foundation of the therapeutic relationship.

Treatment Planning

THE RATIONALE BEHIND STRUCTURING THE THERAPY

In our society, there is an ongoing attempt to operationalize psychotherapeutic treatment (creating systematic steps to follow, like a recipe) in order to provide consistent and predictable results over a prescribed period of time. This is an important and noble effort if we are actually doing this in order to provide people with better care and accurate information that describes what is involved in treating mental health problems. Sadly, we feel that there is a level of disingenuousness at work here. Of course it would make anyone, especially parents, feel better to believe that if we just followed these steps, all would be better. It provides a level of reassurance that parents understandably seek. This effort of operationalizing is called **evidence-based** or **best practices.** The "evidence" on which these treatment plans are based is collected through funded scientific research studies.

These studies have created significant changes to diagnosing and treatment models over the past decade (Visser et al., 2013) and so we suggest that parents spend some time evaluating studies that produce the mental health techniques that may impact their child's treatment.

• Who is funding the study/research and why? (this impacts why this material is being researched and not others)

- Who benefits most from the study results? (this impacts what results are being sought by the designers of the study)
- How many subjects were in the study? (this impacts how results represent a larger group of people)
- How were they chosen? (this impacts how results can be applied to a larger group of people)
- How were they studied? (this impacts whether the results can be used under different circumstances)
- What multicultural groups (gender, geographic location, race, ethnicity, age, socioeconomic status, family makeup, etc.) are a part of the study subjects? (this impacts how results represent a larger group of people)

As an example, we will provide a cursory assessment of a study that the National Institutes of Mental Health (NIMH) funded in the 1990s on ADHD. This study, called the Multimodal Treatment of Attention Deficit Hyperactivity Disorder, became the cornerstone for creating the medication treatment model for ADHD. This study did not allow funding from pharmaceutical companies in order to maintain the perception that it was uncontaminated by corporate money. A flaw, as we see it, was that the tested treatment models were organized into four groups: (1) medication, (2) behavioral therapy, (3) a combination of medication and behavior therapy, and (4) no additional treatment beyond what the child is already receiving (Jensen, 2001). Looking at the treatment models that the researchers chose to study and the ones they seemed to exclude or at least under-represent (i.e., psychodynamic therapies, etc.), does this seem like this was an impartial study that was designed to test the *best* ways to treat ADHD, or was it a study designed to test how medication and behavioral interventions treat ADHD? And if this ended up being one of the main driving forces behind how these "best practices" were identified for the treatment of this disorder, do parents know about it?

In addition, in the study's summary, the researchers acknowledge that "[p]arental attitudes and disciplinary practices appeared to mediate improved response to the behavior therapy and combined medication/behavior therapy interventions" (Jensen, 2001). In other words, we found that these practices work, but not for a vaguely described cross section of "real-life" parenting circumstances (i.e., parents who may use corporal punishment or criticism, etc.). Ultimately, we support you selecting any therapeutic intervention that you choose for your child. We also support you having accurate information that is necessary to make an informed decision. The treatments that you are offered should be what they purport to be. If you are told that psychotropic medication is a key treatment intervention for your child, but that it only works under a specific set of conditions (when your "parental attitudes and disciplinary practices" are just so), then you should know this prior to making your decision regarding this intervention.

Since the NIMH study, subsequent research studies were conducted on the efficacy of psychotropic medications in treating ADHD, and their findings present many differing points of view—some positive (adolescents on stimulants may be less likely to use drugs) and some negative (possible problem if a child already has a heart condition, growth rate issues, more side effects in younger children). How are parents, or therapists for that matter, to know what research result is valid or reliable? To trust any result, we suggest that you first do your own research on the offered treatment, and second, ask questions of the individuals on your child's treatment team. We suggest some questions for you to ask later in this chapter. If you cannot find reliable answers to these questions yourself, how will you be able to explain them to your child when she asks?

Evidence-based practices and the studies that they are developed from have a couple of notable limitations that we think it is important for parents to know. First, they limit the number of variables being tracked to enhance the reliability of the studies. A variable is a fact, situation, or characteristic that could affect the results in such a way as to make it unclear if the intervention or idea being studied is responsible for the study's results. Variables that may be too difficult to measure because of their inherent complexity—like impact of a child's life stressors, family dysfunction, or the level of a parent's confidence—are excluded. Variables that may create too much variation in the results—like the number of students in the child's class, the experience level of the child's teacher, the number of clients in a therapist's caseload, single parent versus two-parent home, the financial circumstances of the family, or the cultural norms of a child's family—are excluded. Thus, transmitting these practices into real world situations requires that these techniques be modified and adapted to individuals and families with specific needs, contrasting clinic and private practice structures, varying environments like schools and homes, and differing cultures and belief systems. Second, the results from these controlled studies have created therapeutic practice recommendations that focus heavily on behavioral modification techniques. Behavior modification, as discussed earlier in this book, is a well-documented therapy that typically de-emphasizes the need to know the origin of a child's behavior, the underlying meaning, and the possible alterative purposes of that behavior—its latent content. Obviously, this runs contrary to our holistic therapeutic philosophy.

Methods from these studies are often developed and described in treatment "manuals" and books. This documentation is said to provide structure, theoretical limits, and direction to therapists practicing certain types of treatment. They can lay out for the therapist (and parents) instructions on what to say, when to say it, what questions to ask, and how to respond to the answers. These instructions can range from cursory and broad to highly detailed and specific. They can define the number of sessions provided to accomplish a given therapy goal and how long after these sessions have ended that a child may expect a follow-up.

Evidence-based practices provided through these manuals and books, in effect, ration treatment—highlighting certain services and limiting and/or excluding others—based on the targeted behavior modification research. The research-backed philosophy behind these therapies and the institutions that maintain them make it difficult—at times impossible—to incorporate differing opinions, alternative methods, or the myriad nuances of a child's mental health presentation. By their existence, the manuals also reinforce, for the therapists that use them, the principles of uniformity of interventions and adherence to the treatment (Addis & Cardemil, 2006). This follows the idea that the insurance companies that pay for these sessions require that therapists remain true to these guidelines, regardless of the aforementioned limitations. Insurance companies follow up on therapists' (and agencies') adherence through audits and enforce adherence through denial of payment for sessions.

Certainly, medical insurances, both private and public, have the right to set up reimbursement formulas and to require the appropriate documentation for any treatment charges. Standardizing and controlling treatment as a containment of healthcare costs is not in itself irresponsible. However, we do not think it is appropriate for these entities to make decisions on the length or type of your child's therapy. We are especially concerned when these decisions are made and justified by a mental health professional in the insurances companies' employ who has never met you or your child or indeed may have no specialized training in working with children.

We do not want to leave you with the impression that these evidence-based therapies are invalid or unhelpful. Anecdotally, there are many child therapists who report having success with these types of therapies. We have found this is particularly so for therapists who use treatment manuals as part of their treatment plan in addition to using other techniques based on alternate theories. This type of usage reflects the therapist's creativity and retains the therapist's personality. By doing this, the relationship with the child remains the key factor of the psychotherapy—not the manual. So, as you move through the treatment planning process, in order for you to retain transparency into your child's therapeutic process, you may want to ask some of the following questions of your child's therapist (regardless of his or her theoretical slant):

- How did you choose this therapy process for my child?
- Did you consider another, and if so, which one?
- How often have you ever been involved in a treatment of a child with this process that did not work the way that you anticipated?
- What would be some indications that this treatment is not working?
- How much time is needed to determine whether this prescribed treatment is working?
- What contingency treatment plans are available if this treatment does not work?

An open-ended treatment structure, as we propose, puts control in the hands of the parents and the therapist of their choice, with the parent having the ultimate decision-making responsibility.

The contention from the financial power brokers in mental health (psychiatry, pharmaceutical companies, health insurers, politicians/legislators) is that evidence-based or best practices are "innovative" and that mental health practitioners who do not use them are involving their clients (*and the insurance companies*) in outdated, lengthy, and costly treatments that are not "quantifiably" effective. There are contentions that mental health practitioners who are not inclined to incorporate these "new and innovative" therapeutic techniques do so out of apathy or even a lack of the skills necessary to assimilate these new techniques into their practice—as opposed to a wariness about using behavior modification as a primary therapeutic framework for helping children. Looking at these studies and the rhetoric associated with them as a recent trend in mental health, it also seems possible that the establishment wishes *to gain more control over the options* that psychotherapy practitioners have in making decisions for these children and, ultimately, to shift the treatment options (and their revenue streams) away from these practitioners. Unfortunately, anxious parents looking for information get swept up into this ongoing clash that on the surface (manifest) looks like a "real" debate over which type of mental health treatment is best for a child, but, under the surface (latent), is actually about money and control within the mental health industry.

While abuses of the system can always happen, we believe that putting more knowledge in the hands of parents is a more trustworthy and balanced way of managing a child's treatment (and possible abuses) than relying on treatment protocols that are often dictated by insurance company profits and research funded by sources with potentially biased priorities. This is not a new conflict within healthcare. Individuals and health professionals have been battling insurance companies (and indirectly, pharmaceutical companies) for years over influencing treatment decisions. Being aware of possible external influences enables you to make informed decisions when planning your child's treatment.

If you are covered by a government-funded medical insurance, the options for treatment for your child may be confined to specific programs and clinics. These programs or clinics may be obligated to follow evidence-based practice approaches as dictated by your state Office of Mental Health or Behavioral Health. There are books available at book outlets that are often used by these agencies, programs, and individuals in developing child treatment plans. These books can provide you with more information regarding treatment decisions being offered to you and your child. The titles are

1. *The Child Psychotherapy Treatment Planner* (PracticePlanners)
2. *The Adolescent Psychotherapy Treatment Planner* (PracticePlanners)

Douglas Ends Treatment Early

Douglas was a 10-year-old boy who was in treatment for severe anxiety. He also presented with low self-esteem and suicidal thoughts. Sadly, Douglas's home life was a significant source of his distress. He had experienced the sudden loss of his mother at the age of 5, and his father, continuing to grieve, had his own psychiatric problems. The nature of Douglas's father's mental health problems made it very difficult for him to participate in Douglas's treatment in any meaningful way. Just getting him to his sessions, which he did, was a difficult task. This structural treatment dynamic slowed the progress of the treatment significantly, but progress was being made. After a year, Douglas was more verbal and more able to articulate the feelings associated with his traumatic life. It was at this time that the insurance company psychiatrist informed the therapist that based on best practices, one year should have been sufficient to address Douglas's anxiety and depression more appreciably. The therapist discussed the extenuating circumstances of the father's mental health problems, but the insurance company would not compromise. The insurance unilaterally altered coverage. The change and the ongoing uncertainty it caused became enough of a stressor for Douglas's father that he ended his son's treatment.

As we mentioned earlier, these evidence-based approaches fail to integrate the idea that psychology and psychological problems are complex and subtle and do not fit into a neat box like many medical problems do. The way a child manages a trauma, for instance, must take into consideration a child's temperament (innate personality), developmental stage, family system (culture, relationships), coping skills, intellectual functioning, the nature of the trauma, and the history of any other traumas—just to name *some* of the main factors. In this case, trying to develop a one-treatment-fits-all approach to Douglas's trauma was simply too limiting and did not acknowledge the uniqueness of this child's psychology and life. Unfortunately, there is little that can be done to alter circumstances such as these. Awareness of these is the best antidote, as it allows you the opportunity to create (with your child's therapist) contingency plans and thus retain a level of clinical control.

We want to caution that often, if the evidence-based program is not working for a child, the explanation by the professional involved is that the program is not being adhered to correctly by parents and child. This explanation of the problem places parents (and child) in a **double bind**—a no-win situation (Bateson, Jackson, Haley, & Weakland, 1956).

1. *This treatment option is not working because of you and your child.*
2. *There are other treatment options for your child's problem other than this one.*
3. *However, this is the best treatment option for your child's problem.*

This double bind makes independent decision-making very stressful. Getting a "second opinion" is one of the ways that we can get clarity and manage the potentially authoritarian nature of the medical model of mental health treatment.

Ill-conceived treatment decisions, evidence-based or holistic, do not stand up to scrutiny and questions from a committed and well-informed parent. Continually advocating for your child, being very knowledgeable and involved in your child's treatment decisions, can make the difference between receiving a one-size-fits-all treatment versus a treatment that is tailored to his or her unique needs.

Luke's Father Has an Idea

Luke was a 16-year-old boy who lived with his adoptive parents. They had adopted him when he was 5 years old, after years of going from foster home to foster home. He had been sexually and physically abused and suffered from depression and trauma-related disorder that led Luke to have difficulty (rage, fear, and anxiety) in social situations. After years of treatment, initially at an agency and then with a private therapist, Luke was feeling emotionally stronger, was becoming more self-aware, and was functioning much better in school and at home. One day, his father was talking to a friend about a new type of therapy that was being researched. He looked it up on the Internet and then called the therapist. He asked if the therapist would look into this and try to incorporate the methods into Luke's treatment plan. An individual in-person session with the father (arranged with Luke's permission) explored his thinking about the new therapy. The therapist saw that the father's research and subsequent request were clearly a sign of the father's acceptance of his son's struggles and a validation of his commitment to and love for him.

OUR VIEW ON TREATMENT PLANNING

This brings the conversation to the nuts and bolts of creating a plan of action to address your child's problems. Going back to the house metaphor, so far we have agreed on an architect (chosen a therapist), drawn up the tentative blueprint (identified strengths, symptoms, and possible causes), and have laid the foundation and placed the struts (established the frame, set the rules, roles, and individual responsibilities). Now we are going to build the walls of the house (decide on what to do to address the problems)—this is the part of therapy that is typically called a **treatment plan**.

We would like to expand the definition of the treatment plan to include your original decision to seek out therapy. We believe that parents initiate treatment plans by calling a therapist and that the therapist is simply a part of that plan.

Like any construction project, there is the plan and then there is the reality created once the plan begins to move forward. We say this in order to acknowledge and discuss the matter of expectations. There is an inherent unpredictability in any treatment. There are ideas that have been tried for others, but your child is unique, and we want your expectations to be hopeful and realistic. So a therapy is simultaneously unpredictable and methodical. We create a plan and then are prepared to alter it as new situations dictate. The treatment plan reflects this flexibility.

A treatment plan is the progression of steps that are intended to address your child's problems. The steps are determined by the **treatment goal(s)**. A major component of the engagement phase is to structure the treatment around this set of goals, which are the focus in direct and indirect ways over the duration of the therapy. A goal is a milestone or a level of achievement. It can be an ability, skill, understanding, insight, idea, concept, or awareness that is consistent with the strength-based model.

Tanisha's Losses

Tanisha was a 14-year-old girl who recently relocated to a new city with her family due to a natural disaster in their hometown. Her family sought psychotherapy for her because she was pulling out her hair, gaining weight, and cutting school. She did not like her new city and wanted to return to her original home. As most of her community had moved away and the considerable devastation there still remained, her wishes to return home hid (and denied) the sad truth that her home, as she knew it, no longer existed. Tanisha wrote poetry in a journal and was willing to share it with her therapist. The poems were full of anger, hurt, confusion, suicidal thoughts, and plans to run away from home. As concerning as the content of the poems were, they were beautifully written, lyrical, descriptive, and were accompanied by detailed drawings. Rather than immediately reacting to the content, the therapist first talked about Tanisha's obvious talent and asked her if she would be willing to recite some of her poems in a joint session with her parents.

Tanisha was grieving many losses—school, friends, church, and neighbors. Her parents' efforts to normalize their daughter's life by creating a new structure for her did not diminish Tanisha's feelings of loss. The therapist identified and validated Tanisha's strength of being able to communicate the depth of her depression in original poetry. Her recognition, further development, and use of this strength were the basis of her ultimate recovery from her traumatic displacement.

Combined with her grief over her loss were trauma-related and depressive symptoms. *Decreasing her depression* would be the stated objective of the overall treatment, with the goals being generated from the list of typical symptoms for a child with depression—decrease isolation, decrease withdrawal, decrease suicidal thinking, and so on. Because each child has unique "components," each child's depression presents distinctively, as do its causes. Thus, we focus on a combination of strengths, symptoms, and possible causes in order to identify treatment goals and develop a plan of action.

TREATMENT GOALS

Just like behaviors, thoughts, and feelings, all treatment goals have manifest and latent elements. This is especially important when we are creating goals for children because often these goals, as expressed by other professionals, are typically articulated in a purely manifest form. Here are some examples:

1. The treatment goal of *speaking up on behalf of oneself*
   a. Manifest goal is developing the language necessary for verbally articulating a message to another person;
   b. Latent goals are building confidence, managing vulnerability, developing a sense of security, and learning about self-care.
2. The treatment goal of *sitting still in class*
   a. Manifest goals are developing the ability to sit in one place without moving, managing basic impulses, learning ways of focusing;
   b. Latent goals are building awareness of the body, identifying internal tension and frustration, enhancing a sense of control, mastery, and self-esteem; and coping with rules and structure, and learning about self-care.
3. The treatment goal of *medicating a child's symptom or symptoms*
   a. Manifest goals are making the choice to be evaluated for medication, creating the relationship with a psychiatrist (who will evaluate your child and prescribe), identifying the correct medication, taking the medication, monitoring for effectiveness, and managing side effects;
   b. Latent goals are building sense of control in child and parent(s), processing thoughts and feelings about medication, augmenting therapeutic support structure, and learning about self-care.

Our use of *manifest* and *latent* treatment goals refers to the terms "short-term goals" and "long-term goals," respectively, that you may hear used by health insurance companies, Offices of Mental Health, agencies, and other professionals. **Short-term goals** tend to focus on the concrete issues of the here and now. Therefore, they focus on the surface manifest content. **Long-term goals** tend to focus on the foundational issues that are obstacles to your child's ability to function or the underlying strengths of your child that need to be supported. Therefore, the focus of long-term goals is on underlying latent content.

Kareem Dances

Kareem was 6 years old when he began to see a therapist, and he had just started first grade in his local public school. He lived with his adoptive mother, who had taken custody of him from his aunt several weeks after his birth. Kareem had been born addicted to cocaine. His new teachers had indicated that Kareem could not sit still, was jumping around, was talking a lot, and had great difficulty concentrating. These issues affected his current functioning at school (class disruption, teacher complaints) and at home (mother's difficulties with getting him to do simple everyday tasks). In his therapy sessions, Kareem did not appear anxious or agitated—he simply could not sit still. There was always a part of his body that was moving, even when asked to sit perfectly still. In addition, he moved from topic to topic, game to game, never staying very long at one—except he would concentrate and focus when dancing to music, which became a part of his therapy sessions. He was well coordinated and had a level of skill of an older child. Once physically tired from dancing he was able to settle down and draw. The therapist felt that the short-term goals were to address Kareem's hyperactivity and diminish his distractibility. The long-term goals were to focus on helping Kareem accept and like himself—to see his strengths and his resilience. If viewed exclusively as a problem, his presentation at home and at school was likely to lead to issues with his self-esteem, feeling different and isolated.

Having provided the multiple meanings of treatment goals (short/surface/manifest and long/underlying/latent), for ease in cross-referencing with other publications, we are now going to use the terminology (short-term and long-term) utilized by the other parts of the mental health world.

THERAPEUTIC INTERVENTIONS

A **therapeutic intervention** is a purposeful clinical response to a child's strength, symptom, behavior, and so on. It is what a therapist chooses to say or do in session, and it is made for the express purpose of creating change. It can be verbal or nonverbal, play-based or art-based, within the physical realm or the intellectual realm—a smile, a nod, a frown, losing a game, describing personal space, exhibiting empathy—there are many forms. These therapeutic interventions correspond with the goals that have been determined by the therapist and the parents—both short-term and long-term.

For Kareem, psychotropic medication was a necessary therapeutic intervention. His hyperactivity and distractibility were physiological and stemmed from the medical issues he had endured during his mother's pregnancy. Other short-term interventions focused on concrete skill building—what to do with his feet and his hands, how to remind himself to pay attention, and strategies for his adoptive mother to manage her frustrations. The long-term goals were addressed through inventions focused on finding a series of activities that were consistent with his body processes, such as dance lessons, karate, and so on. These high-action activities allowed Kareem to use his strength of well-coordinated body movements and control. The therapy discussions were centered on reframing concepts in his life. *Difficulty sitting still* in school became *his need for and enjoyment of activity* rather than a failure. Learning patience and managing frustration became a goal to diminish his urgent/immediate needs for activity but did not dampen his many ideas that were an aspect of his intelligence.

THE TREATMENT PLAN

Abraham Maslow was a theorist who developed a concept called the hierarchy of needs, which stated that a human being needs some basic items in order to be able to develop and grow (water, air, shelter, etc.). Once these basic necessities for survival are acquired, a human being then moves on to seek and attempt to acquire the next level of "needs" (security, stability, etc.). If levels one and two are satisfied, then, building on this foundation, a human being can have relationships, work, and so on (Maslow, 1943).

Clifford's Treatment Goals

Clifford's parents were in the process of getting a divorce caused by his father's increasing alcoholism and violent behavior. Always considered a "quiet" child, Clifford at 13 years of age was withdrawn, had no friends, and was doing poorly in school. He was a sad, soft-spoken, and teary-eyed boy who seemed to be younger than his age. His increasingly worried parents agreed to a referral from Clifford's school psychologist for psychotherapy for their son. His parents believed that Clifford was having trouble coping with their divorce. Clifford's problems seemed worse as some of his issues intensified because of puberty.

The short-term goals focused on the issues of safety, school, and friends—maintaining his security, improving his grades, changing his study habits, and spending more time with his peers. Clifford and his parents understood the short-term goals as they reflected the current problems that Clifford experienced. When the therapist presented the long-term goals to Clifford and his parents, there seemed to be more reluctance from all those involved to agree to engage in the process. The long-term goals focused on issues of low self-esteem, sexual confusion, and his fears of being like his father. The long-term goals were more abstract and less outwardly visible.

Initially, the therapist needed to determine that Clifford was not in any immediate physical danger due to his father's drinking and temper. This short-term goal impacted all the others. While the other issues were a valid source of concern, Clifford's safety was primary. When his father moved out of the home and began receiving treatment for his alcoholism, Clifford was no longer in any danger and the other short-term and long-term goals could be addressed.

Becoming aware of Clifford's low self-esteem helped his parents to understand the need to alter some of the ways they communicated with their son and how to provide him with effective support and encouragement. The issue of Clifford's concerns about his sexuality remained private, as agreed between Clifford and his therapist, and was identified as a long-term goal focusing on his identify and his sense of self.

When we use Maslow's framework as a guide, treatment planning follows a logical progression that builds upon and is dependent upon what came before—like building a house from the ground up. This is important for two reasons: (1) it is difficult to move therapy forward optimally without laying a solid groundwork first; and (2) if the information and/or decisions regarding the treatment change, the therapy is required to take the time to integrate the new element(s) of the treatment before moving forward again.

This type of plan also incorporates a flexible, adaptable, and shifting view of your child's mental health treatment—a child can improve and/or backslide based on the interplay between the different components of his or her life and the therapy. This occurs because the therapeutic process is not linear and does not occur in a vacuum. Progress and regression are functions of the dynamic reality of every child's life—a new event, new information, a new developmental stage, a new behavior, a new reaction, a new therapeutic intervention, or a new therapy goal.

Changes also occur with parents as the therapeutic process moves forward. This has a significant bearing on treatment planning. Since Maslow's philosophy places parental needs and actions solidly within the foundation of a child's life, any changes within the parenting dynamic would have an effect on the child's therapy. When any change occurs, the treatment plan follows, slowing down, speeding up, or altering course. It is an ever-changing process, not a set plan of action. Imagine that the "walls" of this treatment plan are those of a traditional Japanese home—the sliding walls, called *fusuma*, can be rearranged to accommodate for the changing lives of those who live within.

DISCUSSING TREATMENT PLANNING BY AGE GROUP

We want to focus on treatment planning and its meaning and usefulness during treatment to children of different age groups. This closely follows the trajectory of discussing diagnosis with children of different ages. We also want to remind parents that the ideas of manifest and latent material are complex, and that if it is necessary to discuss these ideas with your child, it is important to confer with the therapist. Often latent content is beneath the level of awareness, and consequently, discussing it without preparation and planning can be confronting to a child.

Toddlerhood through Pre-latency or Early Childhood (Age 3–7)

Since children of this age are not connected to the meaning of a diagnosis or aware of symptoms, discussing how to address these symptoms does not apply. The older children in this category may begin to be curious about the workings of therapy and the activities, but, typically, they will ask their parents about the process and will see all activities in a manifest fashion—playing with a doll, shooting a basketball, reading a book, talking about feelings.

Latency or Childhood (Age 7–11)

Children this age are typically aware of how they are feeling, and they may want to understand how the therapist is going to "help" them feel better. These children can understand the manifest details of their symptoms and will have usually heard basic ways (therapeutic interventions) of addressing difficulties—count to 10 when you are angry, talk about your feelings, take deep breaths when you are nervous, and so on. This age group often *chooses* to see therapeutic activities manifestly. These children are able to follow a treatment plan and specific short-term goals if these are presented to them. That said, we feel that parents and therapists should allow this age group to take the lead in exploring all aspects, including the plan of treatment. Developmentally, these children are focused on controlling and mastering their surroundings and abilities. Discussing the treatment plan can be a helpful way of increasing a sense of control over the process.

Early Adolescence (Age 12–15)

Because of the onset of puberty, this age group includes children who fall all along the continuum of maturity level, cognitive and physical development, and identity formation. That said, it is important for this age group to begin to take some ownership over the plan to address their problems and the setting of treatment goals. The **regressive pull** of early adolescence (the tendency to rely on parents) may complicate this process of shifting some responsibility (Blos, 1970). While we suggest that children in this group increasingly be pushed to generate treatment decisions, children in this group will continue to participate in therapy dynamics—attendance, following up with interventions, disclosure of session material, and so on—while parents maintain an ongoing and influential role in treatment planning.

Late Adolescence/Teen Years (Age 15–17)

Subject to maturity level, teenagers should be actively participating in the treatment planning process. Short-term goals and even long-term goals are well within their cognitive and intellectual capacities. These individuals have the capacity to develop a level of insight that allows for the processing and integrating of latent material. Treatment planning transitions away from parents during these years.

Young Adulthood (Age 18–Mid-20s)

The therapist and the young adult discuss all aspects of treatment. The preservation and nurturance of your adult child's sense of independence, mastery, and competence is a crucial aspect of effective treatment with this age group. The treatment plan is governed by patient-therapist confidentiality, but the adult child can share it directly with his or her parent(s) if they wish. The decision to discuss the treatment plan with the parent is part of a thoroughly explored plan/negotiation between your adult child and his or her therapist. This is true even if you as the parent may be paying for the treatment, either directly or indirectly.

If your adult child is dependent on you economically, and/or lives in your home, because of his or her mental health difficulties or other disabilities, maintaining control over the details of his or her therapy establishes a sense of autonomy. This is particularly important because the realities of the living situation may challenge these feelings. In fact, the greater the level of the adult child's concrete dependence on their parents, the greater the need for her to control process of her psychotherapy treatment.

CHAPTER SUMMARY

CHAPTER 9: TREATMENT PLANNING

A treatment plan is the progression of steps that are intended to address your child's problems.
 The steps are determined by the **treatment goals**.
 A treatment goal is a milestone or a level of achievement. It can be

- An ability
- A skill
- Understanding
- Insight
- An idea

- A concept
- Awareness

Short-term goals focus on the concrete issues (at home, at school, with family, with peers, etc.) based on what is happening in the here and now with your child.

Long-term goals focus on the foundational issues (sense of self, anxiety, confidence, control, impulsivity) that are obstacles to your child's ability to function and the underlying strengths of your child that need to be supported.

A therapeutic intervention
- is a purposeful clinical response to a child's strength, symptom, behavior, and so on;
- is what a therapist chooses to say or do in session for the express purpose of creating change; and
- corresponds with the treatment goals.

CHAPTER 10

The Parallel Process of Child Psychotherapy

There is a concept in psychotherapy called **parallel process**. It is the name given to a dynamic that occurs in therapy in which *each* of the people involved (client, parent, and therapist) undergo their own personal transformations (Searles, 1955). Change is often taking place within everyone involved, whether directly or indirectly. For instance, it would difficult to cultivate one part of a garden and not have the process impact the whole garden in some way.

The concept of parallel process can help you understand how important you are to the success of your child's therapy. We return to the sentence from the synopsis of the NIMH study, Multimodal Treatment of Attention Deficit Hyperactivity Disorder: "Parental attitudes and disciplinary practices appeared to mediate improved response to the behavior therapy and combined medication/behavior therapy interventions" (Jensen, 2001). It may not be the writer's intent, but what this quote concludes is that parents' thoughts and actions are a crucial component to how a child responds to a therapeutic intervention. A child's mental health treatment that does not attend to parent(s) as a primary focus is not an effective therapy model.

Your child's growth is connected to your own growth as a parent and as a person. What this looks like exactly may not be what you expect, and so our goal in this chapter is to break this down for you.

Everyone Can Do Things Differently

Barry was 16 years old and was born with epilepsy. When he was younger, his seizures were very poorly controlled. The many medical emergencies caused great stress on his parents. He worried that he would never be "normal," would never have a girlfriend or be able to get a "good" job. His parents' overprotectiveness came from managing the numerous medical emergencies, some of which were life-threatening. They expressed their fears by being very strict and supervising all of Barry's activities. Barry felt more and more socially isolated. His attempts to feel more grown-up were expressed by getting into fights at school and using alcohol. This created a family crisis that resulted in Barry entering treatment.

The parallel process in this treatment involved helping Barry find healthy ways to demonstrate his maturity and helping his parents find healthy ways to express their fears and concerns. This established an environment of change for the family, resulting in Barry taking driver's education at school and practice sessions with his parents using the family car. Barry and his parents established ways to negotiate the reality that Barry was no longer a sickly child, but an adolescent with a chronic condition for which he was going to have to be increasing responsible. His epilepsy and his parents' overprotection increased the feelings of difference and exclusion that are typically experienced by most adolescents. His parents also experienced feelings of difference and exclusion as their worries about Barry's life and health were more intense than the typical worries of parents of other adolescents.

Everyone Says Goodbye

Tiffany's treatment was ending. She was 17 years old and she, her therapist, and her mother all agreed that she had accomplished many things in her treatment. It was time to make a change, as Tiffany wanted to experience life without psychotherapy. Tiffany and her therapist spent several weeks working through her termination, enumerating her accomplishments and discussing what might be her next steps. At the same time, the therapist and Tiffany's mother also were terminating and saying goodbye. While Tiffany had made a therapeutic connection with the therapist over the years, so had her mother (parallel process #1). While Tiffany's work had been about understanding herself, her strengths, and her limitations, her mother's work had been about focusing on responding to and understanding the changes to the mother-daughter relationship as Tiffany moved through adolescence (parallel process #2). So as the treatment was ending, yet another parallel process presented itself—that of growth through separation (daughter from therapist; mother from therapist; and daughter from mother) (parallel process #3). Tiffany's mother told the therapist that she was nervous. She said that she was unsure about her parenting skills going forward. What would she do without being able to consult with the therapist? She indicated that she was sad and she was going to miss their work together.

The experiences of Tiffany's mother and Barry's parents are constructive in understanding the potential of a parent's role in his or her child's therapy. Because you and your child are linked, what happens to your child when she is in therapy has an effect on you, and visa versa. Even if the goals of therapy are focused on your child's needs, the shared experience makes each individual stronger. Tiffany's mother spent the last session examining the progress she had made as a parent, the changes in her understanding of her daughter, and the changes in her skills. Barry's parents came away from his therapy having made progress in providing him with some independence (short-term goal), which created a sense of security about their son's future (long-term goal).

This involvement looks different from child to child, parent to parent, therapy to therapy. The decisions and choices regarding the extent and nature of your participation are based on a variety of factors that we will discuss in this chapter. First, though, we want to give you another rationale for thinking about your own part in this therapy.

It centers on Erik Erikson, who advanced the idea of interconnected and progressive stages of maturation and developmental formation. He identified nine milestones that start at birth and move through end of life. Each of these milestones has a goal or goals—trust, autonomy (making one's own choices), control, creativity, and so on. He believed that if a person navigates the goals of these stages successfully, then that person continues to flourish psychologically and emotionally. If a person does not navigate a stage successfully, then this will affect her experience of each subsequent stage of development. A part of her will be developmentally "stuck," while she continues to progress with difficulty through the other stages. Being stuck in the trust stage leaves one feeling mistrustful; being stuck in the autonomy stage leaves one doubting oneself; and so on. Erikson contended that feeling stuck engenders a variety of "negative" feelings and symptoms: discomfort, sadness, depression, and anxiety, to name a few. And, above all, being stuck affects one's ability to function optimally.

For our purposes, we want to focus on Erikson's fourth stage of his nine. This stage is called Industry versus Inferiority. Its goal is **mastery**. This concept is about attaining a sense of confidence and efficacy in connection to a task that one undertakes. Erikson felt that this goal of mastery was never more present than at the beginning of elementary school, when children are experiencing a new environment (school), new relationships (teachers and classmates), and many new concepts (math, science, writing, reading, etc). As a child accomplished this goal, Erikson believed, she would develop the ability to be *industrious*—productive and active in her life. If not, that child would feel *inferior*—ill-equipped to manage life's challenges and questioning herself.

The concept of parallel process can be applied here as well. As your child goes through the stages of development, so do you as parents. In Erikson's fourth stage, parents are encountering a new environment, new relationships, and new concepts each time they have a child. The addition of a child changes the family structure. Having a first child cannot completely prepare parents for all the new dynamics involved in having a second child or a third. Each new child, whether it is your first or fourth, requires the details and processes of parenting to be (re)examined, (re)learned, and (re)calibrated based on that child's unique characteristics and how that child fits into the new family structure. Feeling industrious and competent about being a parent can easily slip into feeling inferior and incompetent. There is always a learning curve, and we change with each parenting experience.

Martha's Parents Discover Temperament

Martha was a 3-year-old girl who threw many tantrums that worried her parents because she would "blow up" at any moment. Their son, who was 8, never threw tantrums. They thought something was wrong with Martha. When they consulted a therapist, he suggested that the parents meet with him for several sessions. If they still believed that Martha needed to be seen, he would meet Martha and they could discuss treatment. During the next sessions, the therapist described the typical course of child development—that Martha needed control. The parents could respond and understand these tantrums as moments of "needing control." He also discussed the concept of the different temperaments presented by both of their children. One was cautious and the other, Martha, was not. These discussions aided the parents in seeing Martha from a new perspective. Martha's behavior was just something new, not

something bad. Understanding Martha's need for control meant that it was impor-
tant to offer her choices and options about decisions she could make.

In addition, parenting can often feel like a time machine bringing us back to our own childhood when we were parented. The fact that our children often look like us, sound like us, and react like us serves as a constant reminder of those days of the past. If our child presents aspects of ourselves that we are uncomfortable with, we struggle with how to react. When we revisit our own childhoods, we recall both the struggles and triumphs that we experienced. It can bring to mind what we ourselves did not get as children, for one reason or another, with hope that it will be different for our own children.

What Can Beverly's Mother Do With Her Anger?

Beverly was an 8-year-old girl whose mother brought her to therapy because of her various symptoms of depression. Beverly cut her legs, pinched her arms, and hit herself in the head. Beverly's family lived in a home with Grandpa (that he paid for). The therapist had met Grandpa early in Beverly's therapy, because Grandpa had been yelling at Beverly in the waiting room. Beverly's mother often cried in her parent sessions, expressing how parenting in a home with her father around was impossible. Her father would question her in front of the child, call her a bad parent, and threaten to call child protective services. She worried that she would never be the parent that Beverly needed. She admitted that she often took her anger out on Beverly and her siblings when her father criticized her. The therapist and the mother agreed that she and her children could no longer live in a home with her father. Beverly's mental health outlook was contingent on finding a new place to live. Moving became a priority treatment goal. Within a year, Beverly and her family moved into an apartment of their own.

Typically, parents bring their children to therapy when they are feeling unsure about some aspect of this parenting dynamic, and the primary contribution that a parent can make to his or her child's therapy is to work toward being a more secure parent. Secure and confident parents, especially when confronting problems, have a containing and calming effect on a child—the child feels that whatever he is struggling with, it is within the parent's capabilities to contain it and to help him, providing comfort, support, and love.

We are acutely aware that the goal of secure parenting is not a straightforward or simple one to achieve. It is a process, with starts and stops, backward and forward movements, and mistakes and successes—similar and parallel to your child's development and maturation.

Your child's therapy can put you on a path to feeling like a stronger, more confident parent. It can also function as a conduit for a new set of recollections from your own childhood. The process of asking for, receiving, and accepting help are themes that we all experience in life to one degree or another. Placing your child in therapy focuses on these issues. It often serves as an access point to our own experiences relating to needing help. Your child's therapist can direct you toward ways of incorporating these memories into your parenting choices.

Pablo's Father Asks for Help

His parents noticed that 6-year-old Pablo was often nervous and tearful when he did not feel he had control. His parents were concerned about these intense expressions of emotion and took him to see a therapist to help him find ways of better managing his worries. During the second appointment between the therapist and the parents, she asked Pablo's father about his own childhood. His father shared that he had been physically abused himself from a very early age. His father also shared that when Pablo would cry as an infant, that he would imagine himself hitting his son. This would scare him and he would withdraw and ask his wife to help Pablo. His father asked the therapist if it was possible that this was why Pablo was so nervous, because he himself was so nervous. The therapist thanked the father for sharing this sad piece of information and acknowledged the possible connection between the feelings. Then she added that it was possible, even though Pablo was not in any danger, that his father (by withdrawing from his son and involving Pablo's mother) was protecting his son the way he had once wanted to be protected as a child. She concluded that most likely Pablo's crying was accessing the father's childhood memories.

In this instance, the father ultimately obtained psychotherapy for himself, realizing that as Pablo developed, that additional painful memories might arise for the father. This demonstrated the father's mental health, his devotion to his son, and his wish to be the best father possible.

It is important that you are a part of and are aware of the reasoning behind your involvement in your child's therapy. How exactly your involvement looks is based on agreements with your child's therapist that begin during the engagement phase of treatment. It will change over time, based on your child's therapeutic needs and developmental changes. It will also change as you inevitably become more secure in your parenting.

TAKING CHARGE OF THE PARALLEL PROCESS

The parallel process does not take place magically. It begins with you and continues by way of your various contacts with your child and your child's therapist. These contacts can take many forms and serve different purposes in conjunction with the parallel process.

Having discussed and described the theory, we wanted to provide you with a practical way of actively starting the process. If you engage in your child's therapy, what we have described above is going to move forward in any event. To this end, if you choose, you can take on a more proactive role in it. The proactive role is twofold: (1) accumulate information about yourself as a child, paying specific attention to your reactions to your relationships with your parents; and (2) share this information with your child's therapist. We will say that the more your child's therapist knows about you, the more complete her or his understanding of your child can be. Obviously, sharing personal information with your child's therapist takes place when sufficient trust has been established.

Looking back into the past can be challenging, so we want to provide you with focus questions as a way of structuring your recollections. Answer these to the best of your memory. If you cannot recall answers, feel that your memories are confusing or uncomfortable, or have any other intense feelings when you are reading these questions, feel free to not answer those questions. You may want to make note of these feelings and/or thoughts.

CHILD-SPECIFIC ISSUES

- How would you describe yourself as a child? As a teenager? As a parent?
- What would you say were your strengths as a child? As a teenager? As a young adult?
- How did you communicate your feelings to adults as a child? As a teenager?

- Were there any times in your life that were particularly difficult? Happy? Sad? Frightening? Confusing? Complicated?
- What were your friendships like in early childhood? Elementary school? Middle school? High school? Beyond?
- Did you ever have acute or chronic medical problems as a child? If so, what? When? Duration? How did your parent(s) respond to your acute or chronic medical problems?

PARENT-SPECIFIC ISSUES

- How would you describe your parent(s)?
- If you had siblings, what were your relationships like with your siblings?
- Did you feel that your parent(s) treated you and your siblings equally?
- How would you characterize your relationship with your parent(s) during early childhood? Elementary school? Middle school? High school? Beyond?
- How would your parent(s) describe you as a child? As a teenager? As a young adult? As a parent of your own child?
- What were your parent(s)' strengths?
- Did your parent(s) ever get angry? Sad?
- Did you feel your parent(s) were overprotective of you? Not focused on you?
- What was your parent(s)' disciplinary style?
- How did your parent(s) respond to crying?
- How did your parent(s) respond to loud noises?
- How did your parent(s) respond to anger?
- How did your parent(s) respond to sadness?
- How did your parent(s) respond to loss and separation?
- How did your parent(s) respond to nervousness?
- How did your parents feel about your friends?
- How did you and your parent communicate during your childhood? During your adolescence? During your young adulthood? As you became the parent of your own child?
- What was your family structure as a child? Distant, connected, overly connected?
- How would you characterize your parent(s)' relationship?
- Did they get along with and/or support one another?

- Did they argue and/or disagree with one another? How would you characterize these issues?
- Did your parent(s) see parenting as a joint task, or did they have different approaches to parenting that did not connect with one another?

TREATMENT-SPECIFIC ISSUES

- Was anyone in your family in therapy when you were a child?
- Were you ever in therapy as a child? If not, disregard the additional questions in this section.
- If you were in therapy, what were the reasons for you being placed in therapy?
- What did your parents tell you about therapy?
- What were the short-term goals of your therapy?
- What were the long-term goals of your therapy?
- How did you feel about being in therapy?
- How did you feel about your therapist?

This is not a questionnaire that you are required to complete in order for your child's therapy to be successful. It is not supposed to be onerous. It is supposed to elicit memories from our lives that we believe have connections to the way we see ourselves as parents. It is supposed to create a bridge from the past to the present that we can use to become more self-aware and effective parents.

CHAPTER SUMMARY

CHAPTER 10: THE PARALLEL PROCESS OF
CHILD PSYCHOTHERAPY

Parents bring their children to therapy when they are feeling unsure about some aspect of parenting.

The primary influence that a parent can have on his or her child's therapy is to work toward being more secure as a parent. Your child's growth is connected to your own growth as a parent and as a person.

Parallel process is a dynamic that occurs in therapy in which all of the people involved (client, parent, and therapist) undergo their own personal transformations.

The extent and nature of your transformation are based on two main factors:

- Accumulating information about yourself as a child (specifically about your childhood, relationships with your parents, siblings, school, friends, any therapy history, etc.)
- Sharing this information with your child's therapist.

The more your child's therapist knows about you, the more complete her or his understanding of your child can be.

Contributing to Your Child's Psychotherapy

TYPES OF CONTACT WITH YOUR CHILD'S THERAPIST

A parent can always have contact in various ways with his or her child's therapist. Having direct access to your child's therapist is an important factor in preventing misunderstanding and miscommunication. Your contact with the therapist models productive relationship dynamics for your child.

1. *In-person psycho-educational session*—this interaction is often called a **collateral session**. The word "collateral" refers to supplementing, being connected to, but not being the focus of. A collateral session, sometimes called a parent session, or a family member session, is the primary point of contact between a caregiver and a child's therapist. If possible, as a way of maintaining a solid frame and boundaries, we recommend that most of your discussions with the therapist take place in this session. In addition, meeting with your child's therapist models an important message: that therapy is something that you do, too. So, whether you are in your own therapy or not, meeting with your child's therapist declares your acceptance of the therapeutic process.

   Within these sessions, all the work of the parent-therapist relationship takes place. They are typically structured in the following manner (this can vary based on age, developmental stage, and severity of the problem). The therapist

a. asks about the child's current status;
b. asks for an update since the last time the parent(s) and therapist met/communicated;
c. asks parent(s) to identify any progress or regression;
d. asks generally what parent(s) are noticing (trends, patterns, themes);
e. asks what is concerning parent(s) specifically;
f. asks parent(s) if they have any questions.

Each of these questions is geared to generate discussion and to increase the parties' awareness and understanding of the child's strengths, symptoms, actions, communications, and so on. Within the context of your child's life, you are the expert regarding what your child is doing. What the therapist contributes to these collateral sessions is his or her expertise and perspective on children in general. Putting these two sets of expertise together is the goal of collateral work. We call this psycho-educational work, or teaching parents to think like therapists while retaining the emotional connection of a parent.

Psycho-education refers to a therapeutic process of addressing psychological concepts to create better understanding and awareness and to set expectations. It can include a review of a number of topics relevant to your child's treatment.

Child-Specific Issues

- Psychological developmental stages
- Social developmental stages
- Biological developmental stages
- Your child's temperament
- Your child's strengths
- Forms of your child's communication.

Bernard Takes Care of His Mother

Bernard was a 13-year-old boy who was brought to therapy by his mother, who felt that Bernard, who was always "a sensitive child," "had an attitude" and was increasingly disobedient, defiant, and antagonistic. She was concerned that Bernard was acting more like his father, who had moved out of the home years ago. Bernard still spent vacations with his father, and his mother was worried that this contact was having a bad influence on Bernard. Bernard's home life was complicated for him. He was very protective of his mother after witnessing years of arguing and fighting between his parents. He was also an adolescent, going through puberty, and had a developmental need to have some space from his mother. The therapist worked with his mother to understand that, far from becoming his father, Bernard was very devoted to his mother. What he was really struggling with (the "attitude") was how to manage his feelings about being her protector and her teenage son at the same time. His mother indicated to the therapist that she did not need a protector, and the therapist agreed. Their work together then centered on how to help Bernard use his strengths (his loyalty, his sense of family, and his intelligence) to start to understand what had happened between the two key adults in his life and how he fit into this family dynamic as a teenager.

Bernard's mother was used to his "sensitive" temperament but was unprepared for the changes in her son caused by puberty. As Bernard continued to develop as an adolescent, his communication patterns with his mother changed as well. Some of the changes in communication were a source of friction between mother and son. His mother's fears about Bernard becoming "like his father" made it difficult for her to "see" her son's strengths (loyalty, sense of family, and intelligence) that made her son quite different from his father.

Parent-Specific Issues
- Parent reactions/feelings
- Your strengths
- Parent-child relationship
- Parent to child communication
- Family communication

Maxwell Needs to Leave Home

Maxwell, a 15-year-old boy, had been seeing his therapist for several years as a part of court-mandated treatment related to his difficulties in middle school and a suspension because he brought a knife to school. By the time he reached high school,

Maxwell and his father were getting into an increasing number of physical altercations. When the police were called after one fight, the therapist began discussing residential treatment for Maxwell. Initially, both Maxwell and his father rejected the idea. His father indicated that he would feel like a failure as a father and could not imagine having Maxwell live elsewhere. Over the next month, with Child Protective Services involved in maintaining safety in the home, the therapist focused the father on the idea that placing Maxwell in a residential facility (creating some distance) would, in fact, protect the father-son relationship. Keeping them together at this time would jeopardize the relationship. Being able to see the separation as a "safety measure" and not an "end" helped Maxwell and his father feel more secure with this decision.

It is always difficult to cope with a child's serious mental health problems. Maxwell's father struggled with feelings of confusion and guilt. He hoped that things would get better but was also burdened by feelings of loss and separation. Maxwell's mother abandoned the two of them when Maxwell was 2 years old. His father feared adjusting to another loss, even though he knew his relationship with his son was crumbling under the weight of Maxwell's problems.

Treatment-Specific Issues

- Treatment planning
- Short-term treatment goals
- Long-term treatment goals
- Causes and symptoms

Talya Throws a Fit

Talya was a 5-year-old girl, whose mothers described her as a "troublemaker." They described a pattern of behavior that included temper tantrums, ignoring rules, and annoying other children in her class. Talya was born via in vitro fertilization (IVF). The therapist noticed during the intake that the biological mother expressed more worry about Talya than her non-biological mother. Her biological mother made statements indicating that she was at fault for Talya's behavior. The therapist began working with the family, meeting with Talya in individual sessions and her parents in collateral sessions twice a month. In addition, the therapist asked to see

the biological mother by herself. During the individual collateral session, the thera-
pist then asked her mother why she blamed herself for Talya's behavior. She stated
that she was weak because when she said "no" to Talya, her daughter would scream
and throw a tantrum. She was embarrassed about giving in. She believed she was
causing her daughter's distress, something she wanted to avoid because of her own
lonely childhood. The therapist responded by saying that her love for her daughter
was obvious, first, by her wish to be a stronger parent and, second, by her seeking
out help to be a stronger parent. The therapist then added a treatment goal for the
mother—understand the concept of limit setting as a caring, containing, and loving
act, instead of punishment, denial, and rejection.

Often parents know "what not to do" because of their own histories as children. Wanting to be different from your parents and wanting your child to have a "better" childhood than yours are treatment goals based on love and devotion. Collateral sessions with your child's therapist can help parents express their love and devotion in ways that can help their children have "better" childhoods.

2. *In-person informal contact*—by informal we mean unplanned or spontaneous. This typically takes the form of talking before or after a child's session. It can occur in a waiting room, or the therapist can suggest that you meet in a private office. These can be important contact moments for the purpose of providing updates, relationship building, and so on; however, we want you to be aware of how unstructured these types of contacts can be. The amount of time available for these types of interaction is unpredictable and can be limited by a variety of factors. If the matter that you want to discuss is urgent in nature, then a different choice of contact is recommended. The last thing we would want is for an important matter to not be given an appropriate amount of time. In addition, in these informal meetings, there may be some difficulty regarding maintaining confidentiality and boundaries. Your child's curiosity about the subject matter may challenge this type of communication.

We recommend that you prepare your child for this type of interaction by letting them know that you intend to speak to the therapist before or after the session. Your child may have questions about what you intend to say or ask. Be aware that by choosing to contact the therapist in this way and at this time (manifest) you are also choosing to have your child be aware of your communication (latent). Your communication is geared to affect that day's session. Be prepared for the therapist to suggest that the contact happen at another time. If you choose to use this form of contact, the *brief* material can be limited to the following:

- Recent occurrences of note
- Recent conversations
- Recent statements
- Third party communications
- Recent parent observations.

Alexandra's Mother Was Worried

Alexandra was a 6-year-old foster child. She witnessed a significant level of domestic violence during her infancy. She lived with this foster family for several years now and exhibited mild depressive symptoms and anxiety. All children at the foster agency were seen in therapy as part of their care, and Alexandra had seen several therapists at the agency that she came to for therapy. One day, Alexandra's foster mother brought her to session and at drop-off began to speak to the therapist in front of Alexandra. Her foster mother told the therapist that she was concerned that Alexandra did not trust her as much as she should and then turned to Alexandra and asked her, "Why don't you trust me?" Before Alexandra could answer, the therapist stopped the interaction. The therapist indicated that although this was very important, because it was time for the session, they could set up a time to talk about it soon. During the session, the therapist asked Alexandra if she understood what her foster mother had asked. Alexandra did not speak. The therapist asked Alexandra if she knew the meaning of the word "trust." She again did not speak. The therapist asked her if it would be okay for all three of them to sit together and figure out what her foster mother meant. Alexandra nodded.

The therapist needed to address Alexandra's foster mother's anxiety, as it was a crucial aspect of their relationship. The therapist debated what the most helpful way of accomplishing this would be. In the waiting room there was no privacy, and Alexandra did not seem prepared at that moment for a weighty conversation about trust. The therapist judged that this was not an emergency (an issue of safety or imminent danger), which would have dictated immediate therapeutic intervention. There were three options: (1) a collateral session to help the foster mother with ways to discuss the issue of trust; (2) a joint session in which the therapist could meet with them together; and (3) both.

3. *In-person parent-child session* (called a **joint session**)—in this type of session, parent(s) and the child meet with the therapist together. A misnomer exists that the purpose of this session is to have the therapist communicate a message from parent to child or from child to parent. The actual purpose of this type of session is to enhance the parent-child relationship by improving communication and understanding between you and your child. This is accomplished through mediation, educating, increasing openness, modeling empathy, and re-characterizing statements made by each participant. We want you to see a joint session as an opportunity to work on how you communicate to and listen to your child.

The dynamics of this session are complex. We have established that the therapist and the child have a therapeutic relationship that is governed by rules (confidentiality, boundaries, etc.). The joint session has a completely different set of rules that do not erase the rules that govern the child-therapist relationship, but must coexist. The goal is not to undermine the therapeutic trust that has been built with both your child and you by having a new type of session with different rules. The therapist accomplishes this in two main ways:

   a. All information from the individual sessions remains confidential unless your child decides to share the information in the joint session. What this means is that if there is information that is important for parent(s) to know, there will have been a prior discussion/negotiation between the therapist and your child about what can/will be disclosed. You may want to discuss certain material, but if your child does not want to or if she changes her mind while in the joint session, the confidentiality rules remain in effect.

   b. During the joint session, the therapist's identified client shifts from being your child to being the parent-child relationship. Since the goal of the session is communication between you and your child, the therapist's focus will be on *the interaction between the parties* involved, not the individuals or the facts they are presenting. In fact, during joint sessions, the interaction is far more important than the content. Children and parent(s) often request joint sessions with a specific purpose in mind. This purpose is typically manifest content, having to do with a problem that is occurring in the family. The joint session focuses on the "space" between the participants and what is happening there: not experiencing empathy, not feeling heard, not being understood, not having control, and/or not feeling safe are some of the latent communications.

Josyline Stays Out

Josyline was a 15-year-old girl who was adopted from Ethiopia when she was 3 years old. Her fathers brought her to a therapist when she entered high school because she started to skip school. They reported to her therapist that Josyline was arguing with them all the time, yelling and then leaving the apartment. She would stay out late into the evening and her parents would become more and more worried. They had even called the police one evening to report her missing. The police came to the apartment after Josyline had returned home and had told her to be respectful and that she should listen to her parents. It was after the police involvement that her parents asked for a joint session. Her therapist discussed it with her, explained the differences between her own individual session and the joint session, and Josyline agreed, adding that it wouldn't do any good, that nothing was going to change. Joysline, her parents, and her therapist met in a joint session soon after. During the session, one of the fathers was empathic and tried to understand what was happening with Josyline, while the other indicated that he was hurt and frustrated by her behavior. Josyline sat quietly with a frown on her face. Her parents asked her questions and she did not answer. The therapist commented on how much tension there was between Josyline and her parents, but also between the two parenting styles of her fathers. The therapist asked how a teenager could figure out how to respond to two such different parents, who both were expressing concern, but in very different ways. The work of the joint session centered on managing the triangle that had developed between Josyline and both of her fathers and how in many ways she was forced to choose between the two of them and found it easier to leave.

Focusing on the parent-child relationship also reduces the chances of the perception of favoritism. A joint session creates a triangle made up of the therapist, the child, and the parent(s). This triangle is a relationship dynamic that can become problematic if one of the angles (child or parent) of the triangle feels that he or she is being teamed up against during the session. The therapist minimizes this possibility by seeing the child and the parent as a unit for the purposes of the joint session. The functioning of the unit is what is what is central; the needs of each specific parts will follow.

Your child's psychotherapist may not agree to engage in joint sessions. The thought behind this decision is typically concern about creating a conflict of interest, specifically a **dual relationship**. A dual relationship exists when the same individuals participate in two different types (in terms of the rules and roles) of relationships at the same time. A therapist cannot be a friend. The rules of friendship and rules of therapy may have some overlap, but the ways in which they differ make managing these two relationships at the same time very difficult.

Similarly, your child's therapist cannot be your therapist while being your child's therapist. Although the comfort of familiarity is there between parent and therapist, the decision can affect your child's therapy. If attempted, how information is used, trust issues, partiality, bias, confidentiality, and privacy concerns can create anxiety and decrease the effectiveness of your child's psychotherapy.

The therapist may feel that the rules of joint therapy are just too different from individual therapy. He or she may make the clinical decision that therapeutically, requiring your child try to manage these two different sets of rules with one therapist will not be helpful. In some cases, your child's therapist may recommend that joint sessions be part of a family therapy format with a different therapist.

4. *Out-of-session communication* (telephone call/voice mail, e-mail, text, snail mail)—in this form of communication, information is passed between parent(s) and the therapist without in-person contact. As more people carry out much of their daily communications via telephone, the telephone has become a ubiquitous extension of our lives. We talk on the telephone on the street, at work, in our car, on the bus, anywhere really, and because of the frequency, we have become desensitized to its use. We just do not think about it as much. We say all this, because if you are going to use the telephone to communicate with your child's therapist, we recommend that you find a quiet place that allows you to focus and think about it. Any information that you request from or provide to your child's therapist over the telephone (whether discussion or voice mail message), from scheduling to updating, is important and requires concentration. Most therapists do not answer their telephones, but allow the callers to leave a message on voicemail. This message will allow you to describe the specific type of telephone contact you are looking to have.
   - "I want to discuss scheduling, please call me back."
   - "This is a message updating you about David, you do not need to call me back."
   - "I have some questions about what is happening with David at school, please call me back."

When you receive a call back, be prepared for the therapist to indicate that this material can or should be discussed in-person informally or as a part of a collateral session.

Telephone communications can be divided into three categories:

a. The telephone collateral session—this structured time on the telephone follows the same rules as the in-person collateral session. Depending on your child's therapist's views, he or she may be reticent to participate in this type of contact because of the inherent difficulties regarding participants not being able to respond to nonverbal cues. Typically, this type of contact is restricted to emergencies or urgent moments that cannot wait until an in-person session can be scheduled to review the material. These sessions follow the same payment format as in-session collaterals.

b. The telephone discussion—this unstructured time on the telephone is typically used for scheduling or logistics coordination of some kind. In certain situations, the therapist may agree to a "brief" discussion that includes material of a clinical nature—recent updates about your child or clarification questions about his or her situation. Some child therapists, especially those of younger children or children who typically disclose less information in session, find these types of contact helpful. If you have a question for the therapist, be prepared for the therapist to indicate that the answer may be too complex to be discussed over the telephone in an unstructured fashion.

These conversations may have a set end time and may not. Because of the informal structure of these types of contact, at times the duration may not be sufficient to complete the discussion in a way that feels settled.

c. The telephone voicemail message—this type of unstructured telephone-based communication should be as clear and concise as possible. Remember that all messages are subject to confusion and misunderstanding as there is no in-the-moment ability to clarify the communication. This type of communication is primarily for scheduling or logistics coordination of some kind. Clinical updates regarding your child can be left on a voicemail message if your child's therapist agrees previously to this format. If the therapist has not agreed to receive updates on voicemail, the message you leave can indicate that you would like to have a conversation with the therapist in which you will provide an update.

Dirk's Mother Will Call Back

Dirk, a 10-year-old boy, had only been seeing his therapist for a month when the therapist received a message from his mother late one evening. The message indicated that Dirk would not be coming to his session the following week because of logistical issues and the mother's need to focus on another important school issue related to Dirk. The mother stated that she was feeling overwhelmed and ended the message with the statement that she would get back to the therapist when "the situation was more settled." The therapist did not know how to understand this message and was unclear whether the mother had indicated that Dirk would miss one session or more based on the mother's statement. The therapist called back to clarify.

It is also important to be aware that at times you may *not* want to discuss something with your child's therapist—like a session cancellation or ending treatment or an upsetting circumstance. Reticence and avoidance are normal, protective, and often useful human responses. Within your child's therapy, these responses can sometimes create confusion. Acknowledging that we sometimes may have occasional discomfort about making direct contact with our child's therapist is important. With this awareness, we can then make conscious choices about the contact. Should I leave a message with the material? Should I ask for a return call so that we can discuss the material directly?

5. *Out-of-session third-party meetings*—these are moments that take place in other settings such as school, hospital, home, court, or other agencies. At times, the treatment plan that you and/or your child therapist create will include in-person contact with the therapist outside the typical session setting. These types of contact may be ones that are requested by you, such as attending a school meeting or visiting your child during a psychiatric hospitalization. They also may be ones that are driven by external demands on the therapy, such as testifying in family court proceedings or meeting with Child Protective Services.

The therapist will navigate these contacts with you carefully in that there may be individuals involved in the meetings who are not part of the typical therapy frame. For these contacts the frame must be expanded to include new elements. There may be different rules that govern confidentiality, disclosure, and responsibilities. For example, whereas in session the therapist has significant authority over decision-making, in family court, the judge wields that power. It may feel disorienting to experience these changing features of the therapy.

As with joint sessions, the therapist will attempt to maintain his or her therapeutic relationship with you while integrating the needs of the third-party participants. Because of your relationship with the therapist, you are entitled to ask for time and space to speak with the therapist alone.

FREQUENCY OF YOUR COLLATERAL CONTACT

Based on the initial discussion regarding symptoms, causes, strengths, and the other components of your child's presentation, your child's therapist will have a recommendation regarding how often he or she wants to see you. This parent contact will be described as frequency of collaterals. It can be once a week, twice a month, or less frequent, depending on a variety of factors. Like the structure of your child's sessions, having a routine for collaterals is important. The regularity will enhance the integration of parenting concepts and will allow for timely steady sharing of information.

The frequency of collateral contact will change over the course of your child's therapy. For most age groups, except for late adolescence and young adulthood, parent contact at the start of therapy will be more frequent as the relationships are structured and the situation that initiated therapy is stabilized. The collaterals then settle into a routine. The rule of thumb on parent contact with a child's therapist is (1) the younger the child, the more frequent contact with parents can be; and (2) the more severe and urgent the problems are, the more frequent the contact can be. The following is a list of factors that can affect a therapist's thought process regarding how often you may have contact.

- Age of the child
- Developmental stage of the child
- Treatment goals
- Severity of the current problems
- An emergency or crisis.

If your child is struggling with a severe mental health issue—problems that significantly affect his or her daily functioning, such as hearing voices (psychosis), suicidal thoughts (suicidality), self-harming behaviors, harming others, or severe developmental delay, among others—then regular collateral contact is imperative, regardless of age group or developmental stage. The increased structure that the therapist-parent contact provides conveys to your child that you are keeping him safe and secure. Similarly, an emergency or crisis requires the same containing message to your child. In such a situation, collateral contact is increased until the crisis has resolved.

We want to focus on collaterals and how they function for children of different age groups.

Toddlerhood through Pre-latency or Early Childhood (Age 3–7)

The children in this age group typically share information during their sessions—play, actions, behaviors, and so on, that have yet to be expressed in words. Your participation in collaterals can be helpful in interpreting this material. In fact, sometimes material that comes out in therapy has, until that moment, never been expressed to anyone. This type of information is considered **un-symbolized**. Collaterals with children at this age involve you providing information from home and school and the therapist providing feedback regarding possible meanings underlying the information provided, making connections between the various components of your child's life and developing therapeutic interventions. These collaterals are most helpful if they happen regularly. At this age, your child is told that therapists and parents meet and talk about children, ways of helping them feel better, and ways of being helpful parents. Typically, children will have little or no feedback with regard to their parent(s) meeting with their therapist; in fact, it feels containing.

Christopher Opens the Door

When Christopher, age 5, began therapy, his adult-aged brother (who was made his foster father) reported to the therapist that Christopher had been born to their drug-addicted mother and was severely neglected as a infant and toddler—often left alone for hours at a time, not fed, and not cleaned. The first day that Christopher was supposed to come to the therapist's office, he would not leave the waiting room and so the therapist interacted with him there. At the next session, he ran off and hid. At the third session, with the brother's help, Christopher was able to enter the therapist's office. When the therapist tried to close the door, Christopher screamed and ran out. When the therapist met with the brother, they discussed Christopher's reactions. The brother informed the therapist that Christopher had said to him that the therapist had locked the door and had not let him leave. They speculated together that Christopher's fears indicated that he had possibly been locked in a room by someone, or maybe worse. The brother reported that he did know that there had been men in and out of the apartment. The therapist suggested that both in therapy and at home, Christopher would be told that he could be in charge of the doors, that no one would lock them without his permission. In therapy, the door became a significant part of the frame, with Christopher being in control of whether it was open (which it often was) or not and knowing that he could leave the office and see his brother when he needed to. The therapist decided that Christopher's sense of safety outweighed his need for confidentiality and privacy.

Latency or Childhood (Age 7–11)

As children in this age group increasingly are able to verbalize their thoughts and feelings, collaterals shift from your help with interpretation of session material to updates from school, home, relationships, and any information that your child has conveyed to you that has a connection to the treatment goals. The therapist will provide feedback regarding possible meanings underlying the information that you share, will make connections between the various components of your child's life, and will assist in developing therapeutic interventions. Your latency-age child may be increasingly aware of collaterals and may begin to ask about what is being is discussed. Confidentiality does not apply to material discussed in collateral sessions, and so as your children develops, you may choose to share more of what you discuss with his or her therapist. The therapist may also share material from collateral sessions with your child if he or she feels it is therapeutically helpful. Please ask your child's therapist if you have a question regarding how a therapist chooses what to share and not to share with your child. Regular collaterals remain important, but they can be scheduled less frequently.

Artie Wins the Game

Artie, a 10-year-old boy who had been adopted as an infant by his two fathers, had been crying often and getting very frustrated. This in and of itself was not out of the ordinary, but his fathers felt that Artie's emotional outbursts were often connected to seemingly minor issues. For example, if their son got a B on a test, he would tell them that it was actually a B+. When they would refute his statement, he would become upset and cry and argue with them. His parents were having relationship issues, which included Artie often witnessing his parents criticizing each other. When the treatment began, Artie never discussed his home life, except to say that it was "fine" or "okay." He would engage in play, specifically basketball, in which he would alter the score by adding points to his score or removing points from the therapist's score. Inevitably, Artie would win the therapy game through his actions. He would be angry if the therapist ever questioned the score. When asked about his anger, Artie would declare that the therapist was not in charge of the score, that the therapist had told Artie that as long it was safe, Artie could be in charge of the games. The therapist could see the possible connections between Artie's need for control and stability and the effects of his parents' changing relationship. During collaterals, which the therapist requested to have separately because the fathers' in-session conflict hampered discussions, the therapist discussed the different levels of control that a child needs and how a shaky home life can leave a child grasping for any kind of control he or she can get, and that it was possible that changing things like scores and grades was Artie's way of acknowledging his actual changing reality (his parents disengaging from each other). Soon after, Artie's parents separated. After the separation, with a significant decrease in the amount of constant tension that the family members were under, Artie stopped crying at home and began to feel more secure. He started to discuss living with only one of his fathers and visiting the other. The therapist continued to see Artie's parents in individual collaterals until the therapy ended about six months after the separation.

Early Adolescence (Age 12–15)

Collaterals with parents with children in this age group must account for the varying levels of autonomy and independence seeking. The function of collaterals remains the same as the previous age group—underlying meanings, connections, developmental material, and therapeutic interventions—but the significance of the collateral to your child becomes a central issue. How much do you know? What do you talk about? Your early adolescent child can begin to feel diminished (younger) by the existence of your relationship with her therapist. Erikson saw the struggle of this developmental stage as the attempt to create an identity separate from the parent. Collaterals can be interpreted by your child as you being overly involved. As parent-therapist contact remains a part of the treatment plan, if your child is struggling with collaterals, then a clear description of the purpose of the collateral can address the latent feelings of uncertainty and confusion. With the older children in this age group, collateral sessions are scheduled on an as-needed basis.

De'kwan Changes His Tune

De'kwan was 9 years old when his father and mother called a therapist and brought him to therapy for the first time. They were very worried about his anxiety—De'kwan appeared to be nervous about everything: grades, friends, death, and so on. Because of his parents' significant level of concern and its possible connection to De'kwan's symptoms, the therapist chose to see them regularly in collateral, twice a month. The thought was to help the parents feel more secure and competent and that this would help their son feel safer and more contained. De'kwan's anxious symptoms (and depressive ones that became apparent as the therapy progressed) did not resolve quickly and, in part because of the slow progress, the collateral work with his parents remained at the same level. At age 12, with the onset of puberty, the severity of De'kwan's symptoms worsened and his parents became increasingly concerned. In one session, De'kwan seemed to be more withdrawn, and when asked about it he stated, "Why don't you just ask my parents?" The therapist asked how he felt about the therapist working with his parents and he said he did not care. For several sessions, they continued to explore his feelings about this material. The therapist, with the parents' agreement, then made a series of therapeutic interventions centered on the collateral appointments and De'kwan's safety and autonomy: (1) De'kwan would be more proactive in reporting how he felt to his parents; (2) his parents would wait for De'kwan's report instead of preemptively asking him how he was doing; (3) collaterals would decrease in frequency to once a month, depending how this new system worked; (4) everyone involved would look at how this was working in three months and re-evaluate.

Late Adolescence/Teen Years (Age 15–17)

Collaterals sessions are scheduled with explanations and a request for your child's permission by way of assent. The therapist's work is focused on obtaining the assent of your child in non-emergency situations. "Assent" is the term used to describe the agreement of a child who is under the age of consent but who is old enough to participate in the decision-making process. Assent is crucial to preserve the trust of the holding (caring, supportive) environment created by the relationship between your child and the therapist.

These contacts will have a specific purpose (to go over some agreed-upon material) and can, as always, include therapist feedback regarding meanings, connections, developmental material, and therapeutic interventions.

Making Room for Rachel's Rage

Rachel was a 16-year-old girl who lived with her grandmother following her mother's death when Rachel was 8 years old. Her grandmother had wanted her to be in therapy because Rachel was easily enraged and had been acting out in school and at home for years. Her grandmother was concerned that Rachel would get into more trouble and possibly not graduate from high school if she did not get help. Rachel liked therapy and was very communicative with her therapist. She discussed her early childhood when her mother was alive and her father lived with them, as well as his drinking and his anger. She remembered the times when her father hit her mother and hit her. The father's problems resulted in Rachel's placement with her paternal grandmother. She indicated that she saw her father from time to time, even though she hated him. She said that he still wanted a relationship with her and so she agreed to visit with him. With Rachel's assent, the therapist asked the grandmother if she would agree to a meeting between the therapist and her estranged son. The therapist indicated that he had been a key figure in Rachel's life and that part of who she is has a direct connection to him. The therapist explained that it would be helpful to her therapy if the therapist could meet with her father. The meeting with the father focused on exploring his description of his life with Rachel and ways that he could work to improve his relationship with his daughter in the future.

Young Adulthood (Age 18–Mid-20s)

The preservation and nurturance of your adult child's sense of independence, mastery, and competence is a crucial aspect of effective treatment with this age group. In this instance, your child is of the age of consent. Therefore, contact with parents is scheduled only with the explicit permission of your adult child. The decision and plan to meet with the parent is part of a thoroughly explored plan/negotiation between your adult child and his or her therapist. In emergency situations, the therapist must still obtain your child's explicit consent to have contact with you. However, the therapist is ethically obligated to obtain additional help for your child from other professionals even without your child's consent—specifically, if your adult-aged child is a danger to herself or others.

Indira Is Not Grown

Indira was 19 years old and lived at home. She was held back twice in high school because of her depression and the resulting hospitalizations. Her father was very involved in her treatment and since she started therapy a decade earlier. Before Indira turned 18, the therapist had a conversation with her about the changes to the therapy frame. At that time, Indira was stable and was finishing high school. As a legally consenting adult, the therapist was no longer going to be allowed to speak with her father without her permission. When the therapist discussed these changes with Indira's father, he became understandably agitated, indicating that he worked hard for all these years to keep her safe, and that she was not ready for this type of independence. He was worried that she would be back in the hospital. The therapist acknowledged the complexities of Indira's psychiatric problems and the difficult nature of this moment for many parents. The joint sessions focused on creating a legally and developmentally sound plan that addressed the realities of her age and maintained Indira's safety.

THE MUTUAL NATURE OF COLLATERAL WORK

Regardless of age, developmental stage, or specific mental health problem, it may be that you feel that a different level of contact with your child's therapist is necessary. If the frequency or type of contact is not what you find effective or justified, then we recommend that you have a discussion with the therapist. As we have indicated, therapists are human, and there are no absolute right or wrong answers in certain aspects of this type of work. Even when the therapist's opinion may differ, your views as a parent are an important part of a mutual decision-making process.

CHAPTER SUMMARY

CHAPTER 11: CONTRIBUTING TO YOUR CHIILD'S PSYCHOTHERAPY

Types of contact with your child's therapist:

Parent updates refer to the following:

- The child's current status
- An update since the last time parent(s) and therapist met/communicated
- Any progress or regression

- What parent(s) are noticing (trends, patterns, themes)
- What is concerning parent(s) specifically
- Any questions that parent(s) have.

Parent **collateral sessions** are organized as psycho-educational sessions. Psycho-education refers to a therapeutic process of addressing psychological concepts to create better understanding and awareness and to set expectations.

Child-specific issues:

- Psychological developmental stages
- Social developmental stages
- Biological developmental stages
- Your child's temperament
- Your child's strengths
- Forms of your child's communication

Parent-specific issues

- Parent reactions/feelings
- Your strengths
- Parent-child relationship
- Parent to child communication
- Family communication

Treatment-specific issues

- Treatment planning
- Short-term treatment goals
- Long-term treatment goals
- Causes and symptoms

The Work of Child Psychotherapy

The work of psychotherapy is to help children grow emotionally, to enhance existing skills, to learn new coping methods, and to achieve the long-term goals of their lives. The work phase is a process that promotes these changes, even as your child is developing and growing older. Change occurs both within the psychotherapy in the moment and long after the psychotherapy has ended, through your child's memories of the therapy and the therapist. These memories (of receiving help) are activated by times in the future when your child seeks help from you, another professional, a friend, a partner, or a family member. By having your child in therapy, you have provided a new lifelong model for getting help.

Logically, the work phase begins when the engagement phase ends. The length of the engagement phase varies from child to child, and it is sometimes difficult to establish when trust and rapport are sufficient to begin the process of actively working on treatment goals. We recommend that you engage the therapist in identifying and describing the current phase of your child's psychotherapy in order to maintain an awareness of the overall progression of your child's therapy.

THE SESSION-TO-SESSION PROCESS

What does the work phase actually entail? Understanding that it takes time and that the exact end is often unclear, is there a road map that helps guide the journey so that it does not seem so open-ended? We think it may be helpful to understand the work phase process as a series of **therapeutic cycles**. These cycles tend to occur concurrently, meaning that the therapy may address several issues at a time but at different rates of time and at different frequencies. Each therapeutic cycle addresses a specific issue or treatment goal.

The following is a breakdown of one of these cycles:

1. *Therapist identifies a treatment goal*—having prioritized the treatment goals with you (and your child, if age appropriate) as part of the treatment plan, the therapist now selects a goal to address. Sometimes this takes place proactively—the therapist has a plan in place prior to the start of a session—or this takes place reactively—the therapist chooses to address an issue that has presented itself. It is possible that the therapist will select multiple goals to address simultaneously (i.e., safety, limit setting, and improving frustration tolerance).

2. *Therapist makes a therapeutic intervention*—the therapist uses the treatment goals to develop a clinically based communication to your child. This can take many shapes and forms, and is created with your specific child in mind. The therapist may not typically share with you the specific details of this aspect of the therapy, regardless of age. That said, some therapists might be more forthcoming about the details of a specific intervention. Typically, this is because the therapist may want parents to duplicate the intervention at home with their child.

Jackson Won't Break

Jackson was a 7-year-old boy treated for issues related to a spectrum disorder. Jackson's developmental delay made him act controlling and rigid as a way of compensating for feeling out of control and scared. The therapist worked with his parents and teachers to understand this as a strength that allowed him to remain in school. At the same time, the therapist was working with Jackson in session to understand that there were situations in which he could not be in control yet still be secure.

Jackson loved to play with blocks and would build towers and forts. He built these structures and demanded that the therapist keep them and not take them apart. The therapist agreed, but indicated to Jackson that there were a limited number of blocks. When, after the third building, they ran out of blocks, the therapist asked Jackson what they should do about this situation. Jackson replied, "You can buy more blocks for next time." The therapist deciding that working within this limit was going to be the focus of this part of the therapy. The therapist told Jackson that this was all the blocks and that he could choose how he wanted to handle this construction with just these blocks in the session. Jackson was distressed and responded that he would bring blocks from home. The therapist acknowledged that this was a very creative idea, but that blocks for home were blocks for home and that only session blocks were for therapy sessions.

The therapist shared this rule with Jackson's parents as a way of coordinating rules at home and at therapy. Jackson decided to leave the building partly constructed. The therapist continued to discuss the partial building with Jackson each week, with Jackson becoming less and less distressed about the unfinished nature of the building. Eventually, Jackson broke the building himself. The therapist acknowledged his feat, and feeling secure, he expressed pride in his accomplishment.

3. *Child reacts to therapist's intervention*—the therapeutic intervention causes your child to communicate to the therapist. This communication can take on many forms (verbal, nonverbal, behavior, emotion, etc.) and can recur several times throughout the work phase. It includes manifest content and a latent content.

4. *Therapist responds to child's reaction*—the therapist communicates to your child based on your child's responses and reactions to the intervention. Your child's therapist employs a therapeutic skill called the **observing ego** (Hunt, Corman, & Ormont, 1964). The idea of the observing ego is that a therapist can be engaging in a conversation, playing a game, or another interaction with your child, and at that same moment the therapist is "observing" and thinking about the interaction with your child and gathering clinical information. The observing ego enables the therapist to think about your child's latent communication and how to respond to that communication. This generates a therapeutic response, rather than a superficial one focused on manifest content.

5. *Therapist reflects on the exchange between therapist and child*—the therapist considers what has transpired within the relationship. This can take place during the session or after the session. As we mentioned, some reflection is in the moment, but what we are referring to here is the evaluation of the usefulness, success, or lack thereof of each therapeutic intervention. This part of the therapeutic cycle allows for therapists to alter the approach to a child on an ongoing basis and also informs the reworking of treatment goals.

The exact nature of each therapeutic cycle greatly varies. It can be the give and take within a form of play that the therapist is using; it can be a discussion or a series of questions and answers; it can be how the therapist and your child sit in relation to each other; it can include an interaction with you—just to name a few. The cycle can also include a repetition of the reaction and response steps, with a therapist responding to your child's communication and your child reacting to that response. What each of these has in common is that they follow the same fundamental structure. They each examine latent and manifest content, and are all put in place to create change.

LENGTH OF THE WORK PHASE

We typically know how long things will take. It is how we organize our lives and those of our children—both logistically and emotionally. We can, as a way of addressing a child's sense of control, give her or him an idea of when something will be finished or will end. Morning will come when the sun comes up; the doctor's appointment will be over when she checks your weight and height; we will get to grandma's house after we stop for lunch. Using words like "soon," "later," and "eventually" as responses typically does not address the latent struggle. Even if she or he has not developed enough to comprehend time and may not be old enough to be a decision-maker, it is empowering and empathic to provide a child with a tangible way to manage his or her frustrations at times like these.

Neville Questions Therapy

Neville was a 13-year-old boy whose parents were getting divorced; they had separated around the same time his mother referred him to therapy. His mother was in therapy, and she saw that Neville seemed nervous all the time. Neville did not want to talk about anything in session, and definitely not his feelings. When the therapist asked him questions, he would answer with nonverbal head/shoulder movements or one-word responses—yes, no, fine, okay. Neville's frustration about therapy was apparent, and his mother would report that Neville would consistently ask her why he had to go and when he could stop. As per the parent-therapist discussion in collateral meetings, his mother would respond that she felt it was a good idea for Neville to discuss his feelings about the separation and divorce and that therapy could end when he talked about his feelings. After 5 months in weekly therapy, a session began with the therapist asking Neville how he felt about his parents getting divorced. Neville's anger flashed and he shouted at the therapist, "STOP ASKING ME ABOUT THAT, WHEN YOU ASK ME IT MAKES ME ANGRY!" The therapist responded by saying calmly, "I am sorry that you are angry about what I asked. I wonder if you were already angry. Any kid would be angry that their parents were getting divorced. It is totally unfair." This exchange began the work phase of Neville's therapy.

Your child's therapy is a process that consists of the relationship, the connections made between past and present, the discussions about the here and now, and the questions about feelings, thoughts, and actions, the separations, the reunions, the achievements, and even the temporary setbacks. In the words of Ralph Waldo Emerson, "Life is a journey, not a destination," and in some ways the same can be said of the work phase of child psychotherapy.

We are all a work in progress, and your child, with many years of life ahead, will continue to develop throughout her or his lifespan. The ability to cope, adapt, manage, and thrive over a lifetime is based on the flexibility and fluidity of being able to grow and change. Naturally, we all want our children to be happy and successful, although we may define what that entails very differently from each other, and indeed differently even from our children. How long will it take for my child to reach this point in her life (When will it be "done"?) is our parental version of the ubiquitous travel question, "Are we there yet?" Within the context of our children being in therapy, this question is typically asked of the work phase and the length of psychotherapy.

Time is an essential concept when thinking about therapy. If you think about it, it shapes everything we do. It structures our sleep, our work, our school, our socializing, and our relaxing. It can provoke a variety of feelings. Time can make us nervous, excited, and afraid. We respond to it almost without thinking; we rush, we slow down, we panic, we rejoice. Within this context, most of us have a linear concept of the progression of time—seconds, minutes, hours, days, weeks, months, and years. We mark the passing of time on our watches, phones, computers, and calendars, and with birthdays, anniversaries, and holidays.

Children usually learn about time from their parents and schoolteachers starting when they are about 5 years old, but they cannot accurately describe the passage of time until they are older, when they achieve more abstract thinking. Let us examine the latent content of the question, "Are we there yet?" This childhood question relates to two fundamental developmental milestones: (1) learning to wait, and (2) learning that we do not always have control (together called **frustration tolerance**).

Frustration tolerance is the ability to manage negative feelings associated with having to wait (often for another person's decision-making). This is a particularly difficult milestone with which all children (and their parents) must contend. All parents have stories about their children wanting something "NOW!" Manifestly, a child wants what they are demanding. In actuality, the latent communication informs us that the intensity *underlying* the word is giving voice to the child's frustration about his or her *lack* of control and power. For a child to navigate this developmental milestone, he or she learns to cope with the feelings of vulnerability associated with being dependent on someone.

It is the intersection of the two factors, time and frustration tolerance, that is so important in understanding the nature of the **work phase** of your child's therapy. We do not really know the amount of time that will be required to address a child's unique circumstances, how long it will take until you feel more secure in your parenting, and/or how long it will be until your child feels more stable. The work phase of treatment can be relatively short (months) or more extensive (years). It can also be in segments separated by short or long intervals of no treatment. It can take place with different therapists, with each new therapy building on the previous therapy's work phase once the engagement phase is completed. The exact amount of time depends on many factors (**components**) and these factors evolve and change over the course of the work phase.

Maeve Moves On

Maeve was a 5-year-old girl when her mother first brought her to therapy. Maeve was the child of a single mother diagnosed with rapidly advancing pancreatic cancer. Her mother felt that Maeve should see a therapist before she died. The focus of the work was on Maeve's anger, sadness, and adjustment to life with her aunt, who would take custody of her at the mother's request. Her mother informed the therapist that Maeve survived brutal beatings by her biological father at age 2 but has no memory of this. Maeve's mother died and she began to live with her aunt permanently. During their two years of work together, the therapy focused primarily on the illness-related issues—both before and after her mother's death. The therapist also noted that Maeve exhibited symptoms of trauma (nightmares, flashbacks causing fearfulness of being hurt/attacked, disturbing violent memories) unrelated to her mother's illness and death. The therapist discussed with the aunt that Maeve had processed her mother's death with this therapist and that it would be helpful for Maeve to see a different therapist to address the trauma symptoms.

The different therapists' styles and locations allowed Maeve to develop a new relationship that would be specifically created to both contain and explore her symptoms of trauma. With Maeve approaching the age of 8, she would engage this new therapist in a different way than she had her current therapist. The loss of her mother would always be a part of Maeve, and she would discuss it with her next therapist, but it would not necessarily be the focus their work together. The aunt agreed, and the therapist worked to find a child trauma specialist for Maeve, and she began her work with a new therapist.

THE WORK PHASE AND CHANGE

The change that you experience in your child when he or she is in therapy occurs gradually and retrospectively. The change can be gradual in that small subtle improvements may escape your notice. For example, we do not often notice our children growing taller because the growth is so incremental and difficult to see on a day-to-day basis. Our experience of retrospective change occurs when these small improvements add up over time, and we look back to see the distance our children have covered—like seeing an old photo of your child and feeling the nostalgia from a time past. Your collateral involvement and input in your child's therapy (modified for your child's age and developmental stage) can provide you with an ongoing sense that time is passing, that the therapy *is* "moving" forward—even in its subtle and gradual nature. The importance of this is that you will have the information necessary to aid in the management of your child's inevitable frustrations and even your own.

Parents may at times become understandably frustrated with the process of child therapy. Parents are living every day with the situations that therapists engage with one or twice a week. The speed of the work phase can be frustratingly slow. That said, we want to prepare you for the idea that, in child psychotherapy and in mental health in general, the concept of sudden change does not exist. It is an understandable wish. Who does not want a child to have relief as quickly as possible? The reality is that children do not learn how to do anything *suddenly*. In therapy, there are moments of understanding and comprehension along the way, but all transformation—the true integration of the therapeutic concepts that lead to healing—is gradual. It comes from consistent repetition, just like learning letters, numbers, and any life lessons. Learning a new way of understanding takes time.

Ubaldo's Grandmother Wants Answers

Ubaldo was an 11-year-old boy from Argentina who was living with his paternal grandmother in the United States. His divorced father and mother both lived in Argentina. His father had sent Ubaldo at age 9 to the United States "to get him away from his mother." His grandmother was worried that Ubaldo never wanted to leave the home and was having difficulty going to school. After several months of working together, Ubaldo was able to share with the therapist that he missed his parents, specifically his mother. He stated that he was very unhappy, felt like crying, and that he did not like spending time with his peers because they reminded him that he was not in Argentina anymore. The therapist and Ubaldo worked on ways that he could feel connected to his parents, even with them living apart. While Ubaldo was expressing his sadness about his parents, he was attending school only slightly more regularly. His grandmother began to express frustration with the lack of progress in therapy in this area. The therapist shared his concerns and counseled that time was needed to build more trust. Ubaldo's feelings remained raw and painful to him. However, soon after, she decided to remove Ubaldo from therapy.

Ubaldo's grandmother expected that once her grandson cried over his parents and the loss of all things familiar to him, that he would be fine. When the treatment did not meet this unrealistic expectation, she no longer believed that psychotherapy would be helpful. In a follow-up discussion, his grandmother reported to the therapist that as Ubaldo's behavior became more problematic, he went back to Argentina to live with his father. At Ubaldo's request, his father was able to find a therapist for him in Argentina.

CHANGE AND AMBIVALENCE

As much as you want things to improve for your child, change is an unknown that can cause mixed feelings for you and your child. Change can create feelings of pride and confidence. At the same time, it can create unfamiliarity, uncertainty, and feelings of discomfort. We value the feelings of comfort, but sometimes these feelings are arbitrary and are based on familiarity rather than true satisfaction. For instance, we each have a typical way of folding our arms across our chest. If we reverse the position of our arms when folding them over our chest, many of us will feel uncomfortable to the point where we must reverse our arms back again. Whether the right arm is over the left, or the left arm is over the right, is arbitrary—it is what we believe is right, but it is neither right nor wrong—just familiar. If we practice, the position of arms would be equally comfortable in any order. We need time and practice to gain comfort from change and to be able to compare it favorably or unfavorably to what was original.

Let us look at an example:

You allow your child to sleep over at a friend's house for the first time. The following elements may emerge:

1. Your child's pride in herself that she can do it, she is growing up;
2. Your child's worries, nervousness about being away from her parent;
3. Your pride that she is maturing, growing up;
4. Your sense of a loss of control that she is not your little girl anymore.

With growth (a positive) comes loss of the familiar (a negative). This can be upsetting, even if what was familiar was ineffective, unsatisfying, and/or distressing. These conflicting feelings are a mainstay when it comes to managing change.

Life's changes that are considered positive, such as getting married, going to college, becoming a teenager, becoming a toddler, passing a class, or going on vacation, are all accompanied by loss—single life, high school, childhood, classmates, home. It is understandable and reasonable, then, that feelings about change can be contradictory. When we have feelings that are contrary to one another, we experience ambivalence. Which feeling do we use to determine our actions or decisions? Realistically, we know that change is typically good—growth is healthy, and stagnation and feeling stuck are not—but that is our intellectual understanding of change. The visceral feelings we can have about change are often the ones that dominate our thoughts.

- I want my child to grow and be happy; and
- I am sad that she will not be that little girl I remember.

This ambivalence can lead to confusing and complex thoughts, questions, and actions, as we try to make sense of and navigate these often opposing views.

- Maybe my child is not ready to sleep over at a friend's house; or
- Maybe I am the one who is not ready for my child to sleep over at a friend's house?

It is important to understand that both parent and child have these reactions to change. Child therapy is a constant battle within the two levels of this ambivalence, our child's and our own. This is due to the fact that child therapy is structured to create change. It is important to address the ambivalence that parents and children experience in therapy. In order to assist in the identification of ambivalence, we examine actions and requests regarding the therapy process as both manifest and latent communications.

a. Some possible manifestations of a child's ambivalence

Verbal
Your child may convey his or her feeling of ambivalence about change in the following verbal ways:

- "I don't want to go anymore."
- "I want a vacation/break from therapy."
- "I don't want to go today."
- "I don't feel well."
- "I want to be with my friends."

Non-Verbal
You child may also convey his or her feelings of ambivalence about change with the following nonverbal patterns:

- Coming late to sessions
- Forgetting about sessions

Henry Changes His Mind About Therapy

Henry was 14 years old and had been in therapy for 2 years. When he came to therapy, he was hurting himself (scratching his arms up) due to his depression and anxiety. Henry and his therapist spent a great deal of time playing games and talking about his life at home. His father would get high on a variety of drugs before coming home from work. He would criticize Henry for the way he looked, his grades, and his social isolation. The parents separated when Henry entered high school. At the same time, he began to miss sessions—sometimes calling to cancel and sometimes not. When he would see the therapist again, he would indicate that he had too much homework. After several months of this pattern, the therapist asked Henry if he wanted to stop coming to therapy. Henry indicated that he liked therapy and liked coming, but that he wanted to hang out with his friends. He said he felt bad and believed the therapist would be angry. The therapist stated that he was glad that Henry felt comfortable enough to share these complicated thoughts. To the therapist, Henry's stance made sense developmentally, and his wish to spend time with peers indicated a move toward health and a decrease of his depression. Together, Henry, his mother, and the therapist made a plan to stop therapy. Because Henry was still managing symptoms, they agreed that this was a break from therapy and not an end—that Henry and his mother would touch base with the therapist in two months and provide the therapist with an update. Henry and his mother maintained this plan for six months and then ceased contact with the therapist.

Two years later, in March, Henry called the therapist and asked if he could come back to therapy. The therapist agreed with Henry to begin therapy again and only discussed with Henry's mother the matter of payment. Henry began weekly sessions with the therapist that focused on problems that he was having with his girlfriend. Therapy continued until summer vacation. When school ended, Henry told the therapist that he was too busy to come to therapy because of a job that he had gotten for the summer. They agreed to stop therapy again.

---

b. Some possible manifestations of a parent's ambivalence

Parents may convey their feelings of ambivalence about the process with the following nonverbal patterns:

Schedule
- Canceling sessions (child and/or collateral)
- Rescheduling sessions
- Forgetting about sessions
- Coming late to sessions
- Collateral inconsistency
- Wanting to alter the session frequency

Fee
- Letting the private medical coverage lapse
- Not following the procedures to maintain public medical coverage

- Feeling the therapy has become too expensive
- Delaying payment
- Forgetting about payment

Issue
- Not reporting problems
- Not implementing mutually agreed-upon strategies

Relationship
- Not returning calls
- Feeling that the therapist is inaccessible
- Feeling that the therapist/child relationship is too secretive
- Feeling that the therapist is not your ally
- Not feeling like the therapist sees you as a parent

Beth Chooses Health

Alice, a 10-year-old girl, had been in therapy for a year when her parents told her therapist that they wanted to reduce her session frequency to once every other week. They informed the therapist that they could not afford therapy on an ongoing basis. Alice was being seen for mild depression and problems with her behavior at school. Alice had just started doing better in school, according to her teachers. The therapist was concerned about the abrupt shift in the frame and its impact on Alice's progress. The therapist asked the parents if altering the fee would be helpful and also discussed a second option of altering the therapy by building in breaks at school vacation times. Her parents added that the change to the therapy was also a matter of the time commitment. By their thinking, Alice was doing better and so therapy could be cut back. The intensity with which Alice's parents were insisting on change elicited a feeling in the therapist that there was a latent communication at work. The therapist agreed to the change with the stipulation that everyone would monitor Alice closely.

Two months later, Alice's parents and the therapist received reports from her teachers that Alice was having difficulties again. Beth, Alice's mother, contacted the therapist. They discussed changing the session frequency back to once a week. Beth and her husband considered this and declined. Beth did, however, inquire about therapy for herself. She shared with the therapist that she felt that maybe some of the problems centered on her own issues. The therapist made a referral and Beth began therapy. Alice's therapy remained at twice a month.

Beth was feeling ambivalent about Alice's therapy. It turned out that one aspect of these conflicting feelings was that she believed that she needed to address her own problems. In this case, Beth being in therapy was a benefit for Alice (and her therapy). A parent who feels stronger creates a stronger parent-child relationship.

For the purposes of this book, we do not want to focus on interpreting the latent meaning of a parents' ambivalence. We do want parents to be aware that their ambivalence exists and that it can impact the flow of the child's therapy if the parents and the child's therapist choose not to attend to it. All the above potential manifestations of ambivalence are just that— communications that can be heard and responded to. When unrecognized and unexplored ambivalence guides our decision-making, parents often tell us that they feel bad or guilty. While we acknowledge the inherent difficulty in examining and voicing ambivalence, it is when we do not talk about these areas of possible conflict that children's therapy can lose its focus.

PROGRESS REPORTS

School begins, then there is the holiday break; school reconvenes, then there is a spring break; school reconvenes again, then there is the summer break. These natural points of change in routine are opportunities for you, the therapist, and your child to take stock of the work phase of your child's psychotherapy and are convenient intervals of time to engage in a review of the treatment progress. Private practitioners typically do not have a standardized progress report. They can discuss your child's progress at any time; however, we do recommend examining progress at somewhat set intervals because the time allows for therapeutic interventions to be integrated and the effects to be seen (or not, as the case may be).

Ernesto's Summer Vacation

Ernesto was a 15-year-old boy who was having trouble concentrating in class, not doing homework, and getting into fights before school. His mother believed the transition to a new school and missing his friend were causing his behavior problems. In addition, his parents were having marital difficulties the previous year and had separated briefly over previous summer. Ernesto's father spent two weeks out of the home in July. Ernesto was able to explain to the therapist how stressful his home life was over the summer. He indicated that he was happy that his father was home, but that he was nervous everything would fall apart again. The therapist worked with Ernesto to come up with ways of explaining his concerns to his parents.

The therapist met with Ernesto's mother in April, just before spring break, for a collateral session, and she felt Ernesto was doing better and asked about ending therapy. The therapist agreed that he was doing better and indicated that it was imperative that she and his father continue to be available to hear what Ernesto felt about the problems in the home. They agreed that they would make a decision about therapy before summer vacation. By the end of the school year, Ernesto was feeling much better. His parents were still arguing, but Ernesto was talking to them. The therapist met with Ernesto's mother toward the end of the school year, and they agreed that Ernesto would take the summer off. They would speak to each other at the end of the summer to see how Ernesto was doing.

Some states require that mental health clinic therapists review a progress report with the child's parent(s) at designated intervals. These are externally imposed time frames on the child's psychotherapy. They typically occur on January 1, April 1, July 1, and October 1. They are called quarterly progress reports and include the following:

1. Previous diagnosis;
2. Any changes to diagnosis;
3. The previous treatment objectives and goals;
4. New and continued treatment objectives and goals (with time frames for achieving the objectives and goals;
5. The reasons for these changes;
6. A statement about overall progress of the treatment, typically written in narrative form;
7. Outside therapeutic services (if used) and any changes;
8. Psychotropic medications (if taken) and any changes; and
9. Goals for discharge.

This quarterly progress report would be reviewed by you and your child's therapist, who would explain what was included and why. If you agree to what appears in the report, you would be asked to sign the document acknowledging this.

CHAPTER SUMMARY

CHAPTER 12: THE WORK OF CHILD PSYCHOTHERAPY

The work phase process is a series of **therapeutic cycles**. These cycles tend to occur concurrently, meaning that the therapy may address several issues at a time but at different rates of time and at different frequencies. Each therapeutic cycle addresses a specific issue or treatment goal.

The following is a breakdown of one of these cycles:

1. *Therapist identifies a treatment goal*—a treatment goal to address is selected.
2. *Therapist makes a therapeutic intervention*—based on the treatment goal, a clinically based communication is made to the child.
3. *Child reacts to therapeutic intervention*—the therapeutic intervention causes your child to communicate in some way.
4. *Therapist responds to child's reaction*—the therapist communicates to your child, based on your child's responses and reactions to the intervention.
5. *Therapist reflects on the exchange between therapist and child*—the therapist considers what has transpired within the relationship.

The exact amount of time depends on many factors, and these factors evolve and change over the course of the work phase.

- The work phase of treatment can be relatively short (months) or more extensive (years), affected by the various goals of treatment.
- It can also be in segments separated by short or long intervals of no treatment.
- It can take place with different therapists, with each new therapy building on the previous therapy's work phase once the engagement phase with the respective therapist is completed.
- In this way, your child does not necessarily "start over" or from the beginning in therapy when she or he sees a successive therapist.

- The previous therapy's work phase is not lost but becomes a part of your child.

Natural points of change in routine (vacations and school breaks) are opportunities for you, the therapist, and your child to review the progress of your child's psychotherapy.

- Changes to diagnosis
- New and continued goals
- Overall progress of the treatment and progress on specific goals

Hurdles, Obstacles, and Snags

The overarching goal of your child's therapy is for your child to feel better and for you to feel more confident as a parent. This process is not linear; it is not a direct line. There are bumps, setbacks, forward moves, breaks, and so on. Think about it like traveling to a destination, for example, the supermarket. First, the route is not a straight, unimpeded line. There are twists and turns, lefts and rights, ups and downs, stops and starts. Second, and more important for the planning of the trip, although you may know the route, the exact nature of the route cannot be known from day to day. There could be bad weather; if you are driving, there could be a problem with the car; if you are taking mass transit, there could be delay in the system. All these could alter your route in some way. There is no way to prevent issues from altering the route, but we can prepare ourselves and be ready for their inevitable occurrence.

MISSED SESSIONS

One of the differences between child psychotherapy and adult psychotherapy is that in a child's life there are typically breaks from the day-to-day routines. There are many reasons that your child's therapy session may not take place on any given day in any given week, both planned and unplanned—vacation, illness, planned break, another appointment, logistical conflicts (siblings, weather, etc.), cancellations, no shows, among others.

The impact on your child's therapy of missing sessions can vary based on how you and your child's therapist plan for these gaps. Rescheduling sessions for a different day, if possible for parent(s) or therapist, can maintain some level of consistency. If rescheduling is not possible, most missed sessions can be planned in some fashion, allowing the therapist to introduce a variety of therapeutic cycles. These cycles can include therapeutic interventions centering on the "natural" process of missing and then returning to therapy.

Obviously, some cancelled sessions are due to unpredictable illnesses (children do get sick) or other unforeseen circumstances. Contact with the therapist as early as possible in these situations allows for a therapeutic cycle that reinforces communication and transparency—the therapist knows and responds to what is happening in your child's life. The therapist could speak to your child briefly or convey a message to your child through you. This maintains a bridge from session to session, even with the gap. For example, your child's therapist could express over the telephone that he will "miss" seeing your child or that he "hopes" your child will feel better. This action of leaving and returning, of separating and reconnecting, is a fundamental dynamic of child development that affects a child's sense of mastery, confidence, and identity.

Missed sessions become a more complex matter as children get older and may travel to sessions on their own. The therapy frame expands to include a new set of rules—a clear plan that describes the communication that occurs if your child is exceedingly late to a session or seems to be in the process of missing a session. Until your child reaches the age of assent (and possibly later if the therapist and you determine that based on the clinical situation, it is necessary), your child's therapist can contact you and can establish a therapeutic cycle that includes you.

Marius Makes Contact

Marius was 17 years old. He was in therapy because he had been suspended from school several times for fighting, would skip school on a regular basis, and was at risk for being held back. He was depressed and often described feelings of being tired of having to deal with school and his family. Marius did not like the idea of therapy and told the therapist and his parents that it was a waste of time. He told his therapist that he was going to be a professional skateboarder and that he did not need school or therapy, just time with his skateboard friends. The therapist listened to Marius's point of view and proposed that they try therapy for three months. Marius agreed.

Marius came to therapy by himself after school. He attended his first three ses-
sions and then missed the fourth. The therapist called his home (Marius had not
wanted to give the therapist his cell phone number) looking for Marius; his mother
indicated that she did not know where he was. She left a message for the therapist
later that evening that he had returned home and had indicated that he had forgot-
ten about his session.

Marius's depression required the therapist to be concerned about the
self-destructive and isolating nature of Marius's choices. A child "forgetting" and
missing a therapy session is a latent communication that means a need for more
structure and security.

At his next session, Marius and the therapist discussed the missed session
and what had happened. The therapist indicated that, because he had been com-
ing regularly, having not heard from Marius had made the therapist concerned.
Without any information or way of contacting Marius, the therapist made the
choice to call home. They discussed whether this should be the process for future or
if there were other options. In the end, Marius decided to give the therapist his cell
phone number. They agreed that if Marius were going to be late, he would call; if
the therapist was concerned, he would call Marius's cell phone first and the home
phone second.

The therapist's therapeutic interventions focused on identifying which method of staying connected would be most helpful for Marius while acknowledging both his developmental stage and his depressive symptoms.

EMPATHIC BREAKS

Therapeutic interventions do not always inspire the response that therapists predict—they can be misused (delivered incorrectly), premature (used too soon), insufficient (needing more), and/or not empathic (not connected to the child's feelings). A therapeutic intervention that does not work for any reason can lead to an **empathic break**. An empathic break is a rupture (disruption) in the relationship/connection between the therapist and child. The rupture centers on the idea that the therapist has not responded to the child in the way that the child feels he or she should have. The rupture can be characterized by the child's feelings of anger, sadness, or anxiety that accompany his need to either lash out at the therapist or his need for distance from the therapist. At times, children are unaware that an empathic break has occurred.

Micah Does Not Like Leaving

Micah was a 7-year-old boy who was in therapy to address his anxiety. His parents reported that during the day he ripped the edges of his clothes, in addition to chewing on the sleeves and collar of his shirt. At night, he was having difficulty staying asleep. He awoke with nightmares and came to his parents' bed. When they tried to return him to his room, he became distraught and cried. The therapist believed that his communication—the anxiety—was an expression of frustration connected to feeling insecure. He seemed to have these difficulties when separated from his caregivers. Consequently, the therapist remained thoughtful about how Micah felt when sessions were ending and he was leaving. During the engagement phase of treatment, Micah often became upset at the end of the session. He either left immediately when the therapist indicated that therapy would end soon; or he refused to leave the session when the therapist indicated that the session was over.

Imagine feeling emotionally injured or betrayed by someone with whom we are very familiar—a family member or a close friend. Our feelings are hurt; we are in "pain." We are angry and sad. We typically choose one of two ways of addressing this hurt: (1) we lash out, attacking and attempt to hurt that person back; or (2) we withdraw, retreat, and back away from the person. This is sometimes called the **fight or flight** reaction (Cannon, 1915). These types of incidents (which happen all the time) can put a great deal of pressure on a person's personal relationships. Trying to stay emotionally present in a relationship with someone who has "hurt" you is very challenging. We can imagine it would probably be easier to just get angry and leave. When we feel emotionally wounded by another person, it takes time to repair the damage. Primarily, the repair work focuses on rebuilding trust—the most fragile of all the aspects of a relationship.

All of our relationships are subject to unfortunate, and at times inadvertent, moments of hurt and disappointment. In our closest personal relationships, time, proximity, and familiarity often enable the rebuilding process to take place. Addressing "hurtful" statements or actions as quickly and directly as possible is the most beneficial way of maintaining a healthy therapeutic relationship.

The child therapy relationship is a more complicated relationship to rebuild if an empathic break occurs. This is due in large part to the fact that this relationship is founded on contact that does not occur daily and does not have the established familiarity of a family member or friendship relationship. If your child feels uncared for (it might look like upset, anger, or reluctance in your child) due to something that her or his therapist did or said in a previous session, typically a week passes until the material can be addressed within the frame of a session. This gap in time is often too long to address a child's hurt. After a week, the problematic situation or dynamic can become latent material and can be much more difficult to address and heal.

Micah Feels Abandoned

After a few sessions, Micah did not want to go to therapy, but his parents insisted. They told the therapist, who realized that the way sessions ended may have been contributing to Micah feeling unprotected (and as a result, feeling angry and nervous about therapy). To address this, the therapist instituted a 10-minute notice. The manifest content of the notice was about cleaning up and finishing the activity or discussion of the session. The latent content was about feeling prepared and more in control. Micah was not going to be in control of when the session ended or the session's duration. But he could be in control of how he left. Abruptly ending a session had the potential of reinforcing the sense of uncertainty that seemed to hamper Micah's daily functioning. The ritual 10-minute notice (done at the end of every session) provided Micah with enough time to express his feelings both verbally and nonverbally about his appointment ending. The therapist responded to these feelings, and helped to shape Micah's departure from the session.

Micah found this therapeutic intervention to be useful (empathic). Having integrated this ritual, Micah was able to use a version of it in other parts of his life—leaving for school, going to bed, and so on. His parents worked on how to respond to the various feelings that he would express during these rituals.

IDENTIFYING EMPATHIC RUPTURES DEVELOPMENTALLY

We want to focus on empathic breaks by children of different age groups. Situations that involve empathic breaks between your child and his or her therapist can feel confusingly intense to everyone participating in the therapy—your child, the therapist, and you.

Toddlerhood through Pre-latency or Early Childhood (Age 3–7)

Children of this age have only a basic ability to manage frustration. Their feelings associated with being upset with their therapist are difficult to put into words and usually are communicated behaviorally. Parents experience issues such as these as a profound and sudden desire by the child to not go to therapy. Because the younger children in this age group may not have language to express this hurt, they may act this out in nonverbal ways—tantrums, crying, and/or outbursts—seemingly unrelated to the therapy. It is the sudden change of the child's reactions that provide the clue that an empathic break may be present within the therapeutic relationship. The older children in this age group are beginning to be able to express themselves verbally and may begin verbally protesting about going to therapy—asking why, saying no, and so on.

Latency or Childhood (Age 7–11)

Children of this age are more facile with language and relationship dynamics. Since these children are still, for the most part, being brought to therapy by their parent(s), being upset with or feeling let down by a therapist can lead to bargaining with parents about not going. The more internalized children will express feeling sick on the day of therapy or the days leading up to therapy. This is different from the more subtle attempts of a child to evade therapy (or any other required activities) on a given day.

Early Adolescence (Age 12–15)

Because of the onset of puberty, empathic ruptures are ubiquitous in treatment with children in this age group. Early adolescents are struggling to understand themselves, to be understood, and to explain themselves to others. Because of the frequency of these empathic breaks, we think it is more helpful to examine empathic breaks for this age bracket by its level of intensity (longevity) and the related behaviors and statements. How long it lasts will determine to what extent it needs to be addressed. Dynamics, such as protesting therapy, missing sessions, getting sick on session day, and/or coming late to sessions, that last more than a month can be seen as an empathic break. Maybe we can call issues that resolve more quickly empathic lapses.

Late Adolescence/Teen Years (Age 15–17)

Subject to maturity level, teenagers who have experienced an empathic break will express their displeasure directly with the therapist, will refuse to go to therapy, or both. They may express a negative view of the therapist and/or the therapy. They may say that therapy is a waste of time.

Bertram Feels Unsafe

Bertram was a 15-year-old who was in therapy for four months because he was experiencing panic attacks. He was sexually abused as a young child and was in therapy on and off since he was 6. During the session that Bertram discussed the sexual abuse, the therapist became teary-eyed. At the time, the therapist believed that his emotional response was empathic—an acknowledgment of Bertram's own sadness. When the session ended, Bertram left. That night, the therapist received a call from Bertram's father that Bertram no longer wanted to come to therapy. When the therapist asked the reason, the father indicated that he did not know, but that Bertram was very anxious. The therapist suggested to the father that he offer Bertram the option to come in to see the therapist one more time, just to try to explain what had happened. Bertram agreed because the session did not represent him making a commitment to continue therapy. When Bertram came in the following week, he told the therapist that he did not know if the therapist could handle seeing him, that the therapist was just too emotional. The therapist apologized to Bertram for any additional pain he had caused him, indicating that this had in no way been his intention. They agreed that when the therapist was moved by Bertram's words that the therapist would tell him, and they could discuss it.

The therapist now understood that his own feelings had been too intense for Bertram to manage and it had made Bertram feel unsafe. That this had been inadvertent is the unfortunate nature of empathic breaks. Telling the therapist about his feelings turned out to be helpful for Bertram, and he remained in therapy with the therapist. The therapist, in turn, became more aware of when and how to use emotional expression in a therapeutic cycle with Bertram.

Young Adulthood (Age 18–Mid-20s)

The individuals in this group will experience empathic breaks and will address them directly with their therapist. Parents will most likely not know about the empathic break until after the fact—and most likely the ending of therapy.

The consequences of empathic ruptures can feel sudden and unexpected. It can have been building for some time, simmering under the surface, and then manifest with great power. *In all cases, discussing these matters with your child's therapist is your first step.* We recommend a calm and patient response toward your child, as your child is most likely expressing hurt feelings. Rejecting the individual (or the institution) responsible for the feelings is an instinctive way of protecting oneself. It is understandable and natural. The work for your child and her or his therapist is to come to an understanding that there are other ways to protect one's self from hurt feelings, other than ending the therapy. For you, when your child experiences an empathic break, it might help to imagine that your child is on a roller coaster. The best place that you can be during these times is on the ground, paying close attention to your child, allowing the ride to come to a natural end, comforting your child, but not directly experiencing the ups and downs that he or she is going through.

ANGER AT OR DISAPPOINTMENT WITH YOUR CHILD'S THERAPIST

In child psychotherapy, empathic breaks can also occur within the therapist-parent relationship. This is a particularly complicated aspect of your child's therapy because the therapist has less contact with you, and less contact can mean less ability to address issues that caused the break.

Arlene Feels Blind-Sided

Lucy was 8 years old and was in therapy with several different therapists for three years. She was being seen in therapy as a requirement of a Child Protective Services case. Lucy had lived in a violent home for the first five years of her life and now she was in a kinship foster care with her aunt, Arlene. Arlene brought Lucy each week and also saw the therapist once every two weeks for collateral appointments. Lucy struggled with her explosive angry outbursts in which she became violent.

The therapist's work with Lucy and Arlene focused on (1) helping her understand Lucy's need for safety, (2) building Lucy's level of empathy for others, and (3) increasing Lucy's frustration tolerance. Lucy's progress was difficult to identify, and her problems appeared to be increasingly frustrating to Arlene. After a particularly intense and dangerous outburst, the therapist suggested to Arlene that she take Lucy to the hospital emergency room to make sure she (and everyone else) was safe. Arlene followed the therapist's suggestion. Lucy remained in the child section of the emergency room for several hours, calmed down, and was discharged. Soon after, Arlene stopped bringing Lucy to therapy, and instead, Lucy was brought to therapy by other family members. Arlene stopped coming to her collateral appointments and stopped returning the therapist's calls. Within two months, Lucy's therapy abruptly ended and Child Protective Services informed the therapist that Lucy now lived with a different foster family.

The therapist understood that Lucy was going to need a significant level of psychiatric intervention and other supplemental therapeutic support as she grew and matured. Her trauma left her with severe psychological injuries. The therapist also understood what an overwhelming job it would be to care for Lucy. The realities of what caring for Lucy would entail were made tangible for Arlene on the night Lucy was taken to the emergency room. Arlene was hurt and unprepared and felt betrayed and scared about the future; the therapist just mentioned the hospital as a possible option. The lack of contact with the therapist after the emergency room intervention made working through this empathic break impossible.

If you feel angry at, betrayed by, disappointment with, and/or unsure about your child's therapist, we suggest that you initiate a discussion with him or her. Empathic breaks are typical occurrences within any relationship, but especially ones that have the sole and crucial purpose of caring for the health of your child. Acting on these feelings is important. Making changes or course corrections to your child's therapy is a vital part of the process. Empathic breaks and the underlying problems that they highlight provide wonderful opportunities for strengthening the therapy relationships. Attending to the hurt, "making up," creates a mutual gain that brings everyone closer. We understand each other better and can move forward based on this improved understanding.

CHAPTER SUMMARY

CHAPTER 13: HURDLES, OBSTACLES, AND SNAGS

Missed Sessions

There are many causes and reasons that children miss therapy appointments:

- Vacation
- Illness
- Planned break
- Another appointment
- Logistical conflicts (siblings, weather, etc.)
- Cancellations
- No shows

The impact on your child's therapy of missing sessions can vary based on how you and your child's therapist plan for these gaps, if possible, and address them if not.

- Communication—planning, rescheduling, and so on
- Transparency—incorporating the child's awareness of the gaps into the therapy.

Empathic Breaks

An empathic break is a disruption in the relationship/connection between the therapist and the patient.

For the child, it centers on the idea that the therapist has not responded to the child in the way that the child feels he or she should have.

A parent feeling anger at or disappointment with the child's therapist is a sign of an empathic break within the parent-therapist relationship.

CHAPTER 14

Supplementing Your Child's Psychotherapy

Establishing your child's psychotherapy as the primary treatment provides you and your child with an organizing principle for all of your options and the resulting decisions. The holistic lens through which we view a child enables us to set the treatment frame wide enough to include family, environment, personality, behavior, and development. When we incorporate all these aspects of your child, we can create a treatment plan, therapeutic cycles, and goals that address as many issues as possible during the therapy sessions and collateral appointments.

We believe that your child's psychotherapy is a hub—a place to manage, consider, and debate all decisions that affect your child's emotional state, strengths, and overall functioning. It is important to acknowledge that, as we view a child holistically, we also recognize that the problems that your child is facing may also respond to therapeutic interventions outside the psychotherapy setting—at school, through medication, within groups, and at other institutions. There may be important interventions that are beyond the specific expertise of your child's psychotherapist and/or the psychotherapist's setting/organization/agency. They can be specialties of other professionals that become a part of your child's psychotherapy. The goal of these supplementary interventions is to improve your child's sense of mastery, control, and confidence. The work of psychotherapy is to assist you and your child in understanding how these additional interventions can be helpful.

With therapy in place, you and your child's therapist may identify that he or she needs additional support with specific aspects of his or her life or functioning. Difficulties in these areas can slow or curtail the therapeutic gains that can be made in therapy. It may even be that your child's emotional state requires introducing a secondary supportive intervention. This, then, becomes the short-term goal of the therapy. Once the supplementary service is in place, the long-term goals of your child's psychotherapy can move forward.

Annika Needs a New Plan

Annika's parents were working with her teachers for more than four years to address problems in school, when they decided that she needed therapy. Annika was now 9 years old, and her parents informed her new therapist that she was in a special class at school for children with behavior and learning problems. They also reported to the therapist that the teachers were overwhelmed and did not know how to help Annika. Annika was being asked to leave the classroom almost daily, and she was beginning to protest in the morning about going to school. When the therapist met with Annika, she appeared depressed and anxious. The therapist and her parents agreed that the problems at school were so significant that the issues were exacerbating her depression and anxiety. They decided that a meeting would be set up for the therapist, the parents, the teachers, and mental health professionals at the school. The meeting focused on reworking Annika's supportive educational plan at school and coordinating it with the plan and goals of her psychotherapy.

Annika's teachers and school mental health professionals were crucial to her care and to her psychological progress. Following the joint meeting, the school staff understood the educational interventions of the plan in a new way. They decided to have her remain in class even when she was having difficulties, added more one-on-one instruction, and established contact with teachers during lunch and recess. These interventions supported the long-term goals of her therapy to enhance her self-esteem and offer her more structure and security.

SUPPLEMENTAL THERAPEUTIC INTERVENTIONS

Secondary interventions that supplement your child's psychotherapy can take all shapes and forms. These are interventions that will add a level of security, consistency, and structure to your child's care. Your child's therapist may suggest some of these secondary interventions and may help you locate and apply for them. The therapist also can help you think through these options and evaluate the results and effects. We have created a list of secondary interventions that you may have already encountered or that you may consider as additions to your child's therapy.

Complimentary Therapy Supplemental Interventions

Complimentary therapies—These are sometimes described as "complimentary" treatments because they are considered non-traditional or unconventional ways to address mental health issues. However, we view this as a biased way of looking at these options. For example, your anxious child may find great comfort in interacting with animals or practicing yoga. Your child's therapist may have some recommendations with regard to these options.

Some examples are:

a. Acupuncture is a therapeutic intervention based on traditional Chinese medicine. It uses extremely thin needles inserted into the skin at various points on the body. These points correlate to specific energy flows in the body that, when stimulated by the needles, work to rebalance the patient. Acupuncture treats depression, stomachaches, and pain.

b. Yoga/tai chi/chi gong are a group of South Asian and traditional Chinese heath-promoting techniques based on movement, physical balance, and emotional focus that are used in Western medicine to decrease stress, tension, and depression.

c. Meditation and guided imagery are similar to the above but do not include movement and are related to self-hypnosis techniques.

d. Animal-assisted therapy involves the use of domesticated animals to provide emotional support, and connection, and to diminish social isolation, due to the animal's affection, responsiveness, and physical closeness. Dogs are often the animal involved, as well as cats, birds, monkeys, farm animals, horses, and others.

Educational and School-based Supplemental Interventions

CTT or ICT classes (collaborative team teaching or integrated co-teaching) are school-based classes that provide support to students with clinical needs. These classes can include children who have specific clinical needs and those who do not. At least one of the teachers has special education training to be able to address the psychological, emotional, and behavioral needs of their students, and there is typically a high teacher-to-student ratio. These classes are provided as a supportive intervention for your child through a board of education psychological assessment process that creates an **Individualized Education Program (IEP)** for your child. Your child can qualify for an IEP if he or she has difficulties in a number of categories that would impact his or her ability to learn—motor, speech, cognitive, learning, emotional, hearing, seeing, and so on. We recommend that you ask your child's teacher if you feel your child may benefit from services from support staff. Your child's therapist can be involved with the IEP creation and updating process if you request.

An information guide about IEPs can be found through the US Department of Education using the following telephone number 1-877-433-7827, or on the Department's website at the address: http://www2.ed.gov/parents/needs/speced/iepguide/index.html. In addition, you can find information about IEPs on your state's Department of Education website under the heading of Special Education.

Your child can also qualify for a 504 Educational Plan. This plan addresses similar issues as the IEP, but involves teacher-implemented interventions such as

a. extra time on assignments/tests;
b. altered seating design to address focus;
c. adjusted schedules;
d. adjusted grading; and
e. aids (verbal, visual, technological).

The evaluation process is similar to that of the IEP, and we recommend that you ask your child's teacher if you feel your child may benefit from services.

Individual school-based counseling is a therapeutic school-based intervention in which your child sees a school counselor, school social worker, or school psychologist. Typically, these sessions are shorter than therapy sessions, and the material discussed can vary from school-related issues to home and personal problems. The reason for school counseling is to improve your child's ability to make the best use of classroom time. This can enhance your child's learning opportunities.

In addition to you, school mental health professionals are often the first individuals to identify that your child is having difficulties. Often these relationships are important to your child and should continue because your child needs the additional support while in school, in addition to individual psychotherapy. Your child's therapist can maintain a working relationship with your child's school mental health professional as a way of coordinating the different environments in which your child receives care.

Coordinating Julietta's Care

Julietta was 12 years old. Her family's financial problems created a great deal of stress in the family. Both her parents lost their jobs over the past year, and although her mother was able to secure another job recently, the family moved in with her father's parents. During these difficult times, Julietta saw the school social worker at her teacher's insistence on a weekly basis. Julietta met with social worker for six months and looked forward to their talks. The social worker met with her parents when Julietta began to draw all over her skin with pen while in class. The social worker suggested that Julietta meet with a psychotherapist, as these issues needed a different type of therapeutic intervention. Julietta began seeing a therapist shortly thereafter and also continued to see the social worker when at school. With the parents' consent and Julietta's agreement (assent), the therapist and the school social worker spoke each month to update each other and to coordinate treatment.

Psychological evaluations/testing are detailed assessments that can be used to gather additional psychological and intellectual/cognitive functioning information about your child. These assessment can be provided within the school settings, completed by a Board of Education–supplied psychologist as part of an IEP of 504 Education Plan, or outside the school with a psychologist that you identify or who is recommended by your child's therapist.

Responding to Valerie's Evaluation

Valerie was a 6-year-old girl when her parents brought her to see a therapist for what they described as "bizarre" behavior at school. They indicated that she had difficulty in school since she was in day care. They reported that the day care could not manage her because of her disruptive behavior, which included yelling and biting. Kindergarten and first grade did not change Valerie's situation; she often hit her classmates and refused to listen to authority figures. Her parents decided to have her psychologically evaluated. The psychological evaluation described Valerie as highly intelligent. It also suggested that she struggled in a variety of areas, including social interaction. The evaluator indicated that Valerie was uncooperative and very difficult to test. She diagnosed Valerie with a spectrum disorder and disruptive behavior disorder. Valerie received an IEP that provided a variety of services, including individual counseling, occupational therapy, and speech therapy. After a school year with the IEP services in place, her parents decided that based on Valerie's lack of significant progress, they would add psychotherapy to her care. The therapist helped Valerie's parents understand the symptoms, the evaluation, and the diagnoses. They set about creating a treatment plan to best utilize all the services that were being provided.

Therapeutic day schools are private schools your child would attend, just like a typical school. They are specifically designed and approved by the state to educate your child within an environment that understands and responds to the psychological needs of its students. They accommodate children with emotional problems, behavioral issues, developmental delays, and/or learning difficulties. The staff, in addition to specially trained teachers, includes a range of mental health professionals. Information on available therapeutic day schools can be found on your state's Department of Education website under the heading of Special Education Approved Private Day Schools or by searching for local Therapeutic Day Schools on the Internet. As always, a referral from a trusted source is our first preference for finding information about these schools.

Penelope's New School

Penelope was 8 years old. She was in third grade and was getting in trouble with her teacher every day for talking and getting out of her seat. At a planning meeting with the parents and her therapist; her teacher, principal, and school psychologist expressed frustration by the lack of progress that Penelope was making in addressing her behavior problems. Penelope's therapist suggested that this was an issue of "fit." Penelope and the school did not seem to fit well together. The therapist understood that in a school setting with a large number of students in each class, the emotional needs of one child may be difficult to meet, especially without staff training and a mandate to address these problems. Penelope's parents, with the therapist's help, found a therapeutic day school for her before the school year ended. In her new class, there were several students managing the same issues as Penelope. The teachers at the new school provided suggestions to her parents for managing her difficulties. The new school worked closely with Penelope's therapist. As Penelope's school and home environment provided her with the safety and limit setting she needed, her psychotherapy enabled her to develop better tools to manage her anxiety and impulsivity.

Expressive Arts Therapy Supplemental Interventions

Expressive arts therapies are interventions that include the use of visual art, bibliotherapy (use of stories and storybooks), drama/theater, movement/dance, music, and poetry, among other art forms. They help your child express and share thoughts and feelings that he or she cannot easily put into words. Art, dance, drama, and music therapy practitioners receive special postgraduate training in these specific modes of treatment. They are certified by professional organizations. These professional organizations also certify college- or university-based training programs. Art therapy can also be part play therapy and is used to learn about your child's conflicts, fears, and worries.

Perry, the Musician, Finds His Voice

Perry was a 6-year-old boy. He stopped talking (elective mutism) or even making sounds after his grandmother died and he entered foster care. He was in psychotherapy where the therapist used play as the form of communication. In addition, Perry saw a music therapist. He would not sing along with the music therapist but was willing to use a tambourine. Soon he used several different percussive instruments while the music therapist sang. He began to make sounds during music therapy sessions, sometimes imitating a trumpet, other times a tuba or trombone. A year after entering foster care, Perry began to make simple verbal requests for food and hugs.

Family Therapy Supplemental Interventions

Family therapy is a specialized mental health intervention in which the therapist considers your family unit itself as the patient/client, rather than each individual family member (similar to the joint child-parent sessions). Your entire family, you and all of your children—not only the child whom you may be most worried about—are together in the session. Family therapy focuses on improving your family's communication and the understanding of each other's communication styles, clarifying family roles and responsibilities, and working on solving family problems using compromise and mutual respect.

Group Support Supplemental Interventions

Group counseling is a form of psychotherapy that focuses on improving your child's ability to relate to and empathize with other people by placing the child in an environment designed to have him or her interact with other children. Within the group setting, there is an emphasis on your child

1. becoming more aware of and changing her or his views and feelings about other people, and
2. coping and managing with stress related to interacting with other people.

Some child psychotherapists also offer counseling groups. You can also find counseling groups associated with local hospitals and in some mental health clinics.

Skills-building groups focus on a specific clinical issue with the goal of change and growth for your child with respect to that issue. Skills-building groups provide tangible plans of action to address certain problems. These groups place your child together with children of the same age and/or developmental stage. This enables the practitioner to shape the interventions appropriately to the needs of each specific group. Some examples of skills building can be anger management, study habits, organizing, self-esteem, public speaking, and so on.

Socialization groups are therapeutic groups that are based on building your child's ability to interact with his or her peers. These groups emphasize relationship building, communication, listening skills, empathy, self-awareness, and trust. Socialization groups can take place within many, but not all, school settings, with a mental health professional, or outside the school. At school, they center on your child's classmate relationships. Socialization groups not affiliated with school typically take place at outpatient mental health agencies.

In addition, clubs, sports teams, after school programs and summer camps all provide important socialization opportunities for your child.

Support groups are therapeutic groups that often focus on a specific issue, dilemma, or situation and establish connections between your child and other group members. The various purposes of support groups are to exchange helpful information, solve shared problems, and establish connections with other children who are experiencing similar difficulties. Relationship building is a primary emphasis. Support groups can be found in schools, local hospitals, community centers and organizations, or places of worship. In addition to your child, there are many support groups for parents that can be very helpful as a way of finding a community that shares some of your experiences. It is a way that you can gather resources, options, and empathy.

Mentoring Supplemental Interventions

Mentoring is a therapeutic intervention organized around one-on-one interactions between your child and an individual with qualities that you would like your child to emulate. Mentors typically are not mental health professionals, but are supervised and are trained in working with children. This intervention is based on a concept called modeling in which behavior, attitudes, and ideas are copied from another person. Because of this, your child's mentor will be the same gender. Mentoring can be helpful with children who may feel isolated or are suffering from the loss or absence of important adults in their life. There are many mentoring agencies, and we recommend that you seek referrals from individuals whom you trust. There should be an extensive screening/intake process that goes into choosing a mentor for your child. You have a right to detailed information about an organization's screening, match-up, and supervision policies and procedures.

Angela Gets a New "Big Sister"

Angela was 7 years old and an only child. She began therapy after her family moved into a shelter following an industrial accident that destroyed their home. No one in the family was home at the time, but several neighbors, including two of Angela's friends, died. Angela was withdrawn and terribly upset over the loss of her friends. The family lived in a motel near the airport with other displaced families. Her therapist suggested to Angela's parents that they consider involving her with the local Big Sisters organization. The Big Sister took Angela on outings on Saturdays, provided her with an important distraction, an opportunity to play with an adult who did not experience the trauma, and time away from the cramped motel grounds.

Psychiatric/Psychotropic Medication Supplemental Interventions

Psychiatric/psychotropic medication is a therapeutic drug intervention that is thought to modify/alter/re-balance the effects of the chemicals ("neurotransmitters") in your child's brain. Psychotropic (psychiatric) medications treat various psychological symptoms in children. Most of these medications are scientifically tested on adults, and their use for children is based on how the medication has been found to help adults with similar symptoms. Currently, we do not know all of the short-term or long-term side effects of many of these medications on children.

It is our belief that medication is not a treatment for a child's psychological problems but rather a symptom management tool that can help improve the effectiveness of psychotherapy. We do not believe that psychotropic medications should replace psychotherapy for children, nor do we believe that psychotherapy replaces psychotropic medications. We believe that for some children, these two interventions work together.

We suggest that parents consider the use of psychotropic medications to help their children in the same way that we suggest you consider any supplemental intervention. Your decisions about psychotropic medication for your child can relate to your child's ability or inability to enjoy friends, manage school structure, sleep, eat, play, and interact with family.

Typical factors that may lead you and your child's therapist to considering psychotropic medication include the following:

1. Difficulty following fair and consistent rules at home, school, and in other settings that is
   a. not responding to typical limit setting techniques; and
   b. creating situations that are significantly unsafe (emotionally and/or physically).
2. Difficulty enjoying and participating in life to such an extent that it is
   a. curtailing engagement in typical child activities; and
   b. impairing the child's ability to develop.

3. Difficulty controlling thoughts and feelings to the extent that it is
   a. affecting the child's ability to function in typical child settings and situations; and
   b. creating situations that are significantly unsafe (emotionally and/or physically).

Even the most effective medications are vulnerable to abuse, overuse, and indiscriminate use. As a consumer and the person responsible for protecting your child, it is important to ask questions. How does an anti-depressant actually work on my child? Why is ADHD being diagnosed and medicated at such a significant rate? Why are the children with ADHD more likely to be boys? How are anti-psychotic medications prescribed for agitation? Can my child handle an anti-anxiety medication? Should psychotropic medication be prescribed for behavior control? Is medication prescribed for certain races and ethnicities more than others?

Is Toby's Medicine Making Him Feel Worse?

Toby, a 12-year-old boy, was prescribed a stimulant by his psychiatrist for his distractibility, disorganization, and lack of focus at home and school. His father was feeling anxious because Toby was having numerous side effects from the medication, including panic attacks, difficulties going to sleep, and stomachaches. After a meeting between Toby's psychiatrist, his father, and his psychotherapist, it was agreed that the psychiatrist would meet with Toby more often (typical frequency is once a month) in order to monitor these side effects closely and possibly alter the medication intervention if it was seen to not be having the desired effect. The psychiatrist acknowledged that it was difficult to know definitively what was causing these new symptoms.

As the parent, you require information about any medication you give your child. You have a right to expect your child's physician or psychiatrist to provide clear and logical information about all medications and to monitor the medication closely. Physicians and psychiatrists base this monitoring on typical time intervals related to their training and the specific medication, but as the parent, you can request a schedule of monitoring that makes you feel comfortable and secure.

Anthony's Anti-Depressant

Anthony was a 12-year-old boy referred to therapy by his mother. This was the second time that his mother looked for a therapist for Anthony. The first time was three years earlier, after Anthony's father died suddenly of a heart attack. Anthony was 9, and he was in therapy for six months. Currently, his mother worried because Anthony started to spend significant amounts of time in his room and stopped talking to her. She knew that Anthony's father had suffered from depression. She also reported that Anthony was mentioning his father more often over the past few months. When the therapist interviewed Anthony for an intake, Anthony reported that he was thinking about dying. When the therapist asked him to describe the thoughts, Anthony said that sometimes when he waited at a traffic light, he thought about stepping out into the street in front of traffic. The therapist informed Anthony's mother about her son's thoughts and feelings and immediately referred Anthony to a child psychiatrist.

The acute nature of Anthony's depression, specifically his suicidal thoughts and plan, and to a lesser degree his withdrawal (time in his room), led his therapist to recommend a psychotropic medication evaluation. Any long-term goals of therapy were overshadowed by the need to keep him safe. The therapist felt that medication (namely, an anti-depressant) would be the only way to provide Anthony with the protection he needed to continue to function safely on a day-to-day basis and to manage the material that was going to be addressed in his psychotherapy (his father and the loss).

The Federal Food and Drug Administration (FDA) has mandated a "black box" warning on all anti-depressants. The warning actually is within a thick black line rectangle. The warning alerts physicians, adult patients, and parents that it is possible for anti-depressants to increase suicidal thoughts. Updates on these warnings are on the FDA website. As parents, you can ask any physician prescribing psychotropic medications for your child if there are any black box warnings for this drug.

It is beyond the scope of this book to explain in a sufficiently thorough fashion the importance and complexity of this issue. We do want to emphasize that *you should always do your own research on any drug prescribed for your child.*

The National Institute of Mental Health (NIMH) created the following website to provide information (classes, uses, side effects) about psychotropic medication for children and adolescents. As always, please read all information with a critical eye toward what is included and what is omitted: http://www.nimh.nih.gov/health/publications/mental-health-medications/index.shtml. Your knowledgeable participation in this supplemental intervention is essential. While the physician may ask you to monitor your child, this does *not* relieve the physician of her or his ethical and professional responsibilities to monitor your child. The frequency of your child's medication monitoring appointments is not solely up to the physician.

Psychiatrist Shortage

As of 2010, there were only 7,000 practicing child and adolescent psychiatrists in the United States. That is one child/adolescent psychiatrist for approximately 10,500 children. The documented shortage appears to be getting worse, as fewer psychiatrists are being trained in this specialty, and those who are continue to retire (Thomas & Holzer, 2006; Childstats.gov/americaschildren2013/index.asp).

New Mexico, Louisiana, and Illinois are the only states in the United States in which psychologists may prescribe medication. Illinois does not allow psychologists to prescribe to children or adolescents. These states have different requirements, including types of training programs and rules regarding collaboration with other medical professionals involved in the care of the patient. The psychologists in Louisiana are medical psychologists (www.nationalregister.org). There is a distinct problem concerning the discrepancy between rural and urban accessibility to medication in mental health. It is much more difficult to find any type of psychiatrist to prescribe medication if you live in a rural area—let alone a psychiatrist with a specialty in childhood or adolescence.

Other states have proposed legislation that considers extending prescription privileges to trained psychologists (see table). They are Hawaii, California, Georgia, Illinois, Mississippi, Montana, Oregon, Tennessee, Alaska, Connecticut, Florida, Maine, New Hampshire, Oklahoma, Texas, and Wyoming.

Why is all this important? Its importance centers on the availability of medication and care for your child if you choose to explore a medication response to your child's problems. You will need to shape your expectations about accessibility and availability issues. It may take you some time to find a child and adolescent psychiatrist. Remember, all psychiatrists do not have the specialty training to prescribe medication to children or adolescents. You may find one with a long waiting list. You may need to look elsewhere for this type of professional input (such as your child's pediatrician or general practitioner). That said, some pediatricians feel comfortable prescribing medication; others do not.

PROFESSIONALS WITH PRESCRIBING PRIVILEGES

	Psychiatrist	Pediatrician/ General Practitioner	Nurse Practitioner	Psychologist
Alabama	X	X	X	
Alaska	X	X	X	
Arizona	X	X	X	
Arkansas	X	X	X	
California	X	X	X	
Colorado	X	X	X	
Connecticut	X	X	X	
Delaware	X	X	X	
District of Columbia	X	X	X	
Florida	X	X	X	
Georgia	X	X	X	
Hawaii	X	X	X	
Idaho	X	X	X	
Illinois	X	X	X	X*
Indiana	X	X	X	
Iowa	X	X	X	
Kansas	X	X	X	
Kentucky	X	X	X	
Louisiana	X	X	X	X
Maine	X	X	X	
Maryland	X	X	X	
Massachusetts	X	X	X	
Michigan	X	X	X	
Minnesota	X	X	X	
Mississippi	X	X	X	
Missouri	X	X	X	

(continued)

	Psychiatrist	Pediatrician/ General Practitioner	Nurse Practitioner	Psychologist
Montana	X	X	X	
Nebraska	X	X	X	
Nevada	X	X	X	
New Hampshire	X	X	X	
New Jersey	X	X	X	X
New Mexico	X	X	X	
New York	X	X	X	
North Carolina	X	X	X	
North Dakota	X	X	X	
Ohio	X	X	X	
Oklahoma	X	X	X	
Oregon	X	X	X	
Pennsylvania	X	X	X	
Rhode Island	X	X	X	
South Carolina	X	X	X	
South Dakota	X	X	X	
Tennessee	X	X	X	
Texas	X	X	X	
Utah	X	X	X	
Vermont	X	X	X	
Virginia	X	X	X	
Washington	X	X	X	
West Virginia	X	X	X	
Wisconsin	X	X	X	
Wyoming	X	X	X	

* Not permitted to prescribe to children or adolescents.

Rehabilitation Supplemental Interventions

Rehabilitation therapies are therapies that help improve specific physical abilities that need attention due to a developmental issue or delay or following an injury.

- Occupational therapists focus on improving fine motor skills development and body control within a variety of environments and situations.

- Physical therapists focus on improving mobility and movement skills.
- Speech therapists help your child with language development and communication problems. Practitioners focus on your child's abilities to verbally communicate and process language. This intervention addresses your child's speech volume, articulation, and patterns, in addition to issues related to the mouth and to swallowing.

These are services that can be provided for your child within the school setting as part of an IEP or sometimes, depending on your healthcare insurance coverage, outside the school with a professional either visiting your home or in an office setting.

CHAPTER SUMMARY

CHAPTER 14: SUPPLEMENTING YOUR
CHILD'S PSYCHOTHERAPY

Supplemental therapeutic interventions add a level of security, consistency, and structure to your child's care.

Complimentary Therapies
- Acupuncture—based on traditional Chinese medicine, uses extremely thin needles inserted into the skin to treat depression, stomachaches, pain, and other conditions. Acupressure uses similar techniques without the use of needles.
- Yoga/tai chi/chi gong—South Asian and traditional Chinese medicine heath-promoting techniques that are used to decrease stress, tension, and depression.
- Meditation and guided imagery—are related to self-hypnosis techniques.
- Animal-assisted therapy—uses domesticated animals to provide emotional support and connection, and to diminish social isolation.

Educational and School-Based
- CTT and ICT classes—collaborative team teaching or integrated co-teaching with at least one of the teachers having special education training to be able to address the psychological, emotional, and behavioral needs of the students

- Individualized Education Programs (IEPs0—provide in-school services, including assistance and interventions with motor, speech, cognitive, learning, emotional, hearing, seeing, and so on.
- 504 Educational Plan—provides interventions including extra time on assignments/tests, altered seating design to address focus, adjusted schedules, adjusted grading, or aids (verbal, visual, technological).
- Individual school-based counseling
- Therapeutic day schools—private schools that are designed and approved by the state to educate children with emotional problems, behavioral issues, developmental delays, and/or learning difficulties.

Expressive Arts Therapy
- Art
- Bibliotherapy (use of stories and storybooks)
- Drama/theater
- Movement/dance
- Music
- Poetry

Family Therapy
- Therapist considers your family unit itself as the patient/client;
- Entire family are together in the session;
- Focuses on improving your family's communication and understanding of each other's communication styles;
- Clarifies family roles and responsibilities.

Group Support
- Group counseling—places child in an environment designed to have him or her interact with other children.
- Skills-building groups—focuses on a specific clinical issue with the goal of change and growth.
- Socialization groups—builds on a child's ability to interact with his or her peers by emphasizing relationship building, communication, listening skills, empathy, self-awareness, and trust; can take place within schools.
- Support groups—focuses on a specific issue, dilemma, or situation and tries to establish connections between group members.

Mentoring
- One-on-one interactions between a child and an individual with qualities that caregivers would like the child to emulate;
- Typically not mental health professional, but supervised and trained in working with children;
- Based on a concept called modeling in which behavior, attitudes, and ideas are copied from another person.

Psychiatric/Psychotropic Medication
- Drugs that modify/alter/re-balance the affects of the chemicals ("neurotransmitters") in a child's brain;
- Not a treatment for a child's psychological problems but rather a symptom management tool that can help improve the effectiveness of psychotherapy;
- The decision to use medication should be considered when a child's safety is in question.

Rehabilitation
- Occupational therapists—focus on fine motor skills development and body control.
- Physical therapists—focus on mobility and movement skills.
- Speech therapists—focus on language development, communication problems, speech volume, articulation, and patterns, in addition to issues related to the mouth and to swallowing.

Higher Levels of Care

When You and Your Child Need More

Conventional wisdom tells parents not to overreact. Of course, as parents, this does not address the reality that we worry about everything—my child is not eating, is not pooping, hit his head, does not sleep, or is crying all the time. Our child's pediatrician, our parents, our friends, and everyone else give us opinions about what to do and attempt to provide us with the reassurance that it will all be OK—and it usually is.

Our worries do lead us to seek some extra professional assistance and intervention from time to time because we want our children to be emotionally and physically healthy, "on-track" developmentally, and able to grow into adults whom we are proud of and admire. When these wishes for our child seem jeopardized by psychological problems, concerns, or unhealthy behaviors, we suggest that it is time to seek professional assistance from a mental health practitioner. We see child psychotherapy and the supplemental therapeutic interventions as examples of these professional interventions. These all fall into the category of outpatient services.

When engaging outpatient services, your child remains under your care—living at home, maintaining the schedule and daily plan that he or she would typically have, with the addition of the extra support and assistance of the services. This involves you introducing people and therapeutic activities into your child's existing daily routines, altering them, but leaving the essentials of your family's life unchanged. This level of supportive structure is usually sufficient for tackling most emotional difficulties that your child is facing. You have the freedom to expand it if your child needs more support and contract it when he or she is doing better and may need less.

There are different levels of outpatient services. These include the therapists in private practice, mental health clinics, and hospital-based outpatient psychiatry services. The determination of what level your child needs is often based on the degree to which your child's problems disrupt his or her ability to attend school, maintain friendships, manage feelings, and organize thoughts.

Clinics and hospital-based outpatient psychiatry services provide care that is more comprehensive to children because they unite psychotherapy and psychiatry in one setting, promoting a greater ease of communication among the professionals helping your child and greater coordination of your child's care. This is more difficult to attain with a therapist in private practice and a separate psychiatrist in private practice. If your child is (1) actively harming herself or himself, and/or (2) experiencing thoughts, feelings, and/or behaviors that could lead to harming herself or himself or others, we recommend the more comprehensive outpatient treatment setting.

Leroy Tries Different Levels of Outpatient Services

Leroy was a 16-year-old boy brought to therapy at an outpatient clinic by his mother. She was worried about his self-harming behaviors. During the intake process, Leroy described that he was having suicidal thoughts, but had no current plan to hurt himself. The therapist diagnosed Leroy with a major depressive disorder. For several months, Leroy was able to continue to manage his outpatient therapy at the clinic and his schooling, but his mother indicated that he was becoming more and more difficult to handle at home—yelling, crying, isolating, and, she believed, cutting his arms (although he denied this). When Leroy had an episode in school (he was scratching a deep cut into his arm), he was hospitalized for a month. His therapist and his mother decided that Leroy needed more structure on an ongoing basis and chose an outpatient hospital-based program for Leroy to continue therapy. This program provided Leroy with a therapist, a psychiatrist, and a counseling group to address his outpatient clinical needs and was a connection to a hospital if, and when, Leroy had another suicidal episode. His clinic therapist visited him in the hospital to discuss the change in his treatment.

This chapter focuses on those complicated times when adding more outpatient services to your child's existing schedule may not be enough. These are times when, due to a variety of circumstances, your child may need more safety than outpatient psychotherapy (and the other supplemental supportive outpatient interventions) can provide. These moments and decisions are difficult because, similar to the choice to begin psychotherapy, they may provoke a sense of failure in us—the idea that we could not do enough ourselves. In addition, the new realization that outpatient services are not enough to help our child can cause feelings of hopelessness. Struggling with our fears about our children "not being okay" can result in delays in getting our children help when they need it. As long as we see our children's problems as either our failures or their stubbornness, we leave ourselves and our children with few helpful options.

We think it is important to consider the idea of changing our point of view by changing the way we think of this type of problem. This process is called **cognitive reframing**—cognitive (for our thought process) and reframing (for changing or altering it). If your child begins to struggle substantially, instead of thinking about your failure, your fear, or your lack of hope, you could think about the bedrock belief that it is your responsibility to keep your child safe.

Safety is one of those foundational necessities of human existence. From safety comes, trust, curiosity, courage, and action. Without safety and protection from danger, it is extremely difficult to grow and develop. How, when, and why we provide this protection for our children become the important questions.

Why are we referring to *safety* in this context? Children rely on the adults who care for them for their sense of safety and protection. We do many things to keep children safe—provide a physical presence, make decisions about the people in their lives, create rules about strangers, chemicals, animals, streets, and so on, and display our love and emotional commitment. We base our decisions about this structure on the idea that our children are living their lives out in the world—going to school, having friends, engaging in activities—and so it makes sense that we provide the structure they need to do this. If our children have specific needs with regard to eyesight, hearing, mobility, and emotional state, we provide for them the structural changes to address these needs with the goal of helping them feel safe and secure enough to keep growing and developing. If a child is having difficulty seeing, we get her eyes checked. If a child is having difficulty hearing, we check his hearing. If a child's feelings are overwhelming and communicated via worrisome behaviors, we can get her emotional health checked.

When we come to understand that the treatment structure created with your child's therapist may not be providing the needed level of safety, then it is important to contemplate reworking it. Let us use the example of a thunderstorm. There are many ways to help a person caught in a thunderstorm to feel safe. We can give her an umbrella, a raincoat, and rubber boots; we can tell her to avoid trees, water, and metal rods; we can even give her an idea of how long the storm will last and empathize with her regarding how it feels to be stuck out in a storm. We do all this because we want her to feel like she can handle storms, in general. We do not want her to fear all storms or to feel that we do not trust her.

However, if the storm is too big, too fierce, and too overwhelming, then providing these guidelines will not give her the needed protection from the storm. They do not provide enough support to keep her out of harm's way and therefore are no longer effective solutions. In the case of this storm, it is just too dangerous for her to be outside in the storm at all. This is a "stay at home, keep away from the windows, and fill the bathtub with water" type of storm.

With regard to mental health, we describe identifying and accessing a safer and more contained system—"staying at home"—as providing a **higher level of care** for your child. By higher level, we mean more structured, contained, and supervised. This enhanced clinical structure provides your child with a sense that you (and their therapist) will provide him with a level of protection and will not allow him to come to harm or be left to manage his overwhelming difficulties on his own. Examples of higher levels of mental health care include the following:

- *Diagnostic treatment center*—a relatively brief-stay residential facility where your child's difficulties are assessed on an intensive and daily basis and recommendations are made for future treatment.

Figuring Out Yvgeny's Rage

Yvgeny was an 11-year-old boy. He began therapy following a report to Child Protective Services of domestic violence in his home. His father was removed from the home by the police, and his mother brought Yvgeny and his 1-year-old sister Yulia for therapy. Yvgeny was quiet and withdrawn in therapy and did not say much to his therapist. After several months of therapy, his mother found several small bruises on Yulia's legs one morning. When asked about the bruises, Yvgeny denied knowing about them. One week later, Yulia was found with larger bruises on her torso. As a mandated reporter, Yulia's therapist called Child Protective Services. The subsequent investigation found that Yvgeny was hurting his sister at night. Based on the recommendation of Child Protective Services, and with the help of his therapist, Yvgeny was sent to a diagnostic treatment center for an intensive psychiatric evaluation. He then went to a longer term residential treatment facility. Yvegny made good progress with the therapist in residential treatment. Two years later, Yvgeny returned home, and he chose to return to his former therapist.

The diagnostic treatment center intervention accomplished several important goals: (1) Yvgeny was kept safe from his violent impulses toward his sister and from the possibility of harming her (or anyone else) in a more permanent way; (2) Yulia was kept safe and hopefully could now maintain a loving relationship with her brother; (3) Yvgeny's mother was helped to take steps to protect her children from a dangerous situation; and (4) Yvgeny was now in a therapeutic environment that could monitor him closely and provide a more accurate understanding of what he was experiencing and how to help him.

In some states, decisions about Yvgeny's care would be made by Child Protective Services or a similar designated state organization. This is a temporary transfer of custody (decision-making regarding legal and physical issues) of Yvgeny from his mother to the state. Children can return home after the completed diagnostic workup or go into a longer term residential treatment center. The parents regain full custody once it is clear that all the children in the home are safe and community-based treatment has been arranged for the child.

- *Drug treatment/rehabilitation center*—a residential therapeutic environment with medical services focused on learning the skills needed to remain sober, identifying the danger signs that threaten sobriety, and making life changes to support sobriety, which can also include schooling. Some drug use requires a hospital-based program to provide safe withdrawal and detoxification prior to entering some drug rehabilitation programs.

Suraj Dries Out

Suraj was 22 years old and lived at home with his parents. The family emigrated from Trinidad, beginning with his father, who was then followed by the other family members. Fourteen-year-old Suraj joined his parents and older sisters in the

United States after a four-year separation from them. Suraj worked in his father's
hotel. His binge drinking increased once he dropped out of a local college. His father
threatened to stop supporting him if he did not stop drinking and get help. Suraj
and his therapist agreed that sessions required his sobriety. Suraj came to sessions
sober, yet by the fifth session Suraj's extreme self-hate concerned the therapist. The
therapist believed that Suraj needed an anti-depressant and discussed a psychiatric
evaluation. Suraj came to the next session intoxicated, suicidal, and detailing how
his uncle had sexually abused him when he was living with him in Trinidad. With
Suraj's permission, the therapist called his parents and, in a joint session, Suraj
agreed to go into a hospital-based detoxification program. Once sober, he was trans-
ferred to inpatient psychiatry and was discharged from there on anti-depressant
medication. Suraj resumed therapy with the same therapist and focused on address-
ing his traumatic past.

- *Hospital emergency room (ER)*—used to obtain an emergency psychiatric
  evaluation because the person may be a danger to himself or to others.
- *Psychiatric hospitalization*—inpatient mental health services, either
  short-term (days) or long-term (weeks to months), depending on the severity
  of the person's psychiatric condition and the complexity of the psychtropic
  medication routine needed to help the individual. A subset of this category,
  mentioned earlier, is a partial hospitalization program that can serve as
  a transition from inpatient services to more typical outpatient services. It
  can also serve as a middle step if outpatient psychotherapy is not providing
  enough structure to maintain your child's safety. In can include intensive
  outpatient psychotherapy, medication management, group services, and
  family services.
- *Residential treatment facility and school*—a therapeutic environment that
  includes on-site psychiatric services, psychotherapy, and school facilities.
  The school facility uses a therapeutic environment and counseling to support learning, intellectual growth, and behavior change, organized along a
  typical school calendar.

Ricky's Sadness

Ricky was a 15-year-old boy who lived at home with his father and his four broth-
ers and sisters. His mother died from cancer when he was 11. He was the oldest, and
since entering puberty he had been getting into trouble—skipping school, staying

out late, and so on. His father, as part of Ricky's probation, had brought him to therapy after he was arrested when he and his friends injured a younger classmate. His typical statements to the therapist were that therapy was for weaklings and that only girls talked about feelings. When Ricky started to miss his therapy sessions, the therapist called his father for a meeting. The therapist told Ricky's father that his son needed much more structure than outpatient therapy could provide. The therapist felt that Ricky's depression and self-destructiveness made day-to-day life overwhelming. The therapist recommended that Ricky be sent to a residential treatment facility and school. The father agreed and Ricky was enrolled shortly thereafter. Ricky did well in the school, which had many rules and regulations. He earned periodic visits home. Without the pressure at home to be the oldest and the "strongest" child and all the reminders of his mother, he was able let go of his "tough" façade and discuss with his new school therapist his feelings about his mother's death.

Our "storm" metaphor enables us to envision supplying a higher level of care as a loving act for a child. Understandably, many parents and children initially view this type of therapeutic intervention as a punishment, rejection, or abandonment. We believe this comes from a societal viewpoint that if your child leaves home or "goes away" to receive psychiatric services for mental health reasons that he or she is "crazy," "weak" and/or severely mentally ill. "Going away" describes entering a hospital for **inpatient mental health treatment** (an admission that typically lasts for more than 24 hours). In fact, higher levels of care are simply for children who need protective as well as therapeutic interventions.

If your child was sick with an unknown fever, you would first try outpatient interventions—home remedies, then a visit to the doctor's office, and next, the doctor's prescribed medicine. If these were not successful, or if the fever worsened while trying these treatments, you would (and your child's pediatrician would agree) most likely take your child to a hospital to be evaluated and to begin an increased level of treatment.

Alma's Anxiety

Alma was a 14-year-old girl in therapy because of her severe anxiety reactions. Her autism spectrum disorder made it very difficult for her to interpret other people's thoughts and feelings. She sometimes misinterpreted people's responses to her as *negative and hostile. One evening, Alma's mother called the therapist to report that Alma was yelling and throwing things at her. Alma accused her mother of thinking that she was making up her anxiety. The therapist directed her to take Alma to the local hospital emergency room. In addition, if she did not feel that she could get Alma there by herself, she could call 911 for help. Alma's mother was able to get her daughter to the hospital. They remained in a child section of the emergency room for several hours and gradually Alma felt more in control. While in the hospital, physicians checked in with her on a regular basis and asked her questions. They also discussed with Alma and her mother the possibility of psychotropic medication.*

CALLING 911

Alma's mother was able to take her to the hospital without help. If you feel that you need assistance in getting your child to the hospital, then we recommend that you call 911. The call will connect you to a dispatcher. The dispatcher will ask you about the nature of the emergency. A straightforward explanation is best (i.e., "My child is yelling and throwing things and will not stop. I am worried that she will hurt herself or me."). The help that arrives will be in the form of police and EMS personnel. The arrival of police officers does *not* mean that your child is in trouble. The police are there to provide a safe structure for your child, and they will take control of the situation. It is a communication that "no one is going to get hurt." The EMS workers are responsible for assessing your child and getting him or her to the hospital. The police may or may not escort your child to the hospital, depending on the how dangerous they perceive the situation to be. Depending on the age of your child, you may be able to travel in the ambulance. You can ask the EMS personnel about how to proceed with regard to accompanying your child to the hospital.

We need to recognize that some communities fear the police due to issues of excessive force. In order to help the emergency response team understand how to prepare and respond to your child, it is important that you clearly indicate that your concerns do not involve a gun or other weapon.

THEMES OF A HIGHER LEVEL OF CARE

Typically, a higher level of care places your child into a **treatment milieu.** This means that the entire environment focuses on providing, treatment, support, limits, and safety. We can break down the various aspects of a treatment milieu by identifying the main themes of a higher level of care in the following ways:

- New environment (not a typical environment in which your child functions; the unfamiliar surroundings provide a focus for your child's attention and create an uncertainty that allows your child to be more open to help);
- More rules (an increase in the number of rules that limit your child's options and choices; this simplifies your child's decision-making that under the current circumstances may have become too difficult and overwhelming). At times, rules reinforcement uses a **token economy**—meaning that one receives privileges for following the rules or denial of privileges due to breaking the rules.
- More contact with clinicians (an increase in the individuals with whom your child interacts who have knowledge of child development, child psychology, and psychiatric problems; your child forges relationships with a variety of people who understand what he or she is going through);
- Focus on consistency and clarity (an adherence to routines and rules, clear communication, and clarity of purpose; the repetition of these elements creates basic trust that your child comes to rely upon and build upon);
- Safety precautions (safety and security become a requirement, not a choice; the unambiguous point of view that your child is important, cared for, and loved sides with the healthier part of your child's ambivalence about him or herself).

Craig's Paranoia

Craig was 17 years old. His parents referred him to therapy when they noticed that he had not slept for the past week. They heard him in his room moving around, but behind a locked door. In the morning, the door was open and he was dressed in layers, although it was hot and humid. When his parents brought Craig to meet the therapist, he would not make eye contact and seemed jumpy. During his session, he stated that staying up all night was part of his plan to stop the men from finding him. He said that the men had found him at school last week and that school was a battle zone. He was late to school because that gave him an advantage over the men, as they would not expect that and he would have the advantage. The therapist met with Craig's parents after the session and told them that Craig needed to see a psychiatrist at the hospital—that he was paranoid and suffering from psychotic delusions. The therapist explained that Craig was not safe because his thinking was not based on reality. He told them that the hospital would admit Craig and that he would remain there, on a locked floor, until the hospital staff completed a psychiatric evaluation and made a plan for Craig's ongoing care (which would include therapy and psychotropic medication). He would continue schooling in the hospital, so he would not miss school. Once situated in the hospital, based on Craig's agreement and his parents' permission, the therapist visited him and continued the relationship to enable therapy to resume following discharge.

Although Craig's psychotic break was terribly sad for him and his parents, their quick action allowed Craig to remain as safe as possible. We wish that serious situations would never occur with our children. If they do, however, we would like you to consider the concept of **harm reduction**. The idea comes from addiction treatment (smoking 2 cigarettes is better for you than 10) and acknowledges the realities of being human, and having flaws. We feel that it applies here in a helpful way. If, as parents, we realistically cannot eliminate harm, then surely limiting its effect, duration, or intensity on our children is good parenting. Getting Craig to the hospital rapidly, and getting him the right therapeutic intervention for his serious condition, allowed him to continue to live his life in the best possible way under the circumstances.

OTHER HIGHER LEVEL OF CARE OPTIONS AND SCENARIOS

Each state has a variety of options when it comes to higher levels of care. The interventions that we have included in this chapter are available in every state, although they may have different names (see Appendix C).

CHAPTER SUMMARY

CHAPTER 15: HIGHER LEVELS OF CARE: WHEN YOU AND YOUR CHILD NEED MORE

There may be times when, due to a variety of circumstances, a child may need more safety than outpatient psychotherapy (and the other supplemental supportive outpatient interventions) can provide.

Higher level of care means more structured, contained, and supervised care.

- New environment
- More rules of daily living
- More frequent contact with clinicians
- Focus on consistency and clarity
- Concrete safety precautions

Types of higher levels of care:

- *Diagnostic treatment center*—a relatively brief-stay residential facility where a child's difficulties are assessed and recommendations are made for future treatment.
- *Drug treatment/rehabilitation center*—a residential environment focused on learning to remain sober, identifying the danger signs that threaten sobriety, and making life changes to support sobriety.
- *Hospital emergency room (ER)*—used to obtain an emergency psychiatric evaluation because the person may be a danger to himself or to others.
- *Psychiatric hospitalization*—inpatient mental health services, either short-term (days) or long-term (weeks to months). This includes partial hospitalization, which provides more intensive outpatient services affiliated with a hospital.
- *Residential treatment facility and school*—a therapeutic environment that includes on-site psychiatric services, psychotherapy, and school facilities.

CHAPTER 16

Separation and Consolidation

Saying Goodbye to Your Child's Psychotherapist

When you finish reading this book, what are you going to do with it? Before you answer that, consider this idea. It is a twofold concept called **separation and individuation**. Margret Mahler had the idea that as children develop, they emotionally begin to "leave" (their parents) and become more independent. She called this change **separation**. Mahler believed that as children separated from their parents, they did not just move off into the world, never to be seen again. Of course, there was a physical component (manifest) to this separation, but the more crucial part was the emotional part (latent). She saw this part as a slow moving progression—with repeated starts and stops, leavings and returns—that continues until a new type of relationship develops between parent and child that is based more on **mutuality** and less on dependency. The child's growing comfort with this new reality she described as **individuation**.

Like Mahler's separation and individuation concept of child development, the goal of child psychotherapy (for child and parent) is increasing self-sufficiency. Your child and you do not achieve self-sufficiency in therapy in one fell swoop. It begins with a process of growing competency that includes feeling more comfortable with the idea of no longer seeing your child's therapist on a regular basis.

From this viewpoint, you and your child actually began separating from the therapist from the moment you said "yes" and started your child's psychotherapy. From that moment when you arrived with concerns and questions, you and your child began the process of learning, understanding, and healing. In psychotherapy terminology, the name given to these steps of separating and individuating—of gaining confidence, leaving therapy, and venturing out on one's own—are called **termination**.

"Termination" is the psychotherapy word that you will most likely hear from your child's therapist. However, we prefer to use the word "separation."

Separation conveys the idea that the psychotherapy experience does not end, but evolves into a new reality whose roots come from the psychotherapy experience. It speaks to the process of leaving therapy as akin to finishing a book that is part of a larger series of books or of graduating from a training program and then moving on to a related job. Second, for most people, and especially children, the idea of just ending contact with someone important in our lives can be painful. Common statements that help us avoid difficult feelings, such as "I hate long goodbyes" (which rush the endings) or "See you soon" (which evade the endings), represent our aversion to the whole idea of not seeing someone again. In reality, ending therapy has little connection to never seeing your therapist again. One can always make an appointment to see the therapist again in a physical sense.

Is it even realistic to think that this significant relationship just ends? It depends on how you define "end." Each therapy relationship includes the manifest connection and the latent connection. When we talk about terminating, we are talking about ending the manifest connection between your child and his/her therapist. We maintain that the conclusion of therapy sessions does represent the "end" of the therapy relationship, because the latent connection continues.

You and your child can continue to "use" the latent therapy experience well after you stop seeing the therapist. It's like remembering a past teacher or coach—someone who has had an effect on us that may last for a long period of time and that we may draw from whenever we choose. We call this process—of finding a lasting place within ourselves for what we have learned in therapy—**consolidation**. Consolidation is the final piece of therapeutic work that we accomplish. It is work completed without the physical contact with the therapist.

Abdul Is Impressive

Abdul was a 4-year-old boy living with his mother and his four sisters. Abdul was the middle child. Abdul's mother brought him to therapy to address what his day care workers described as compulsive behaviors and anxiety. Abdul was very quiet, and his mother worried that without his father around Abdul was becoming timid and weak. In sessions, Abdul built with Legos without speaking. The therapist built next to Abdul and remarked on his play without Abdul responding. When Abdul completed a Lego project, the therapist talked about it and always ended the comments with a statement, "That is impressive; you are impressive." They worked for several years, and this theme continued. Abdul's play changed and he began talking and feeling better. When Abdul turned 7, his mother and the therapist agreed that Abdul would leave therapy. They had several more sessions, and during these sessions, the therapist told Abdul that he was very impressed with how much Abdul had grown and changed, that he seemed stronger and more courageous. Then they said goodbye.

Three years later, the therapist received a call from Abdul's mother. Abdul had asked his mother if he could visit the therapist. The therapist agreed and they met for a session. Abdul was now in fourth grade and was bigger. He sat in the therapist's office and looked around. The therapist asked Abdul how he was doing, and Abdul replied, "I am impressive." He laughed and then they laughed together.

Abdul's therapy had ended years earlier, and yet he had remembered this word. It retained an importance to him that he could call on when he chose. When he thought about himself and his accomplishments, he felt "impressive"—big in a way that conveys strength, mastery, and confidence. Abdul had incorporated the therapist's affirmation that he was impressive. It became a consolidated part of him forever.

We think it is useful that you have an awareness of separation, *and your feelings about it*, because it has such relevance to this phase of your child's psychotherapy. The fact is that much of what we are doing as human beings is separating and individuating from something. We separate from our mother's body when we are born; then we separate from our parent's arms when we crawl and walk. Staying in school without our parents follows this stage. We begin to establish relationships with friends and partners that become as important, but distinct from, the one we share with our parents. We then have our own families and children that, although connected with our parents, are separate and independent from them. We separate so often that you would think it would be simple and straightforward by the time we reach adulthood, but we typically end up having a variety of complicated feelings, concerns, worries, regrets, guilt, and relief. We each have our own set of ambivalent (mixed) feelings about separation.

How would you answer these questions?

- How do you feel about your child leaving therapy?
- Do you feel that your child and you got enough out of your child's therapy?
- Are you pleased about the outcome?
- Are you ready for your child's therapy to be over?
- Are you going to miss your child being in therapy?

We believe that separating from therapy is a *process*, not a moment, and that effective separation from psychotherapy happens over time. We suggest avoiding sudden endings in order to give your child and you time to look back on all that you have been through—the changes, accomplishments, and difficulties.

When a worker leaves a job by choice, it is customary to give notice. The outgoing worker and the employer work out a set amount of time that the worker will remain at the job. This amount of time is a period of transition. During this transition, he is finishing up tasks, training a new worker, having parties, saying goodbyes, and so on. This is the manifest material of leaving a job.

Of course, as you may know by now, there is also the latent material of leaving a job. The memories of the work, the accomplishments and missteps, the time on the job—the worker thinks about all of these during this time of leaving. He may also have a variety of feelings about leaving. He may be feeling nervousness (Did I make the right choice to leave?), excitement (I can't wait for some time off), sadness (I will miss everyone), relief (I am exhausted from all this work), and maybe even anger (they can never replace me). Leaving a job is not just about the physical reality of no longer being at that job; it also is about what that time at his job meant to him and what it will mean to him in the future as he goes on to other jobs. He might receive a gift from his fellow workers. The gift will remind him of the good times, stories, and moments shared. The gift is called a **transitional object** because in a physical sense it bridges the past with the present. It softens the turmoil (loss and vulnerability) of separating from the previous familiar job and committing to a new and unknown job. The gift represents the friendship and warmth of the coworkers from the former job. It provides comfort to him on days when things might not go so well, support when he feels lonely, and encouragement when challenged. You can think about your child's favorite blanket or toy. These, too, are transitional objects, supporting your child as she or he separates and individuates.

Abby Finds Her Way

Abby was 11 years old when she began therapy. She entered therapy because she had a serious facial tic. She refused to go to school. Her mothers were ending their relationship and planning separate homes, but they were still having considerable conflict. She attended sessions for one year during which time she would build an obstacle course with pillows, chairs, tables, anything she could use to climb on or under or step on. At each session, the course would be different, and Abby would make her way around the room. The therapist would time her and they would keep her time on a chart.

A year after she started therapy, everyone agreed (the therapist, her parents, and Abby) that she would "graduate" from therapy when school ended. Her facial tic was effectively gone and only came back slightly when she was very nervous. She had several coping strategies to calm herself when she felt nervous. The mothers settled into separate homes. They retained joint custody and established a regular living situation schedule. Abby was sad to leave therapy and initially protested. Her facial tic returned, and the therapist and her parents agreed that they would say goodbye slowly. Over the next two months (8 sessions), Abby and her therapist discussed all that she had accomplished, looking at how her feelings of confidence steadily improved over the past year. They talked about the obstacle course. They made the "most complicated one yet." They remembered that she was "slow" when she had started and now she was "so fast."

The therapist acknowledged that he would miss her and gave her the obstacle course chart so that she would remember how she "just had to take her time to figure out where to go." The therapist made a copy with her so she could leave a copy with him, too. Both Abby and her therapist had their own transitional objects.

The reasons for ending a child's therapy and the steps of this separation process vary from child to child, from family to family. You and your child's therapist will discuss this process the same way that you have discussed all other aspects of your child's psychotherapy. In this case, the therapy had accomplished its goals, but Abby needed to separate slowly. She had already "lost" a version of her family, and she needed to feel more in control of leaving the therapist. Abby needed to consolidate the growth that she and her parents made while she was in therapy (the coping skills, increased confidence, increased security, etc.). The accomplishments and positive changes that you and your child make during psychotherapy are called the **therapeutic gains**.

THE NUTS AND BOLTS OF SEPARATING FROM YOUR CHILD'S PSYCHOTHERAPY

How do you know when it is time to enter this phase of your child's therapy? The answer is not always straightforward, but as always, communication is essential for this part of the psychotherapy process. Talking to your child's therapist is always the first step. You may have a general idea, based on any ongoing discussions you have been having in collateral appointments, but to make plans, we recommend that you bring it up directly with your child's therapist.

1. The Decision

Many factors influence the decision to start the termination process:

- *Treatment-related* (met goals, changed goals, reached a safe level of functioning)

  The optimal goal is for treatment to end when your child has met his or her treatment goals and has reached a level of day-to-day functioning that allows your child to perform and manage situations at home, at school, socially, and so on. Members of the treatment team can provide you with the input necessary to decide whether your child has reached this point.

Delmon Finally Speaks

Delmon was a depressed and anxious 11-year-old boy. His mother died of complications related to drug abuse when he was 8 years old, and his father brought him to therapy soon after. Delmon worked with his therapist for three years. When Delmon was in therapy, he chose not to speak to the therapist. He rarely spoke at school or at home and never spoke with the therapist. Eventually they figured out that Delmon and the therapist could write notes back and forth, and they did this for two years. One session, Delmon wrote that he was afraid that he was going to die just like this mother. The therapist wrote that having that thought would be very scary and that it was very brave of Delmon to share it. The therapist also wrote that his mother had been sick and that Delmon did not have his mother's illness. Soon after, Delmon began to speak in sessions, and he and his therapist discussed his feelings about his mother's death and missing her. Delmon began speaking more in school and was doing much better. His father and the therapist decided that Delmon's work with this therapist was finished for now. Delmon and his therapist spent four sessions going over their notes from the past three years. Looking back at the notes helped them identify the therapeutic gains that Delmon had made—speaking about his fears and grieving the loss of his mother. As a transitional object, the therapist created a folder of all their back and forth notes and gave them to Delmon at their last session. Delmon wrote a final note to the therapist saying thank you.

- *Logistics-related* (schedule changes, home life changes, environmental changes, financial changes)

When treatment comes to an end with a therapist without the treatment goals having been reached or without your child's situation having been stabilized to a degree with which you and your child's therapist are comfortable, the therapist will typically recommend (and is ethically bound to do so) that your child's treatment continue with another therapist. This process called a transfer, and it happens for many reasons:

a. Family is relocating;
b. Therapist is no longer available (change of setting, illness, pregnancy, life change);
c. Another setting is more suitable to address your child's needs (new facility, a specialty is needed);
d. Various logistical reasons (concrete issues such as money, distance, timing, etc.).

Let us look at a family that is relocating. Under these circumstances, it is the parent's responsibility to access further mental health care for his or her child. Moving is a time of considerable stress for you and your child. The change in environment from living quarters to neighborhood to school can and do place pressure on your child's coping and adjustment abilities. Naturally, therapists assist in identifying resources in the new community, but the required legwork often falls to the parent.

If treatment ends because the therapist becomes unavailable for a variety of reasons, it becomes the therapist's responsibility to identify and facilitate meeting with a new therapist. This can take many different forms.

The therapist can provide a list of names for you as the parent to contact and evaluate who you believe would be the best therapist for your child, following the process detailed in the early chapters of this book. At times, the therapist has a specific person in mind for your child. If this is the case, there are several questions for you to ask concerning this type of recommendation.

a. What is the special skill/training that this person has that you believe my child needs?
b. Why choose this person in particular?
c. Can you provide me with other therapist's names/contact information who are similar to the person you want my child to see?

If you choose to agree to the therapist's selection, the therapist may want to facilitate an in-person transfer. In this instance, you and your child meet the new therapist, introduced to you by the current therapist. This type of transfer often occurs in clinic settings. At times your child's current therapist believes that your child needs this type of **bridging** to enable her or him to connect with a new therapist. This attempts to address any possible feelings of disloyalty to, or abandonment by, the current therapist. The therapist is obligated to explain the reasons that she or he prefers this model of transfer.

Billy's Time to Grieve

Billy was 16 years old when his treatment for cancer was successfully completed. He worked with a therapist throughout his very aggressive medical treatment. The treatment pulled him out of school, away from his friends, and changed how his body functioned in many key ways. Billy was now cancer free and was looking forward to the future. By age 19, Billy became depressed as he remembered the many other children he befriended who had died. His therapist was pregnant and was about to go on maternity leave. Naturally, the interruption of his treatment due to his therapist's pregnancy made Billy more aware of the other losses in his life. His therapist believed that Billy needed the help of a therapist specially trained in helping grieving teenagers and that he could not wait for her to return to her practice. The former therapist explained that she did not have this training and felt that Billy needed to see a specialist, much as his pediatrician had sent Billy to see a specialist about cancer. His former therapist arranged to accompany him and essentially had a joint session about transferring Billy to this new therapist.

There are also times when, based on complex factors in your child's life, a transfer does not occur and treatment comes to an end without the treatment goals having been reached. In these situations, the goal of this stage of the therapy is to help you and your child know that returning to therapy at a later time (with his or her current therapist or another) is always an option.

Jenny Leaves Town

Jenny was a 17-year-old coming to therapy for problems related to her diagnosis of post-traumatic stress disorder. She was severely abused as a child and had been living with various foster families during her adolescence. She had been seeing her therapist for two years when she began having serious arguments with her current foster mother. She acknowledged that her foster mother was too controlling for her and that she was thinking about running away. The therapist knew that when Jenny turned 18 she had a decision to make about whether she was going to stay in foster care or not. Jenny and her therapist discussed her options. With her therapist's help, Jenny decided that instead of leaving abruptly and without warning, she would tell the agency that she was going to leave foster care when she reached her birthday. She had relatives in Florida, and they had indicated that she could live with them for a while. When Jenny turned 18, she left foster care, said goodbye to the therapist, and moved to Florida. For the next three years, on the anniversary of their last session together, Jenny called to give the therapist an update about how her life was going.

- *Child development–related* (refocused priorities, developmental needs have changed)

    Sometimes psychotherapy ends because your child has reached an end associated more with his or her development and less with the problems identified in the therapy. This can be driven by the innate need of the child to move from one developmental stage to the next in a clear and well-defined (in terms of boundaries) manner. The way that a child relates to a therapist in each developmental stage is unique to that stage. Maintaining a relationship with a therapist through the transition from one stage to the next can be too complex to keep the work of therapy moving forward. This is a natural time to end therapy with that particular therapist. Sometimes when the child is "ready" to resume therapy, it makes sense to begin with a new therapist.

Barry's Work Changes

Barry had struggled since he was very young with problems related to developmental delays. He had a therapist since he was 5 years old who initially diagnosed him with **pervasive developmental delay** *and then changed the diagnosis to Asperger's syndrome when he was 8 years old. Barry was in therapy because when he had tantrums, it was very difficult for his parents to calm him down. He liked therapy and played with Legos, building cars, trucks, and buses. He loved building with Legos and constructed creations both big and small. His therapist would ask questions about his cars, trucks, and buses and also would play with them when Barry said it was OK. As he got older, his therapist continued to use play therapy techniques to engage Barry in managing his frustration, communicating his feelings in a more complete way, and understanding the needs of others. When Barry was 11 years old, his therapist and his parents discussed the idea that with Barry moving toward puberty, adolescence, and junior high school, it was time to establish a new therapy frame. The therapist wanted Barry to talk more about his feelings in therapy and to move away from a play-based therapy, and thought that it might be easier to accomplish with a fresh start. The therapist recommended a colleague with a similar background, and over the next several months, Barry's therapist explained to Barry that the new therapist was for older kids and teenagers and that he was "graduating" from one therapy to a new one.*

- *Higher level of care–related* (the need for more structure and safety)

   The need for higher levels of care can result in the termination of treatment with the current therapist. This happens when the child's living situation changes—such as when the child enters a residential treatment center—and therapy continues with an onsite therapist at the center.

   At times, children require that therapy continue with a hospital-based outpatient psychiatry program. This may happen because the child may need hospitalization or re-hospitalization (also called partial hospitalization) because he or she has recurring symptoms that require the protection of an inpatient hospital unit. An outpatient psychiatry program means that your child will meet regularly with a psychiatrist and receives psychotherapy from a psychologist or clinical social worker in the program.

2. The Work
Each element of the termination process is designed to help your child retain the useful parts of his or her psychotherapy experience.

a. *Reminiscing*—examining where your child started compared to where he or she is right now. The comparison of beginning to end highlights progress and gives your child a useful perspective. It is similar to looking at old pictures. We remember how we used to feel "back then." Talking about the journey makes the abstract qualities (the relationships, the progress, the difficulties) of psychotherapy more concrete. The more concrete these elements are, the more they can be consolidated.

b. *Identifying therapeutic gains*—explicitly naming and describing the achievements that your child has made during her or his time in psychotherapy. Tailored for the age of your child, the therapist and your child will discuss and reinforce successes, **affirmations** (praise related to a positive attribute), learned coping skills, increased self-awareness, and self-care strategies. Your child's therapist and your child separately define these elements. It can also be very helpful for you to identify your ideas about the specific ways that your child has changed during his or her therapy and the ways that your relationship with your child may have changed.

c. *Giving the therapy a meaning*—describing what the significance is of your child's time in therapy. A theme or a general description of the overall relevance of the therapy experience can be valuable to your child as another way of retaining the memories of his or her time in therapy. "This made me feel stronger," or "we played with Legos and I made messes," or "I did not let you speak." Your child's therapist can also put meaning to the therapy experience. "You helped me see that children can be brave," or "You helped me understand how unfair it is for children who go through divorce."

Hildi and the Apology

Hildi was 16 years old and was in therapy for several years when her therapy ended because her mother was relocating out of state. Her parents separated while Hildi was in therapy and were going through a vicious divorce and custody fight. Hildi, as an only child, was always in the middle. She was very depressed when she saw her therapist. Her parents agreed to a short termination process and Hildi said goodbye to her therapist over two sessions. Five years later, Hildi called the therapist and left a voicemail message. She said that she did not want a call back, but that she was thinking about the therapist and wanted to hear the therapist's voicemail message again. In her message, she said that she was doing fine, that she was in college. She remarked that what she remembered most about therapy was that the therapist always said the word "sorry" and looked sad whenever Hildi was describing problems with her parents.

The "meaning" that Hildi gave to her therapy was that when people feel distress there are people who will express thoughtful understanding. In short, the meaning that Hildi gave to therapy experience was **empathy**.

d. *Creating a transitional object*—identifying a physical representation of the therapy experience can be a very helpful way for your child actually to hold on to the experience. The transitional object is a tangible thing that retains the essence of the time that your child and the therapist spent together. It is a direct connection to the therapy experience, like something that the therapist and your child used or created during the work. It can also be indirectly connected or representative of the work. In either case, the goal of a transitional object is that when your child handles or views it, he or she will be able to conjure feelings and/or concepts from the therapy as a support. In fact, you may already be using transitional objects with your child. Teddy bears, blankets, and pacifiers, to name a few, are all forms of transitional objects that address the feelings related to the separation from parents that all children experience. Transitional objects can be used at any time during the treatment when separation from the therapist may be complicated (difficult moments, vacations, etc.).

Hussain Plays Ball in Court

Hussain was 14 years old when his mother and his father's custody fight was heard in family court. He was very nervous about the proceedings and was talking about the possible outcomes with his therapist for weeks. He was required to testify about his thoughts about where he should live. He and his therapist discussed that it was important that he speak in court as a way of helping him feel more in control and older. The day before the hearing, Hussain told the therapist that he felt like he was having a panic attack. The therapist and Hussain played basketball with a Nerf ball during the session, and this activity helped Hussain calm himself. The therapist gave Hussain the ball and suggested that he take it to court. The therapist suggested that he hold it while the lawyers and the judge asked him the questions and that he think about their basketball game if he became nervous.

e. *Making the relationship more real*—establishing a more accurate way for your child to know his or her therapist makes the relationship more real. The process involves the therapist sharing some details about him- or herself during the termination stage. We call this act of providing personal information **self-disclosure**. Therapists typically hold self-disclosure to a minimum, as the therapy can lose its focus and boundaries otherwise. Adapted for the age of your child, the therapist can self-disclose some limited personal information that may enhance your child's ability to recall. Your child has created a variety of ideas about his or her therapist during the course of the therapy—ideas about the therapist's life outside the session room and what the therapist may be thinking about your child. These are abstract ideas because the therapist may not have confirmed or denied them. Making some of these ideas real—concrete—makes them, and the therapist, easier to hold on to. My therapist has children. My therapist lives in an apartment. My therapist learned from me that children could be strong and cry at the same time. Like the transitional object, the more real something is, the more a child can retain it.

Arnette Sings One Final Performance

Arnette was an 8-year-old girl when her foster mother and the foster agency decided that Arnette needed to go to a therapist's office that was an easier trip for her family. The trip to the therapist was too difficult for the foster mother to make regularly, and Arnette was missing sessions. Arnette was very sad to be leaving. During her work with the therapist, Arnette informed the therapist that she wanted to be a singer. She said that her foster brother and foster sister thought that she had a terrible voice and that they made fun of her when she sang. In sessions, Arnette asked the therapist to play specific songs from the computer and she sang along. The therapist clapped and praised her performance when she finished. In their last session, Arnette sang a Disney song. When it was finished, the therapist clapped and then disclosed to Arnette that the therapist's daughter loved that song and often sang it, too. The therapist told Arnette that from now on, each time he heard his daughter sing that song, he would also think of Arnette.

3. The Duration

You have choices to make regarding how long the termination process continues. The therapist can make recommendations about the length of time he or she believes will be sufficient to accomplish the work of separating. The choices that we make about time provided for separating connect with how we feel about separating. We can feel sad, angry, excited, or a combination of these emotions, and these feelings can shape our decision-making. If we are aware of these feelings, then we can balance the pull of the feelings with the pull of our children's therapeutic needs and optimize the benefits of the experience and the therapeutic gains.

The rule of thumb is three sessions per year of treatment. This number can change based on your child's situation. For example, if your child has suffered from losses, then we would recommend increasing the duration.

POTENTIAL COMPLICATIONS WITH SEPARATING

As you can see, all your choices have an influence on how your child and you are going to remember the psychotherapy experience. Depending on your child's age, developmental stage, and problems, you and the therapist can make decisions about what to consider when structuring the termination process. There are several situations that require "cautious" thoughtfulness and attention.

Hasty Separation

A separation process that is too brief may not leave the therapist, your child, and you enough time to do to the work of saying goodbye. We model how to say goodbye. Helping them understand the benefits and rewards of a thoughtful farewell can reduce discomfort in the future.

Separation can be disruptive to a child. The internal chaos of a rapid change can destabilize a child. The loss of a known structure causes this distress. We see this at the start of summer vacations and the start of school each year—children struggle and their parents struggle until the achievement of a new balance. A paced termination reduces the possibility of difficulty by building the transition into the separation process. Your child goes through the goodbye process with the support of the therapist and does not have to manage it on his or her own.

Unforeseen and Sudden Separation

It may come to pass that your child's psychotherapy ends abruptly for unfortunate reasons that (1) you may not have planned for or predicted (illness, sudden move, death, etc.), and (2) no other options exist but to end. The repercussions of this type of separation are difficult to forecast accurately, but we imagine that your child will have a reaction. We suggest that you expect both manifest and latent communication regarding the sudden loss of the relationship to occur. Under these circumstances, you can act as proxy for the therapist and engage your child in the process of separating from the therapy, after the fact, taking your child through the steps of reminiscing, identifying therapeutic gains, giving meaning, and creating a transitional object.

Therapist-Generated Separation

Although it may seem obvious, it is important to mention that therapists end child psychotherapy at times for personal reasons. This is similar to a patient-driven termination. The difference is that it typically includes an active hand-over process in which your child's therapist will be involved in finding and transitioning your child to another therapist if you choose to continue your child's treatment.

The Irreparable Empathic Break

At times, despite the therapist's efforts to repair an empathic break, the therapeutic relationship is no longer effective. Whether the original empathic break was due to an error by the therapist, the child's or parent's distortion, or a mis-understanding among all involved parties, sometimes the only remedy is for the parent to seek a consultation with another therapist.

The consulting therapist may

- suggest some ideas of how to heal the empathic break, or
- determine that exploration and resolution needs to take place within a new therapeutic relationship with a new therapist.

It is important for you to continue your child's therapy following an empathic break. Your child's original need for therapy stands separate from the current difficulties with the therapist that you and your child may be experiencing. Moving your child's treatment to a new therapist does not mean that the treatment with the previous therapist is invalid or "a waste." Rather, the new therapy can preserve and build on the gains from the previous therapy. If you or your child experience an irreparable empathic break, it remains important for both of you to have an official last session with the current therapist.

FUTURE CONTACT

We have mentioned this before, but ending the therapy does not necessarily mean the end of contact with your child's therapist. For many reasons, you and your child can have contact with the therapist. Prior to the end of regular sessions, contact with your child's therapist, checking in and evaluating progress and consolidation of therapeutic gains from the therapy meetings, are scheduled. If there are no formal plans, you can informally contact the therapist with questions and updates. You can also re-establish therapy at any time.

Most therapists believe that once they are someone's therapist, then they are always that person's therapist. This is important because the end of the therapy relationship does not mean that the relationship becomes a fundamentally different type of relationship, like a friendship or another type of social relationships. This is a helpful distinction for your child to understand if there are some questions regarding future interactions.

The one rule is that, unless other arrangements are made, you and/or your child are responsible for initiating all contact with the therapist after your child's sessions are concluded. If you and/or your child want or need to contact the therapist, the impetus comes from you. The rule of refraining from initiating contact by the therapist is not a sign of disinterest. It is a respecting of boundaries and an honoring of the inherent power differential in the therapist-child relationship.

So, let us get back to the question of what you are going to do with this book now that you have finished reading it. Knowing what you now know about separating, endings, and termination, how are you going to manage the process of "putting this book down?" Do you feel like you have more control now that you have read it? Can you put it into words? We hope you will keep it around, will use it when you need it, and will pass on the ideas if you think they would be helpful to others. We are both parents and psychotherapists. We wrote this book because we believe that the stronger parents feel and the more they know, the better it is for their children.

CHAPTER SUMMARY

CHAPTER 16: SEPARATING AND CONSOLIDATION: SAYING GOODBYE TO YOUR CHILD'S PSYCHOTHERAPIST

Leaving therapy is called **termination**; however, we prefer to use the word **separation**.

A primary end goal of child psychotherapy (for child and parent) is increased self-sufficiency.

Finding a lasting place for what has been learned in therapy is called **consolidation**.

The accomplishments and positive changes that you and your child make during psychotherapy are called the **therapeutic gains**.

We believe that separating from therapy is a *process*, not a specific moment in time, and that effective separation from psychotherapy happens over time. We suggest avoiding sudden endings to give you and your child time to look back on all that you have been through—the changes, accomplishments, and difficulties.

The Decision—factors that influence the decision to terminate treatment:

- *Treatment-related* (met goals, changed goals, reached a safe level of functioning, empathic break leads to transition to new therapist)

- *Logistics-related* (schedule changes, home life changes, environmental changes, financial changes)
- *Child development–related* (refocused priorities, developmental needs have changed)
- *Higher level of care–related* (where the child's treatment continues with a new therapist associated with the child's new living situation)

The Work—each element of the termination process is designed to help your child retain the useful parts of his or her psychotherapy experience.

- *Reminiscing*—examining where your child started, compared to where you are right now;
- *Identifying therapeutic gains*—explicitly naming and describing the achievements that your child has made during her or his time in psychotherapy;
- *Giving the therapy a meaning*—describing what the significance is of your child's time in therapy;
- *Creating a transitional object*—identifying a physical representation of the therapy experience can be a very helpful way for your child to actually hold on to the experience;
- *Making the relationship more real*—establishing a more accurate way that your child knows his or her therapist.

The Duration—three sessions per year of treatment.

APPENDIX A
Case Studies

Introduction: A Framework and Rationale for This Book
Frank and Henry's Battle at Bedtime
A Child Gets Lost

Chapter 1: A Holistic Perspective of Child Psychotherapy
Max Blames Himself
Jane and Steve Look for a Therapist

Chapter 2: Systems-Based Approach to Child Psychotherapy: Working Together
Talking to Paul's Babysitter
Anxious LaShawn and Her Teachers

Chapter 3: Seeking Out a Child Psychotherapist
Tabitha Needs Her Insurance
Insurance Weighs in on Jed's Therapy

Chapter 4: The First Session: Consultation and Intake Meetings
Talking to Charlie (Age 5) About Therapy
Shannon and Becky (Age 10) Talk About Therapy
Jonathan (Age 15) and His Mother Discuss Beginning Therapy
Reggie Presents Therapy Options to Rebecca (Age 17)
Clarence (Age 22) Listens to His Grandmother Betty

Chapter 15: Higher Levels of Care: When You and Your Child Need More
  Leroy Tries Different Levels of Outpatient Services
  Figuring Out Yvgeny's Rage
  Suraj Dries Out
  Ricky's Sadness
  Alma's Anxiety
  Craig's Paranoia

Chapter 16: Separation and Consolidation: Saying Goodbye to Your Child's Psychotherapist
  Abdul Is Impressive
  Abby Finds Her Way
  Delmon Finally Speaks
  Billy's Time to Grieve
  Jenny Leaves Town
  Barry's Work Changes
  Hildi and the Apology
  Hussain Plays Ball in Court
  Arnette Sings One Final Performance

APPENDIX B

Recommended Readings

Here are several books from the theorists that we make reference to in this book. These are all seminal works, and if you are interested in digging more deeply into some of the concepts that we have presented, these are good places to start.

Erikson, E. (1968) *Identity, Youth and Crisis*. New York: Norton.

Horney, K. (1951) *Neurosis and Human Growth*. London: Routledge and Kegan Paul.

Mahler, M., Pine, F. & Bergman, A. (1975) *The Psychological Birth of the Human Infant*. New York: Basic Books.

Maslow, A. (1968) *Toward a Psychology of Being* (2nd Edition). Princeton, NJ: Van Nostrand.

Rogers, C. (1995) *On Becoming a Person*. New York: Houghton Mifflin (Reprint 1961).

Thomas, A., & Chess, S. (1977) *Temperament and Development*. New York: Brunner/Mazel.

Winnicott, D. W. (1963) *Maturational Process and Facilitating Environment*. Madison, CT: International Universities Press.

APPENDIX C

Child Mental Health Services Contact Information by State

ALABAMA
Website: http://www.mh.alabama.gov/UT/FindServices.aspx
Telephone: 1-800-367-0955 (Toll-free in Alabama)

ALASKA
Website: http://dhss.alaska.gov/dbh/
Telephone: 1-800-465-4828 (Toll-free in Juneau)
1-800-770-3930 (Toll-free in Anchorage)
1-907-451-5042 (in Fairbanks)

ARIZONA
Website: http://www.azdhs.gov/bhs/
Telephone: 1-602-542-1025 (General Information)
1-602-364-4558 (Behavioral Services)

ARKANSAS
Website: http://humanservices.arkansas.gov/dbhs/Pages/ChildrensServices.
   aspx
Telephone: 1-501-686-9164
1-501-686-9176 (TTY)

CALIFORNIA
Website: http://www.dhcs.ca.gov/services/Pages/MentalHealthPrograms-
   Svcs.aspx
Telephone: 1-916-440-7800

COLORADO
Website: http://www.colorado.gov/cs/Satellite/CDHSBehavioralHealth/
CBON/1251578892077
Telephone: 1-303-866-7400

CONNECTICUT
Website: http://www.ct.gov/dmhas/
Telephone: 1-800-446-7348
1-860-418-6707 (Hearing Impaired)

DELAWARE
Website: http://dhss.delaware.gov/dhss/dsamh/mental_health_cmhc.html
Telephone: For Mental Health Services
1-302-778-6900 (New Castle County-Wilmington)
1-302-857-5060 (Dover)
1-302-856-5490 (Sussex)

FLORIDA
Website: http://www.myflfamilies.com/service-programs/mental-health
Telephone: 1-866-762-2237
1-800-955-8771 (TTY)

GEORGIA
Website: http://dbhdd.georgia.gov/office-child-adolescent-mental-health
Telephone: 1-800-715-4225

HAWAII
Website: http://health.hawaii.gov/camhd/
Telephone: 1-808-733-9333

IDAHO
Website: http://www.healthandwelfare.idaho.gov/Medical/MentalHealth/
ChildrensMentalHealth/tabid/314/Default.aspx
Telephone: 1-800-926-2588

ILLINOIS
Website: http://www.dhs.state.il.us/page.aspx?item=29728
Telephone: 1-800-843-6154
1-800-447-6404 (TTY)
1-312-814-5050 (TTY)

INDIANA
Website: http://www.in.gov/fssa/dmha/4450.htm
Telephone: 1-800-901-1133
711 (for individuals who are deaf, hard of hearing or speech impaired)

IOWA
Website: http://www.dhs.state.ia.us/mhdd/
Telephone: 1-800-972-2017 (General Information)
1-800-735-2942 (TTY)

KANSAS
Website: http://www.acmhck.org/about-us/cmhc-directory/
Telephone: 1-785-234-4773 (Assoc. of Community Mental Health Centers of
   Kansas, Inc.)

KENTUCKY
Website: http://dbhdid.ky.gov/dbh/programs-child.aspx
Telephone: 1-502-564-4456
1-502-564-5777 (TTY)

LOUISIANA
Website: http://www.dhh.louisiana.gov/index.cfm/page/97/n/116
Telephone: 1-225-342-2540 (Louisiana Behavioral Health Partnership-
   General #)
1-337-262-4190 (Acadiana Area Mental Health Services)
1-225-922-2700 (Capital Area)
1-318-487-5191 (Central Louisiana)
1-985-543-4333 (Florida Parishes)
1-337-475-3100 (Imperial Calcasieu)
1-504-838-5215 (Jefferson Parish)
1-504-568-3130 (Metropolitan)
1-318-362-3270 (Northeast Delta)
1-318-862-3085 (Northwest Louisiana)
1-985-858-2931 (South Central Louisiana)

MAINE
Website: http://www.maine.gov/dhhs/ocfs/cbhs/index.shtml
Telephone: 1-207-624-7900
1-888-568-1112 (Crisis Hotline Services)
711 (TTY)

MARYLAND

Website: https://mmcp.dhmh.maryland.gov/chp/SitePages/Home.aspx
http://www.montgomerycountymd.gov/HHS/index.html (Health Services ->
Child & Adolescent Mental Health – For Montgomery County)

MASSACHUSETTS

Website: http://www.mass.gov/eohhs/gov/commissions-and-initiatives/cbhi/
cbhi-contact-information.html

MICHIGAN

Website: https://www.michigan.gov/mdch/ (click on Behavioral Health &
Developmental Disability)
Telephone: 1-517-373-3740

MINNESOTA

Website: http://mn.gov/dhs/ (People We Serve -> Children & Families ->
Health Care)
Telephone: 1-651-431-2000
1-800-627-3529 (TTY)

MISSISSIPPI

Website: http://www.dmh.ms.gov/service-options/mental-health/children-and-
youth-services/
Telephone: 1-877-210-8513

MISSOURI

Website: http://dmh.mo.gov/programs.htm
Telephone: 1-800-364-9687

MONTANA

Website: http://www.dphhs.mt.gov/mentalhealth/children/information.
shtml
Telephone: 1-406-444-4545

NEBRASKA

Website: http://dhhs.ne.gov/behavioral_health/Pages/beh_mh_childmh.aspx
Telephone: 1-888-866-8660
1-888-556-5117 (TTY)

NEVADA

Website: http://www.dcfs.state.nv.us/DCFS_ChildMentalHealth.htm
Telephone: 1-775-684-4400

NEW HAMPSHIRE
Website: http://www.dhhs.state.nh.us/dcbcs/bbh/
Telephone: 1-603-271-4440 (Child Youth & Families)
1-800-852-3345 ex 5000 (Behavioral Health)
1-800-735-2964 (TTY)

NEW JERSEY
Website: http://www.nj.gov/dcf/
Telephone: 1-877-652-7624
1-866-896-6975 (TTY)

NEW MEXICO
Website: http://cyfd.org/behavioral-health
Telephone: 1-505-827-8008

NEW YORK
Website: http://www.cmhny.org/agencies.html (NYS Coalition of Children's Mental Health Services
http://www.omh.ny.gov/omhweb/childservice/ (NYS Office of Mental Health)
http://www.childrensaidsociety.org/health-counseling/ mental-health-services (Children's Aid Society)
Telephone: 1-518-436-8715 (NYS Coalition of Children's Mental Health Services)
1-800-597-8481 (NYS Office of Mental Health)
1-212-949-4800 (Children's Aid Society)

NORTH CAROLINA
Website: http://www.ncdhhs.gov/MHDDSAS/providers/childandfami-lymhs/index.htm
Telephone: (919) 715-2774 (Main SOC #)
Local numbers are based on the System of Care Coordinator in client's area

NORTH DAKOTA
Website: http://www.nd.gov/dhs/services/mentalhealth/children.html
Telephone: 1-800-472-2622 (General Info)
1-800-366-6888 (TTY)
Local numbers are based on the Partnership Program Contact Person in client's area

OHIO
Website: http://mha.ohio.gov/Default.aspx?tabid=279
Telephone: 1-614-466-2596
1-614-752-9696 (TTY)

OKLAHOMA
Website: http://ok.gov/odmhsas/Mental_Health_/index.html
http://integrisok.com/children-mental-health (INTEGRIS)
Telephone: 1-800-522-9054
1-405-522-3851 (TTY)

OREGON
Website: http://www.oregon.gov/oha/amh/Pages/child-mh-soc-in-plan-grp/
main.aspx
Telephone: 1-503-945-5763

PENNSYLVANIA
Website: http://www.dpw.state.pa.us/forchildren/omhsas/index.htm
Telephone: 1-800-692-7462 (Department of Public Welfare – General #)
1-717-705-8289 (Bureau of Behavioral Health)

RHODE ISLAND
Website: http://www.bhddh.ri.gov/MH/application.php
Telephone: 1-401-462-3291

SOUTH CAROLINA
Website: http://www.state.sc.us/dmh/center_inpatient.htm
Telephone: 1-803-898-8581
1-864-297-5130 (TTY)
1-866-246-0129 (TTY) Upstate
1-866-246-0130 (TTY) Midlands

SOUTH DAKOTA
Website: http://dss.sd.gov/behavioralhealthservices/community/
Telephone: 1-800-265-9684

TENNESSEE
Website: http://tamho.org/service.php (Tennessee Assoc. of Mental
Health Orgs.)
Telephone: 1-615-532-6500 (Dept. of Mental Health & Substance Abuse
Services)

TEXAS
Website: http://www.dshs.state.tx.us/mhsa/mh-child-adolescent-services/
Telephone: 1-888-963-7111 (Dept. of State Health Services
1-800-735-2989 (TTY)

UTAH
Website: http://hs.utah.gov/overview/youth-services/
Telephone: 1-801-538-4171

VERMONT
Website: http://mentalhealth.vermont.gov/cafu
Telephone: 1-888-212-4677

VIRGINIA
Website: http://www.dbhds.virginia.gov/OMH-default.htm
http://www.dbhds.virginia.gov/LPSS/LPSS.aspx (Licensed Providers)
Telephone: 211 (Toll Free Health and Human Service Specialist)

WASHINGTON
Website: http://www.dshs.wa.gov/dbhr/childrensmentalhealth.shtml
http://www.dshs.wa.gov/dbhr/childrensbehavioralhealth.shtml
Telephone: 211 (Toll Free Health and Human Service Specialist)

WASHINGTON, DC
Website: http://dmh.dc.gov/service/children-youth-and-family-services
http://dmh.dc.gov/node/119532 (Licensed Providers)
Telephone: 1-202-673-7440
1-202-673-7500 (TTY)

WEST VIRGINIA
Website: http://www.dhhr.wv.gov/bhhf/sections/programs/Programs
    Partnerships/ChildandAdolescent/Pages/ChildAdolescent
    BehavioralHealth.aspx
Telephone: 1-304-558-0627 (Office of Behavioral Health)
1-304-356-4811 (Bureau for Behavioral Health and Health Facilities)

WISCONSIN
Website: http://www.dhs.wisconsin.gov/MH_BCMH/index.htm
Telephone: 1-608-266-1865
1-888-701-1251 (TTY)

WYOMING

Website: http://www.health.wyo.gov/mhsa/treatment/waiverindex.html
http://www.health.wyo.gov/mhsa/treatment/MHprovidermap.html (Mental
Health Providers by County)
Telephone: 1-800-535-4006 (Behavioral Health Division)

GLOSSARY

This glossary expands on the definitions the reader finds within the book chapters. The definitions reflect the authors' ideas and points of view and are not meant to be the definitive explanations of these terms. Other books include definitions of these terms that reflect different ideas and points of view.

A

The Affordable Care Act (ACA) = Healthcare reform legislation to assist people without work-connected medical insurance to afford to purchase it on their own. Among the features of the legislation is parity (equality) between medical and mental health coverage. Prior to this legislation, most medical insurance policies covered mental health care at much lower rates and with more restrictions than medical care

Accountable Care Organizations (ACO) = Medical insurance vendors created by the Affordable Care Act

Activity play therapy = A type of play therapy that involves sports, games, and craft projects as a way to assist traditional talk therapy

Adherence/Adhere = In this book, used to indicate following as planned or as discussed; to comply or compliance

Affect/Affective = Feelings, emotions, or the expression of emotions

Affirmation = Identifying a characteristic, aspect, or quality in a person, making them aware of it and specifically praising it

Age-appropriate language = Language that is chosen to be clear and understandable in relation to the child's age and cognitive (thinking) abilities

Ambivalence = A mixture of feelings that may be in conflict with each other

Analytic play therapy = A type of play therapy following the concepts of Sigmund Freud and other therapists who further developed his ideas. Typically, in this type of play therapy, the therapist is an observer of the child's play, providing undivided attention and comments. Play, itself, is the language of the child's communication to the therapist

Analytic psychodynamic therapy = A type of talk therapy following the concepts of Sigmund Freud and other therapists who further developed his ideas. Analytic theory focuses on how one's historical and emotional past shape current feelings, thoughts, and actions

Anxiety = Level of worry that does not respond to a change of circumstance, active comforting, or reassurance. The person is unable to think of anything else but her or his worries, making it difficult for the person to attend to other tasks and/or issues

Assent (age of) = Describes providing under-age (under 18) children with enough information to be aware of decisions made for them by parents and caregivers

Attachment = Level of emotional connection that supports the individual's self-esteem

Autonomy = Separateness and individuality that help an individual make his or her own decisions, plans, and choices

B

Behavioral therapy = A type of talk therapy that believes that learned behaviors and reactions shape one's thoughts and feelings. Helping a person change behavior or reactions can change one's thoughts and feelings to be more productive and healthier

Boundary/Boundaries = Emotional and physical separateness among individuals that respects each as individuals with her or his own thoughts, feelings, and needs

Bridging = A part of some transfer processes whereby the current therapist is present for part of the session when the client meets the new therapist

C

Cognitive behavioral play therapy = Type of play therapy that enables the therapist to refocus and redirect a child's play to more productive and healthier images, symbols, and choices

Cognitive behavior therapy = Talk therapy that focuses on altering thoughts and behaviors as a way of creating a change environment for more productive and healthier reactions and choices

Collateral(s) = Therapist's contact and/or meetings with important non-family individuals in the child's life that can include but are not limited to teachers, other mental health professionals, doctors, and other healthcare professionals with the parent's consent

Cognitive = Referring to thinking or thought process

Compromised decision-making = Choices or options unduly influenced by other people or outside forces

Confidentiality = A concept where material discussed in therapy, including play material, is not shared with others without the individual's written consent, except in situations where the individual is a danger to her- or himself or others

Conscious play material = Play activities that are planned, intended, thought of, and easily explained by the child

Consent (age of) = A person 18 years of age or older has the right to make informed and knowledgeable decisions about his or her life, options, and choices

Consolidation = Final step of integration (*see* integration) of an experience in which the experience becomes a part of the individual. Person's feelings, thoughts, and/or behaviors are changed or altered permanently

Consultation = An exploratory meeting focused on offering an opinion, advice, or suggestion

Containment = Proactive protection of an individual from unhealthy or unproductive feelings, thoughts, and/or behaviors

Cultural norms = Options, behaviors, and expectations of a specific society, group, community, or organization, often enforced by those in power positions on the less powerful

Custodial parent = A parent who has legal rights and responsibilities to provide day-to-day care of the child

D

Depression = A feeling state that can cause a person to neglect one's personal hygiene and to withdraw from relationships and social situations, can cause irritability, impairs day-to-day functioning at work/school, and often is associated with feelings of helplessness and hopelessness. Can often include feelings of self-criticism, self-hate, and/or self-loathing

Desensitization = Individual no longer reacts to a distressing experience, feeling, thought, and/or behavior with the same intensity

Developmental stages = Refers to a child's process of physical, cognitive (thinking), and emotional growth and maturation that is divided into phases that coincide with age ranges in which the maturation typically takes place

Diagnosis/Diagnosing = A label describing (or the process of describing) a condition, problem, or illness using agreed-upon indications and descriptions

Disclosure = Sharing information, typically of a personal and at times sensitive nature

Displacement = Feelings and thoughts about an individual, situation, experience, or event are shifted to/onto another or different individual and/or unrelated situation, experience, or event

Distraction = A change in focus and/or attention away from a person's current thoughts, feelings, and/or behaviors

Double-bind communication = Confusing set of commands, requests, questions, and/or expectations that are contradictory in nature

E

Empathy = Feeling *with* and/or as if you had a similar feeling as the other person, connecting with his or her feelings in a sincere manner. Sympathy is feeling *for* an individual and tends to disconnect you from him or her

Engagement = Establishing and nurturing a relationship based on respect, acceptance, and a non-judgmental attitude

Evidence-based treatment(s) = Research-based process of helping a person, often using a manual, to preserve consistency of the process

Expressive Therapies = Using art (drawing, painting, sculpting), music (playing, listening, singing), movement (dance, posture training), writing (journaling, poetry), and/or other creative activities that enable the individual to express thoughts, feelings, and/or behaviors that may be difficult to put into words

H

Holistic perspective = A way of understanding a person, problem, or situation that is highly inclusive of all related and contributing factors. This is beyond being comprehensive, but rather is a philosophy of seeing and valuing the interconnectedness of mind, body, relationships with others, one's place in the world, culture, faith, and nature

Humanistic model = A way of understanding an individual that focuses on his or her strengths and abilities and seeks to find ways to further enhance them

I

Individuation = Process of becoming a separate individual with his or her own thoughts, feelings, and needs, different from the parents or other caregivers

Intake = A meeting that explores, assesses, and reviews an individual's concerns, thoughts, feelings, and behaviors in order to achieve an initial comprehensive understanding of the individual

Integration = Taking something in, remembering it, and applying it to thoughts, feelings, and/or behaviors, as it is easily found/located in your mind when needed

Intervention = An action, comment, suggestion, and/or recommendation focused on helping an individual with and/or to better understand a problem, concern, thought, feeling, and/or behavior

K

Kinetic = Physical movements of the body

Kinship parent = A foster parent who shares some level of "blood" relationship with the foster child

L

Latency age = Children older than toddlers and younger than the beginning of puberty

Latent (content) = Hidden, underneath, not consciously known

Law guardian = A person appointed by a judge to represent a child's interests during a court proceedings or hearing

M

Manifest (content) = Concrete, actual, surface, consciously known

Master/Mastery = A combination of confidence and ability

Medical model = A way of understanding an individual that focuses on symptoms, diagnosis, treatment, and cure

Mental status = Ability or inability to use good judgment and be in touch with/connected to reality

Mentor/Mentoring = Individual is a role model, demonstrating feelings, thoughts, and/or behaviors different from those familiar to the mentee, enriching the mentee's life with additional positive experiences, at times educational in nature, focused on nurturing the mentee's self-esteem

Mood = Overall emotional state that shifts and changes due to internal and/or external thoughts and feelings, frequently affecting most aspects of daily life

Mutual/Mutuality = Shared by both people in a relationship and/or for the benefit or benefiting both people in the relationship

N

Nervous/Nervousness = Refers to a person who is worried about a recent external event or situation and responds to support, comfort, and/or advocacy

Neurological = referring to the way the brain works

Non-custodial parent = Legal parent who does not have the rights or exercise the responsibilities for the day-to-day care of the child

Nonverbal communication = Sharing information without words but rather by behavior, actions, body/hand movements, facial expressions, and/or sounds

Normalize/Normalizing = Reassurance that a decision, choice, feeling, thought, and/or behavior is typical, expected, or anticipated in relation to an event, situation, or experience

O

Organic/Organicity = Refers to a difficulty, problem, or impairment that relates to some alteration or damage to the brain

P

Parent collateral = Therapist's meeting with the parent to discuss the child and the treatment, to update the current situation while providing education and support to the parent

Person-in-Environment model = Understanding an individual and her or his decisions, choices, feelings, thoughts, and/or behaviors within the context of the family, community, and culture

Phobia = Irrational intense fear of external items (i.e., snakes), and/or situations (i.e., heights) that are seen as a displacement (*see* displacement) from a traumatic (*see* trauma) event

Presenting problem(s) = Initial reason(s), situation(s), and/or concern(s) that resulted in the referral for psychotherapy

Pre-verbal = Refers to the phase of infancy when the child does not have words or language skills but communicates with facial expressions and noises

Primary caregiver = Individual in the child's life who provides the majority of the child's day-to-day care

Progression = Moving forward, spreading, and/or increasing

Projection = Individual assumes the other person has feelings and thoughts that the individual is actually having her- or himself

Projective test = One of the ways psychologists evaluate a person's thoughts and feelings. The individual is shown or draws a set of consistent images and is asked to react to them. Projective tests have a grading key based on large numbers of research subjects to generalize what is a typical or expected response to the image

Psychodynamic play therapy = A type of play therapy where the therapist joins in but does not alter or change the child's play while commenting on and asking questions about the play

Psychotropic medication = Chemical compounds that act on the brain and are thought to alter the chemical balance within the brain and/or decrease/diminish certain thoughts and feelings related to a psychiatric diagnosis

R

Rage = Intense combative and aggressive distress, usually caused by past hurts and pain, projected onto a recent situation, event, or relationship

Regression = Returning to a past and/or earlier time/age demonstrated by thoughts, feelings, and/or behaviors

Relational (object relations) psychodynamic therapy = Talk therapy where the relationship between the therapist and individual is the focus of the therapy as a way of assisting individuals to recover, cope, adjust, and/or adapt to past unsuccessful relationships

S

Self-determination = Able to make one's own plans, decisions, and choices without the interference, biases, or judgments of another

Self-esteem = The way a person thinks of her- or himself, either favorably or unfavorably, in comparison to others and influenced by defining experiences, either positive or negative

Self-referential = Thoughts, feelings, and/or behaviors of the individual based on that individual's needs to the exclusion of others

Separation = Understanding one's self as a different person from the parent, not identical with the parent

Sexual abuse = Use of sexual contact, behaviors, and/or exposure to control, harass, humiliate, hurt, intimidate, and/or menace an emotionally and/or physically less powerful person against her or his will or through seduction or exploitation

Single case agreement = Negotiated rate of coverage for medical or mental health coverage for one individual patient with a provider that is not connected to the medical insurer

Social Security Administration = Federal entitlement program providing financial support to a retired or disabled covered person or the surviving spouse and minor-aged children of a deceased covered person

Splitting = Gathering multiple opinions, suggestions, directions but choosing none of them while, simultaneously creating conflict and confusion between individuals and/or professionals by providing distorted and different accounts of one's situation or problems to each

Stigma = Aspect of a person that is devalued, discriminated against, and/or rejected by others

Strength/Strengths = Aspects of a person, either an ability, characteristic, talent, and/or skill that supports/enables quality of life and healthy/productive choices

Subconscious = Not consciously known, under or below one's awareness

Subconscious play material = Aspects of play under or below the child's awareness

Supervision = Monitoring an individual or process to ensure safety, consistency, and/or quality control

Supplemental Security Income (SSI) = Additional federal entitlement for people covered by Social Security who are under the poverty line. Also for people with disability under the retirement phase

Support = Providing comfort, help, advice, direction, suggestions to another person that helps him or her be more effective/successful

Symbolic = Thoughts, feelings, and/or behaviors that have a hidden or unintended meaning, often without the individual's awareness (*see* latent; *see* subconscious)

Symbolized = Feelings that an individual puts into words for the first time, shares them with another person, and the individual experiences an empathic (*see* empathy) response from the other

System = Organizing principle or entity that often uses a hierarchy with defined roles and responsibilities for the people within it

T

Temperament = Describes the typical emotional expressions and reactions of the child that she or he demonstrated in infancy

Termination = Ending the psychotherapy process without the intention of resuming it again for some time; can either be planned (optimal) or unplanned

Therapeutic gains = Healthy/productive changes in thoughts, feelings, and/or behaviors related to the psychotherapy process

Therapeutic milieu = Specialized environment focused on helping, supporting, and protecting the individual, using policies and procedures that rely on psychotherapeutic concepts

Therapeutic play = educational/instructional play that helps prepare a child for a situation or experience to occur in the near future or helps a child understand and discuss a situation or experience that has recently occurred

Transfer = Psychotherapy continues with another therapist due to the termination of psychotherapy with the previous therapist

Transference = Analytic concept that describes the thoughts and feelings a person develops for his or her therapist based on the person's past experiences with other relationships, particularly those from childhood

Transformation = Results of a significant change in a person's thoughts, feelings, and or behaviors. A person is altered (not the same as before) and establishes a new typical everyday manner of being (new normal)

Transition of care = Period of time granted by a medical insurer to a patient working with a therapist not covered by the insurer until the patient transfers to a therapist covered by the insurer

Transitional object = Item that represents or evokes an emotional connection to another person or experience

Trauma = Event, situation, or experience that overwhelms the emotional coping abilities of the individual, at times resulting in long-term feelings of fear and lack of safety

Treatment goals = Refers to the hoped for and agreed upon short-term and long-term outcomes of psychotherapy

Treatment plan = Outline or "road map" of the steps to be taken to achieve the hoped for and agreed upon short-term and long-term goals of psychotherapy

Treatment team = Group of mental health, healthcare, and education professionals, and the child's parents, working together to help the child

U

Unsymbolized = Unexpressed/unspoken intense feelings often due to trauma (*see* trauma) under the awareness of an individual that negatively affect self-esteem, decisions, choices, options, and thoughts

V

Validation = Recognizing, hearing, and empathically (*see* empathy) responding to a person's feelings

Visitation = Legal agreement for a non-custodial parent (*see* non-custodial parent) to see, share time with, talk to her or his child, who is in the other parent's custody (*see* custodial parent)

BIBLIOGRAPHY

Ackerman, N. W. C. (1958) *The psychodynamics of family life*. New York: Basic Books.

Addis, M. E., & Cardemil, E. V. (2006) Does manualization improve therapy outcomes? In J. C. Norcross, L. E. Beutler, & R. F. Levant (Eds). *Evidence-based practices in mental health: Debate and dialogue on the fundamental questions* (pp. 131–160). Washington, DC: American Psychological Association.

Adler, A. (1959) *Understanding human nature*. New York: Premier Books.

Adler-Tapia, R. (2012) *Child psychotherapy: Integrating developmental therapy into clinical practice*. New York: Springer Publishing.

Ainsworth, M. D. S., Blehar, M. C., Waters, E., & Wall, S. (2014) *Patterns of attachment (Classic Edition): A psychological study of the strange situation*. Florence, KY: Guilford Press Taylor & Frances Group.

Aron, L. (1996) *A meeting of mind: Mutuality in psychoanalysis*. Hillsdale, NJ: Analytic Press.

Axline, V. M. (1947) *Play therapy: The inner dynamics of childhood*. Oxford, UK; Houghton Mifflin.

Baer, R. A. (2003) Mindfulness training as a clinical intervention: A conceptual and empirical review. *Clinic Psychology Science and Practice*, 10: 125–143.

Bateson, G., Jackson, D. D., Haley, J., & Weakland, J. (1956) Towards a theory of schizophrenia. *Behavioral Science*, 1: 251–264.

Beutler, L. E. (1983) *Eclectic psychotherapy: A systematic approach*. New York: Pergamon.

Bandura, A. (1969) *Principles of behavior modification*. New York: Holt, Rinehart & Winston.

Bandura, A. (1977). *Social learning theory*. Englewood Cliffs, NJ: Prentice-Hall.

Bandura, A. (1986). *Social foundations of thought and action*. Englewood Cliffs, NJ: Prentice-Hall.

Beck, A. J., Rush, A. J., Shawn, B. F., & Emery, G. (1979) *Cognitive therapy of depression*. New York: Guilford Press.

Blaustein, M. E., & Kinniburgh, K. M. (2010) *Treating traumatic stress in children and adolescents: How to foster resilience through attachment, self-regulation and competency*. Florence, KY: Guilford Press Taylor & Frances Group.

Blos, P. (1970). *The young adolescent*. New York: Free Press.

Borys, D. S. (1994) Maintaining therapeutic boundaries: The motive is therapeutic effectiveness not defensive practice. *Ethics & Behavior*, 4(3): 267–273.

Bowlby, J. (1969) *Attachment and loss*, Vol. 1: *Attachment*. New York: Basic Books.

Bowlby, J. (1982) *The mind in conflict*. New York: International Universities Press.

Bromfield, R. (2007) *Doing child and adolescent psychotherapy: Adapting psychodynamic treatment to contemporary practice* (2nd Edition). Hoboken, NJ: John Wiley & Sons.

Cannon, W. (1915) *Bodily changes in pain, hunger, fear, and rage*. New York: D. Appleton and Company.

Cassity, M. D., & Cassity, J. E. (1994) Psychiatric music therapy assessment and treatment in clinical training facilities with adults, adolescents and children. *Journal of Music Therapy*, 31(1): 2–30.

Cooper, W. O., Callahan, S. T., Shintani, J. A., Fuchs, D. C., Shelton, R. C, Dudley, J. A., Graves, A. J., & Ray, W. A. (2014, February) Antidepressants and suicide attempts in children. *Pediatrics*, 133(2): 204–210. doi: 10.1542/peds.2013-0923.

Corrigan, M. W. (2014) *Debunking ADHD: 10 reasons to stop drugging kids*. Lanham, MD: Rowman & Littlefield.

Crenshaw, D. A. (2006) *Evocative strategies in child and adolescent psychotherapy*. Lanham, MD: Jason Aronson; Rowman & Littlefield.

Deakin, J., & Lennox, B. (2013, March) Psychotic symptoms in young people warrant urgent referral. *Practitioner*, 257(1759): 25–28.

Ellenberger, H. (1970) *The discovery of the unconscious*. New York: Basic Books.

Ellis, A. (1994) *Reason and emotion in psychotherapy revised*. Secaucus, NJ: Citadel.

Ellis, A. (2001) *Overcoming destructive beliefs, feelings and behaviors*. Amherst, NY: Prometheus Books.

Erikson, E. (1968) *Identity, youth and crisis*. New York: Norton.

Fairbairn, W. R. D. (1954) *An object relations theory of personality*. New York: Basic Books.

Federal Interagency Forum on Child and Family Statistics. *America's children: Key national indicators of well being, 2013* (2014, January 1). Retrieved August 1, 2014, from http://www.childstats.gov/americaschildren13/index.asp

Fenton, M. C., Geler, T., Keyes, K., Skodol, A. E, Grant, B. F., Hasin, D. S. (2013, May) Combined role of childhood maltreatment, family history and gender in the risk for alcohol dependence. *Psychological Medicine*, 43(5): 1045–1057. doi: 10.1017/S00332917/200/79.

Fine, A. H. (2006) *Handbook of animal-assisted therapy*. London: Academic Books.

Frank, J. D. (1973) *Persuasion and healing* (2nd Edition). Baltimore, MD: Johns Hopkins University.

Frankel, V. E. (1963) *Man's search for meaning*. New York: Washington Square Press.

Freud, A., & Burlingham, D. (1967) *The writings of Anna Freud: The ego and the mechanisms of defense*, vol. 2. New York: International Universities Press.

Gold, C., Vonacek, M. & Wigman, T. (2004) Effects of music therapy for children and adolescents with psychopathology: A meta analysis. *Journal of Child Psychotherapy*, 45: 1054–1063.

Gottlieb, T. G. (1994) Ethical decision making, boundaries and treatment effectiveness: A reprise. *Ethics and Boundaries*, 4(3): 295–298.

Horney, K. (1951) *Neurosis and human growth*. London: Routledge and Kegan Paul.

Hunt, M., Corman, R., & Ormont, L. (1964) *The Talk Cure*. New York: Harper & Row.

Jacobs, T. J. (1991) *The use of self: Countertransference in analytic situations*. Madison, CT: International Universities Press.

Jenson, P. (2001) Findings from the NIMH multimodal treatment study of ADHD (MTA): Implications and applications for primary care providers. *Developmental and Behavioral Pediatrics*, Feb; 22(1).

Jones, E. (1953) *The life and work of Sigmund Freud*. New York: Basic Books.

Jung, C. (1968) *The psychology of the child archetype in collected works of C. J. Jung* (Vol. 9, Part 1). Bollinger Series XX (2nd Edition). Princeton, NJ: Princeton University Press.

Kaley-Isley, L C., Peterson, J., Fischer, C., & Pearson, E. (2010, August) Yoga as a complimentary therapy for children and adolescents. *Psychiatry*, 7(8): 20–32.

Klanecky, A., McChargne, D. E., & Bruggeman, L. (2012 May–June) Desire to dissociate: Implications for problematic drinking in college student with childhood or adolescent sexual abuse exposure. *Journal of the Study of Alcohol and Drugs*, 73(4): 549–558.

Klein, M. (1932) *The psycho-analysis of children*. New York: W. W. Norton & Co.

Kohut, H. (1971) *The analysis of self: A systemic approach to the psychoanalytic treatment of narcissistic personality disorder*. New York: International Universities Press.

Krumwiede, A. (2014) *Attachment theory according to John Bowlby and Mary Ainsworth*. Santa Cruz, CA: GRIN Verlag Gmbh.

Lampert, B. (2003) *A child's eye-view: Gestalt therapy with children, adolescents and their families*. Highland, NY: The Gestalt Journal Press.

Landreth, G. L. (2012) *Play therapy: The art of relationships* (3rd Edition). New York: Routledge.

Lazarus, A. A. (1994) How certain boundaries and ethics diminish therapeutic effectiveness. *Ethics & Behavior*, 4(3): 255–261.

Lazarus, A. A. (1993) Tailoring the therapeutic relationship or being an authentic chameleon. *Psychotherapy*, 30: 404–407.

Lazarus, A. A. (1984) *In the mind's eye: The power of imagery for personal enrichment*. New York: Guilford Press (Reprint 1974).

Li, S., Yu, B, Zhou, D., He, C., Kang, L., Wang, X., Jiang, S., & Chen, C. (2011) *Acupuncture for Attention Deficit Hyperactivity Disorder (ADHD) in children and adolescents*. New York: The Cochrane Collection, John Wiley & Sons Ltd.

Lieberman, A. F., & Vanthorn, P. (2011) *Psychotherapy with infants and young children: Repairing the effects of stress and trauma on early attachment*. Florence, KY: Guilford Press Taylor & Frances Group.

Losconcy, L. (1981) *Encouragement therapy*. Englewood Cliffs, NJ: Prentice Hall.

Mahler, M., Pine, F., & Bergman, A. (1975) *The psychological birth of the human infant*. New York: Basic Books.

Mahoney, M. J. (1974) *Cognition and behavior modification*. Cambridge, MA: Ballinger.

Maslow, A. (1943) A theory of human motivation. *Psychology Review*, 50: 370–396.

Maslow, A. (1968) *Toward a psychology of being* (2nd Edition). Princeton, NJ: Van Nostrand.

Maslow, A. (1971) *The further reaches of human nature*. New York: Viking.

May, R. (1953) *Man's search for himself.* New York: Norton.

May, R. (1967) *Psychology and human dilemma.* New York: Norton.

May, R. (1969) *Love and will.* New York: Norton.

May, R. (1975) *The courage to create.* New York: Norton.

McNeill, B., & Worthen, V. (1989 October) The parallel process in psychotherapy supervision. *Research and Practice,* 20(5): 329–333. doi: 10.1037/0735-7028.20.5.329.

Meichenbaum, D. (1977) *Cognitive-behavior modification: An integrative approach.* New York: Plenum.

Menninger, K. (1958) *Theory of psychoanalytic technique.* New York: Basic Books.

Minuchin, S. C. (1974) *Families and family therapy.* Cambridge, MA: Harvard University Press.

Mittenberger, R. (2001) *Behavior modification: Principles and procedures* (2nd Edition). Belmont, CA: Wadsworth/Thomas Learning.

Mooney, C. G. (2013) *Theories of childhood: An introduction to Dewey, Montessori, Erikson, Piaget & Vygotsky* (Redleaf Professional Library) (2nd Edition). St. Paul, MN: Redleaf Press.

National Register of Health Service Psychologists. *Credentialing for Doctoral, Postdoctoral Trainees and Psychologists* (2014, January 1). Retrieved August 1, 2014, from www.nationalregister.org

Raskins, N. J. (2004) *Contributions to client-centered therapy and the person-centered approach.* Ross-on-Wye, UK: PCCS Books.

Reik, T. (1948) *Listening with the third ear.* New York: Farrar and Strauss.

Rinella, V. J., & Gerstein, A. I. (1994) The development of dual relationships: Power and professional responsibility. *International Journal of Law and Psychiatry,* 17(3): 225–237.

Rogers, C. (1939) *The clinical treatment of the problem child.* Boston: Houghton Mifflin.

Rogers, C. (1995) *On becoming a person.* New York: Houghton Mifflin (Reprint 1961).

Rogers, C. R. (1951) *Client-centered therapy.* Boston: Houghton Mifflin.

Rosen, D. (2002) *Transforming depression: Healing the soul through creativity.* York Beach, ME: Nicholas-Hays.

Ross, A. C. (1981) *Child behavior therapy.* New York: Wiley.

Rubin, J. A. (2005) *Child art therapy* (Deluxe Edition, 25th Anniversary Edition). Hoboken, NJ: Wiley & Sons.

Ruhrmann, S., Shultze-Lutke, F., & Klosterkotter, J. (2009, March) Intervention in the at-risk state to prevent transition to psychosis. *Current Opinions in Psychiatry,* 22(2): 177–183. doi: 10.1097/YCO.06013e328324b687.

Satir, V. C. (1972) *People making.* Palo Alto, CA: Science and Behavior Books.

Schore, A (2003) *Affect dysregulation and disorders of the self.* New York: Norton.

Searles, H. (1955) The informational value of the supervisor's emotional experience. *Journal for the Study of Interpersonal Processes,* 18: 135–146.

Slade, A. (2009-October 20) Representation, symbolization and affect regulation in the concomitant treatment of a mother and child: Attachment theory and child psychotherapy. *Psychoanalytic Inquiry,* 19(5): 797–830.

Stern, D. (2004) *The interpersonal world of the infant.* New York: Basic Books.

Stern, D. (2004) *The present moment in psychotherapy and everyday life.* New York: Norton.

Sternberg, R. J. Evidence-based practice: Gold standard, gold plated or fool's gold? In C. D. Goodheart, A. E. Kazdin, & R. J. Sternberg (Eds.), *Evidence-based psychotherapy: Where practice and research meet* (pp. 261–271). Washington, DC: American Psychological Association.

Stettin, G. D., Jianying, Y., Verbrugge, R. R., & Aubert, R. E. (2006 August) Frequency of follow-up care for adults and pediatric patients during initiation of antidepressant therapy. *American Journal of Managed Care*, 12: 453–461.

Stockman, A. F. (1990) Dual relationships in rural mental health practice: An ethical dilemma. *Journal of Rural Community Psychology*, 11(2): 31–45.

Strachey, J. (1966) *The complete introductory lectures in psychoanalysis: Sigmund Freud. Dreams* (1916) VII, The manifest content of dreams and the latent dream thoughts: 113–125. New York: W. W. Norton & Company.

Strachey, J. (1966) *The complete introductory lectures in psychoanalysis: Sigmund Freud. General theory of the neuroses* (1917) XVII, The sense of symptoms: 257–273. New York: W. W. Norton & Company.

Strachey, J. (1966) *The complete introductory lectures in psychoanalysis: Sigmund Freud. General theory of the neuroses* (1917) XXII, Some thoughts of development and regression: 339–357. New York: W. W. Norton & Company.

Strachey, J. (1966) *The complete introductory lectures in psychoanalysis: Sigmund Freud. General theory of the neuroses* (1917) XXIII, The paths to the formation of symptoms: 358–377. New York: W. W. Norton & Company.

Strachey, J. (1966) *The complete introductory lectures in psychoanalysis: Sigmund Freud. General theory of the neuroses* (1917) XXVII, Transference: 431–447. New York: W. W. Norton & Company.

Sullivan, H. S. (1974) *The psychiatric interview.* New York: Norton.

Szente, J. (2007, June) Empowering young children for success in school and in life. *Early Childhood Education Journal*, 34(6): 449–453.

Thomas, A., & Chess, S. (1977) *Temperament and development.* New York: Brunner/Mazel.

Thomas, C. R. & Holzer, C. E. (2006) The continuing shortage of child and adolescent psychiatrists. *Journal of American Academy of Child and Adolescent Psychiatry*, Sep; 45(9): 1023–1031.

Visser, S., Danielson, M., Bitsko, R., et al. Trends in the parent-report of health care provider-diagnosis and medication treatment for ADHD disorder: United States, 2003–2011. *Journal of American Academy of Child and Adolescent Psychiatry.* 2013.

Walsh, R., & Shapiro, S. (2006) The meeting of meditative disciplines and Western psychology: A mutually enriching dialogue. *American Psychologist*, 61(3): 227–239.

Webb, N. B., & Doka, K. J. (2010) *Helping bereaved children: A handbook for practitioners* (3rd Edition). Florence, KY: Guilford Press Taylor & Frances Group.

Webb, N. B. (Ed.) (2007) *Play therapy with child in crisis: Individual, group and family therapy* (3rd Edition). Florence, KY: Guilford Press Taylor & Frances Group.

Webb, N. B. (2007) *Helping children and adolescents with chronic and serious medical conditions: A strength-based approach* (3rd Edition). Florence, KY: Guilford Press Taylor & Frances Group.

Wilkinson, M. (2006) *Coming into mind: The mind-brain relationship: A Jungian clinical perspective.* New York: Routledge.

Winnicott, D. W. (1963) *Maturational process and facilitating environment.* Madison, CT: International Universities Press.

Winnicott, D. W. (1953) Transitional objects and transitional phenomena: A study of the first not me possession. *International Journal of Psychoanalysis,* 34: 89–97.

Wolf, M. M., Giles, D., & Hall, R. V. (1968) Experiments with token reinforcement in a remedial classroom. *Behavior Research and Therapy,* 6: 51–64.

Yung, A. R., & Nelson, B. (2011, Feb) Young people at ultra high risk for psychosis: A research update. *Early Intervention Psychiatry,* 5(Suppl 1): 52–57. doi: 10.111 1/j.1751-7893.2010.00241.X.

Zimring, F. M. (2000) Empathic understanding grows the person. *Person-Centered Journal,* 7(2): 101–113.

INDEX

Note: Page numbers in **bold** indicate glossary entries.

drug treatment/rehabilitation center, 229–230
dual relationship, 169–170

early adolescent child
  books to prepare for therapy, 68
  collateral contact with, 176–77
  connecting to therapist, 69–70
  diagnosis, concept of, 118
  empathic breaks in, 202–3
  informing about therapy, 54–55
  treatment plan for, 149
educational interventions, 208, 210–13, 222–23
educator, as treatment team member, 25
e-mail communication, 131
emergencies, 57–58
Emerson, Ralph Waldo, 184
emotionally injured, 200
emotions, 101, 200
empathic breaks
  definition of, 199, 206
  in early adolescent children, 202–3
  fight or flight reaction and, 200
  irreparable, 250–51
  in late adolescent/teen children, 203–4
  in latency-age children, 202
  relationships and, 200–201
  within therapist-parent relationship, 204–5
  in toddlerhood through pre-latency children, 202
  in young adults, 204
empathic lapses, 203
empathy, 53, 247, **271**
ending phase. See termination phase
engagement, 121–22, **271**
engagement phase, 8, 121–23
environmental component, 114–15, 116, 119–120
Erikson, Erik, 154–55
evidence-based treatment(s)
  definition of, **271**
  limitations to, 137

in mental health, 139
not working for child, 141
to operationalize psychotherapy, 135–36
ration treatment through, 138
success of, 138–39
examination process. See also psychological tests, 104–5, 107–10
expressive arts therapies, 213, 223
expressive therapies, 95, **271**

Facebook, 132
family friend, 23
family member session, 162
family system, 20
family therapy, 213–14, 223
favoritism, 169
Federal Food and Drug Administration (FDA), 218
Feeling Better: Kid's Book About Therapy (Rashkin), 68
fees, 38–40, 127
fight or flight reaction, 200
first meeting. See consultation; intake
fit, 114
504 Educational Plan, 210, 211, 223
flight into health, 76–77
focus questions, 158–160
foster parent, 22
the frame of therapy
  changes to, 133
  confidentiality, 127–28
  daily routine issues, 125
  day and time as, 125
  fees and, 127
  frequency and, 126
  geographic issues, 125
  holding environment, 124–25
  rules and routines as, 123
  trust and, 123–24
frequency of session, 126
Freud, Sigmund, 91
frustration tolerance, 185–86

goodness of fit, 114, 119
group counseling, 214, 223
group support, 223
guided imagery, 209, 222

harm reduction, 234
hasty separation, 249–250
healthcare cost containment, 138
Health Insurance Portability and
    Accountability Act (HIPAA),
    129–130
healthy development of child, 60–61
hierarchy of needs, 146–47
higher level of care
    contained system as, 228
    definition of, 234
    diagnostic treatment center, 228–29
    drug treatment/rehabilitation center,
        229–230
    hospital emergency room (ER), 230
    need for, 245
    psychiatric hospitalization, 230
    residential treatment facility and
        school, 230–31
    themes of, 232–34
    types of, 228–231, 235
holding environment, 124–25
holistic model of treatment, 106–7, 120
holistic perspective, 2, 11–12, 105, **271**
hospital-based outpatient psychiatry
    services, 226, 245–46
hospital emergency room (ER), 230
hospitals, 32–33
humanistic model, 2, **272**

ICT classes, 210
Individualized Education Programs
    (IEP), 36, 210, 211, 223
individual school-based
    counseling, 210–11
individuation, 114, 119, 236, **272**
industry vs. inferiority stage, 155
infant children, communication with, 81
informing child about therapy, 52–58

inner emotional turmoil, 101
inpatient mental health treatment, 231
in-person communication, 130, 166–67
in-person psycho-educational
    session, 162–66
in-person transfer, 243
Instagram, 132
insurance/insurance companies
    diagnosing for, 100
    evidence-based treatment and, 138
    governmental medical, 41, 140
    influencing treatment decisions, 140
    therapist fees and, 38–40
intake. *See also* consultation
    definition of, **272**
    including child in, 49–50
    process of, 46–47
    scheduling, 32–33
intake therapist, 46
integration, 173, 187–88, **272**
Internet-based referral services, 32, 42
interventions
    child reacts to therapist's, 183
    definition of, **272**
    educational, 208
    parental attitudes toward, 136–37
    secondary, 209
    supplemental (*see*
        supplemental interventions)
    teacher-implemented, 210
    therapeutic (*see* therapeutic
        interventions)

joint session, 168

kinetic, **272**
kinetic communication, 86–88, 90, 97
kinship parent, 22, **272**
Knell, Susan M., 93

late adolescent/teen child
    books to prepare for therapy, 68
    collateral contact with, 177–78
    connecting to therapist, 70

paced termination, 250
parallel process
    child-specific issues, 158–59
    definition of, 152, 160
    example of, 153
    focus questions, 158–160
    parents and, 155–160
    proactive role in, 158
    stages of development, 155
    treatment-specific issues, 160
parent-child relationship, 168–69
parent collateral, 127, 180, **273**
parents
    communication between infants
        and, 81
    connecting to children, 7
    defense mechanisms of, 6
    parallel process and, 155–160
    taken back to childhood, 156
    taking care of children, 9
    therapeutic interventions and, 148, 152
    vulnerability of, 7, 156
parent session, 162
parent-therapist relationship, 162–63,
    176, 204–5
partial hospitalization program, 230, 245
patient, as treatment team member, 21
payment for services, 13
perception, definition of, 3
personality component, 113–14, 116, 119
personal referral, 31, 42
person-in-environment model, 2, 106–7,
    120, **273**
pervasive developmental delay, 245
phobia, 96, **273**
physical custody, 22
physical therapists, 222, 224
play therapy
    activity, 93–94, 98
    analytic, 91–92, 97
    cognitive behavioral, 93, 98
    psychodynamic, 92, 97–98
    therapeutic, 94–95, 98
    verbal therapy vs., 90–91

preparation for first meeting,
    47–50, 58–63
preschool children. *See* toddlerhood
    through pre-latency children
presenting problem(s), 47, 61, 64, **273**
pre-verbal, 81, 85, **273**
primary caregiver, 22, **273**
privacy, 127–28
private therapists
    consultation with, 45
    contacting, 32–33
    fees of, 38
    progress reports and, 193
    selecting, 34
    supervision of, 38
procrastination, 74
professional referral, 31, 42
progression, 70, **273**
progress reports, 193–95
projection, 5, **273**
projective test, 108, **273**
psychiatric diagnosis, 106
psychiatric hospitalization, 230
psychiatric symptoms, 100
psychiatrist (MD), 36, 219–220
psychodynamic play therapy, 92,
    97–98, **273**
psycho-education
    child-specific issues, 163–64
    definition of, 163
    parent-specific issues, 164–65
    treatment-specific issues, 165–66
psycho-education sessions, 180
psychological/emotional battery, 108, 109
psychological testing, 108–10
psychological tests, 108–10, 211
psychologists, 36
psycho-pharmacologists, 36
psychotherapeutic drugs, 36
psychotherapist
    cultural background of, 15–16
    defining, 13–15
    educational background of, 13–14
    ethical issues concerning, 16–17